Darrell K...
duselton1@gmail
901-619-8499

Spiritual
NETWORKING

Father Don Mowery
and Youth Service

Darrell B. Uselton & David Yawn

Produced by:

FriesenPress
Suite 300 – 852 Fort Street
Victoria, BC, Canada V8W 1H8

www.friesenpress.com

Distributed to the trade by The Ingram Book Company

TABLE OF CONTENTS

Spiritual
NETWORKING

ACKNOWLEDGMENTS

The authors gratefully acknowledge the following individuals who in particular have contributed to the success of this book. From an editorial standpoint, we commend Mary Beth Uselton, Ginger Guin, Jocelyn Regenwether, and Paola High, for their proofreading and editorial skills through different phases of the manuscript, as well as Corinne Walker and Ruthie Hall for compiling the personal names index.

We credit J. Lester Crain, Jr. for his leadership and for being the persuasive agent who first recommended telling the Youth Service story. Without his advice and support, this book would not be a reality. Brian Pecon provided expert guidance, encouragement and supervisory project management along the way. Bishop Don Johnson of The Episcopal Diocese of West Tennessee supplied encouragement and a workable system whereby the book could be produced with transparency and purpose. Excellent insight and recall of pertinent dates, names and facts by long-time staff member Frank Dawson contributed greatly to our being able to share this story with such accuracy. Additionally, the early history of Youth Service penned by former board member Jay Eberle provided an initial framework for this book.

Cynthia Ham, Jim Boyd and Randy Brown of BRIDGES were instrumental in helping "bridge" the history with the present in the chronicling of this vital account. For that matter, we are indebted to the BRIDGES staff for the usage of the Youth Service archival files. From these materials, we were able to reconstruct important events and interesting anecdotal accounts from the board meeting minutes and other documents from year to year.

We especially thank Don Mowery for his patience and understanding throughout this often complex and tedious process. Don's leadership and dedication to the youth of this country has made a positive and lasting impression on the writers. His vivid recollection of names, dates and facts about Youth Service and its staff is remarkable. A special acknowledgement is given to Julie Mowery for her graciousness, kindness and generosity, which was always evident during our many meetings with Don in their home, and for her editorial assistance, photo selections and design ideas for this book.

Finally, the collective efforts of thousands of people contributed to the success of Youth Service and played a vital role in changing the lives of countless young people across America. Unfortunately, it is impossible to mention everyone and his or her specific roles in this account. However, each staff member, volunteer, social worker, sister agency and donor who committed their time, energy and money to the mission of Youth Service, though not identified by name, will always remain a significant part of this important legacy.

PREFACE

The combined biography of Episcopal priest The Reverend Donald Edgar Mowery and the accounts of Youth Service in Memphis, Inc. and Youth Service, USA are so closely woven together that they are virtually inseparable. One begets the other, as readers of this book will find when opening its pages. Readers will be inspired either by what they view as frequent coincidental episodes or by the evident work of a providential hand. Those close to the subject affirm that the latter was most certainly at work as Don grew through his formative and early entrepreneurial years into a man who devoted his life to serving others.

Father Mowery established key relationships with many individuals through his "spiritual network," which grew to include influential persons and organizations across America. For instance, Elvis Presley grew up in one of the Memphis housing projects served by Youth Service and became a strong supporter of the agency. Youth Service also obtained direct support from four U.S. presidents in its effort to build a national program and three Joint Chiefs of Staff, representing the U.S. Army, Navy, and Air Force, actively supported the agency and served at various times on the Board of Directors for Youth Service, USA. Additionally, Bud Wilkinson and John Wooden were board members and were among the many notable contributors to the development of the youth agency. These people, along with many others, helped forge the success for the Youth Service endeavors.

So many crossroads, challenges and intricacies enter the story of Youth Service that this brief synopsis does not do it justice. Suffice to say that Don Mowery envisioned an organization well beyond the confines of campgrounds for underprivileged and troubled youths. His work became the premier template of how a priest with a mission can create a workable and worthy national program – a program that enjoyed many accolades from the highest levels. Nevertheless, its inception and growth were anything but automatic. Various initiatives were tried and some failed, but all were supplemented with prayer along with a few favors now and again from Don's "spiritual network" of donors and supporters. Most of all, Youth Service was effectively blessed by the ever-providing hand of God, which is evident when tracing the history of this organization

"Father Don," as most Memphians know him, joined Youth Service in Memphis, a social service agency sponsored by The Episcopal Church and supported by United Way, in January 1963. During his 33-year tenure, Youth Service established four major youth programs locally and then expanded three of them to over 100 U.S. military bases across the country. First, came the Camping and Vocational Exposure Program; second, the Job Skills Training and Employment Program for older youths (18 to 24 age group); and third, the About Face Program, marking the first juvenile boot camp to fight drug use among young people, and which operated within a military framework. Finally, the capstone became the Bridge Builders program, which evolved into BRIDGES, Inc. a platform that trains young people in leadership, human relations and community service.

Father Don guided Youth Service successfully from the early 1960s until 1995. His vision transformed the organization into a model for outreach programs, and with the help of staff members, top military brass, key board members, and private donors, built the agency into an organization of broad national proportions.

The growth and expansion of these programs across a myriad of military bases representing all phases of the military service, is unparalleled among civilian organizations. No other civilian organization, before or since, has been awarded the use of military facilities in both the manner and scope that Youth Service was allowed. Father Don proved to the top echelons of the U.S. military how youth development programs and workforce development training can transform young people into productive and positive citizens. Building Youth Service, Memphis and forming Youth Service, USA are accomplishments that remain unprecedented in their scope. These programs attained so many "firsts" in their parade of progress that one would have difficulty selecting a single event that most represents their entire slate of successes. In the process, Don and Youth Service garnered 13 Freedoms Foundation awards for their efforts.

Don Mowery has lived an extraordinary life working with people from very diverse backgrounds. He has devoted his career to helping others find the good in themselves, while helping them reach their life goals. The core mission of Youth Service throughout was to help young people and their families reach their maximum potential by becoming self-respecting and self-supporting citizens. Behind every Youth Service program was Don's Christian concern for the well-being of the fortunate and the less fortunate.

Readers will find a number of distinct leadership qualities in Don Mowery – among these are his perceptive networking abilities, an instinct for innovation, along with unique pastoral and interventionist qualities. These attributes are evident from his first assignment, the rebuilding of a small urban church congregation in Nashville, and from his unique ability to communicate with young people and older folks alike.

His enduring ability to continue broadcasting his near half-century old radio talk show, *Talk It Out with Father Don*, is most commendable. The groundbreaking broadcast, primarily created for teens, hosted thousands of guests ranging from celebrities such as Bob Hope and Ed Sullivan to local citizens and volunteers who share valuable information about their worthy causes.

This book also exposes the turbulent times of the 1960s and 1970s amidst a vastly changing social culture, a time when Youth Service served as a community stabilizer for racial and generational reconciliation during a period of social unrest. As such, Youth Service was a leader in the transition to equality for thousands of young people, as its staff reached out with love and compassion in creative ways to bring about change and opportunity. From the Church Mission of Help at Trinity Church Wall Street in the 1920s, to its development into the BRIDGES program of today, Father Don worked to promote the ideals of these organizations well beyond the local level and into national prominence.

This book holds many lessons for those interested in personal leadership, the development of social programs and the challenges that face the youth of this country everyday. Civic and educational leaders, law enforcement officials, service organizations, community agencies, church laity and clergy, military personnel, and individuals interested in ways to invest in the future of youth in America will all benefit from this book.

Youth Service, Memphis and Youth Service, USA have positively affected the lives of countless young people, many of whom became respected leaders in their own right. Therefore, the fascinating story of Father Don and Youth Service, their mission and legacy should be shared widely. The co-authors of this work are honored to provide readers with this fascinating story of devotion and commitment to the special cause of helping the youth of America.

Darrell B. Uselton and David Yawn, co-authors

CHAPTER ONE

The Formative Years

Donald Edgar Mowery was born the second son to Myrtle Allison Mowery and Clarence Edgar Mowery on August 2, 1931 in Chattanooga, TN. The Mowery family, by the economic standards of the times, was a typical middle class family with their home situated in a neighborhood in the East Lake subdivision between Missionary Ridge and Lookout Mountain. The family would often sit on the front porch and enjoy a panoramic view of the historic Lookout Mountain Hotel and the vast surrounding beauty.

Several miles from the Mowery home in downtown Chattanooga was the Hamilton National Bank, where his father worked for a number of years during the Great Depression. Because of the hard times, the country's economic climate was volatile, but the Mowery family managed to have a normal family life.

Don's only sibling was an older brother, Paul, born in 1922. Though very fond of his brother, the nine-year age difference left a "distance" between them. Fortunately, the brothers established a close relationship during adulthood until Paul's death in 1992. Paul began college at the onset of World War II, attending the University of the South at Sewanee and later graduating from the University of Alabama. With the war in progress, Paul trained as a fighter pilot in the Army Air Corps. Following the war, he settled in Beaumont, Texas and, like his father, made a career in banking and finance. Paul and his wife, Sara, had two sons: Paul Jr. and Dale.

In 1935, older brother Paul was a teenager and his energetic little brother Don, then four years old, shared a heartbreaking and life-changing experience. Their mother suffered a tragic automobile accident while on a winter trip that year in Kentucky. She survived the crash, but her back was broken. Young Don's life changed overnight. For Paul, some changes went along with his being a teenager, but Don, like any other small child, depended greatly on his mother Myrtle's teachings and guidance. For the next five years, their mother was bed-ridden in a plaster body cast that enclosed her small body from the top of her shoulders to the bottom of her torso. Because of the accident, almost all of her physical responsibilities as mother to young Don were immediately suspended. Don recalled, "After the accident, she was no longer by my side like she had always been. I can still see her in that cast, lying on the bed, unable to move, and in severe pain." At first, young Don was confused, but out of necessity, he emerged a more self-sufficient and independent lad. He was nine years old when his mother's cast was finally removed.

Because of the accident, Don's father changed, as well. Don remembered that his father, Clarence, was "all business" and had very little time to spend with him. Therefore, family members and friends cared and nurtured the inquisitive and energetic young boy. Due to his mother's injuries, there was a host of nurses and caretakers in and out of the home. Grown-ups with their business and adult conversations thus surrounded him. During these crucial developmental years, Don gained a sense of independence and emerged with more freedom, wisdom and a keen sense of entrepreneurship.

Don's childhood, in an emotional sense, was brief. The presence of his father's mother, Louella, proved to be quite helpful to Don in terms of overall character development and in building his self-reliance. She herself had been a single parent to Don's father, Clarence, and his brother and two sisters. Her own husband, the children's father, disappeared without a trace after their fourth child was born. Louella became the family's sole provider, and she continued working until her four children completed high school and both daughters finished college.

Don remembered his grandfather's influence:

> My mother's father, Burch Cook Allison, was a great influence on me during my youth. He owned two general stores in the rural areas of Chattanooga and Rossville, GA. I always loved to work and I especially liked merchandising. Maybe I innately wanted a general store like my grandfather. When I was seven years old, I actually built a makeshift store in my parents' garage and sold gum and candy to my neighbors along with various other items. My grandfather was a 'go-getter' and an enterprising person. I remember he would give me 50 cents for Christmas and that was a big deal. I believe I acquired

much of my work ethic from my grandfather Allison. My father's style of work was somewhat different and always had me working various jobs in all of his businesses.

Don's mother, Myrtle, was one of six children. She was thoughtful, selfless, and charitable, always helping people, including strangers. She was also a very hard worker, like her own father. When she was bed-ridden, she had countless visits from people who genuinely loved her. She suffered greatly during her time of rehabilitation, but was determined to overcome her physical condition.

Don spent his primary grade school years at Cedar Hill Elementary and later, at East Lake Junior High School. Don's pleasant demeanor, self-assuredness and a desire to help others developed in him an ability to relate to people of all backgrounds. He also had an uncanny sense for selling almost anything. At age 10, Don sold magazines and Christmas cards door-to-door, and, at 14, he began selling Kay's Ice Cream from a single pushcart. While selling ice cream, Don learned about the Birds Eye Company and their new line of frozen food products. With that bit of information, he created the idea to sell frozen vegetables and ice cream, door to door. Don recalled the experience, "I had approached Birds Eye when the company first introduced the frozen food products line and soon became a distributor. I was then able to have a Bird's Eye logo sign on the side of my truck."

Don remembered working during his youth from sun up until dark most days, except Sunday:

> I gained an exemplary work ethic, modeled after my parents' and grandparents' diligence and determination. I never saw or heard of anyone else my age with a desire to work over play. First, I had a single pushcart for my business, and then I recruited other boys to work for me. I used dry ice to keep the ice cream frozen. Soon, I bought an open-bed pickup truck with the money I had made. I had a box for dry ice to keep ice cream frozen in the back of the truck, so I could carry and sell more merchandise. I was only 15 at the time and before I had a license to drive. I sold three flavors of ice cream and shaved ice to the people around Fort Oglethorpe, GA., and found time to pump gas for my father at a gas station he owned. When I finally received my driver's license at 16, I leased

a larger panel truck, so I could add more products and expand my territory.

To Don, school was equally important as work. When he entered ninth grade, his parents sent him to Baylor School for Boys, a military school in Chattanooga. The majority of the student body was composed of class-mates from affluent families. Though Don's family was not affluent, he had gained valuable life experiences that his fellow Baylor students did not possess. From a very early age, Don taught himself to be an origi-nal thinker and to be self-sufficient. Fortunately, Baylor built upon this foundation.

Don enjoyed school and participated in several sports activities. However, he was not the best athlete, nor was his heart centrally into sports; rather, he simply enjoyed being around others. He had a deep desire for working and seeing the results and rewards of his own actions, and was happiest and most comfortable when plying his social skills.

During Don's stay at Baylor, the school had a serious outbreak of polio. Many students contracted the disease. Several were crippled and two children died during the school year. Because of the epidemic, the health department closed the school for several weeks. The incident ter-rified the students' families and the tragic experience stayed with Don for many years. Later in life, he "adopted" the polio ward of the Vanderbilt Hospital as a part of his ministry when he served in Nashville. Don would regularly visit the children, whose families could not be with them due to work or other circumstances, taking books and magazines on Sundays.

When Don was in the fourth grade, his father became treasurer of Campbell Oil Company, a large distributor of petroleum products. Clarence later expanded into the automobile and transportation business with the purchase of a local service station, followed by the establishment of an automobile dealership adjacent to the station. Don worked in his father's businesses, learning the ins and outs and difficulties of commerce. He recalled that his father worked constantly and instilled in him the serious work ethic that carried him into adulthood. "We rarely engaged in recreational and social activities. My father enjoyed playing golf with my older brother Paul, so I developed other interests. I often found myself on my own, but I was fortunate to be involved with Boy Scouts, which exposed me to their character-building activities."

In the fall of 1947, Don's father accepted a job offer in Atlanta. The job required his parents to move in order to take advantage of a larger income for the Mowery family. Unfortunately, this created more distance between his parents. Later that year, Don accepted an offer from Eugene

Turner, an acquaintance of the Mowery family, to live and work part-time at the Turner Funeral Home in Chattanooga during his senior year of high school. This was a fitting position for Don because he enjoyed the business and had helped at the funeral home at night and on the weekends throughout the previous two summers.

From childhood, the church was a significant part of Don's life. As a teenager, he became a member of St. Paul's Episcopal Church in Chattanooga and enjoyed attending church with friends. Don became increasingly involved with members of the clergy, who were influential in his later decision to go to seminary and become a priest of the church. "I enjoyed everything about The Episcopal Church; the music, the liturgy and all of the activities there. The idea of participating in the liturgy just sort of grew naturally in me."

From an early age, Don always loved to help people and working at the funeral home offered him an opportunity to aid and assist others in many ways. At first, Turner delegated various odd jobs around the funeral home, but soon Don's responsibilities grew. During the 1940s, funeral homes generally operated the local ambulance service and were "on-call" 24 hours a day to pick up injured and the dead from accidents and illnesses. Since Don lived in the dorm at the funeral home, he was always ready for ambulance duty. Though they became good friends, it soon became apparent that Turner would be a difficult man to work for – one who wrenched every ounce of work from his employees.

Don remembered his days at the funeral home:

> I lived in the dorm with six other staff, much like fire-fighters on-call. I also learned to be an embalmer from someone who became my great personal and family friend, John William (Bill) Johnson, who was head embalmer, manager and funeral director at the Turner Funeral Home. I watched him closely and gleaned all of the knowledge I could about embalming. Johnson was a great influence on me. I would probably have become a funeral director and an embalmer for the rest of my life had it not been for Turner's disagreeable nature during my college years.

Turner was quite an unusual man; a strict disciplinarian and one of Chattanooga's most colorful businessmen. Turner only completed the sixth grade, so he was not an academic influence in Don's life, yet he was one of the most influential politicians in the city. His personality was often outlandish and he would sometimes characterize those who disagreed with his political ideology as "sick." Some people referred to him as "One-Way" Turner and he would fight fiercely for any friend or relative in heated campaigns for elected positions such as sheriff or police commissioner. As a result, Turner often found himself in awkward positions. He was once arrested for using a sledgehammer to open the door of a polling place when he was denied entrance to watch the counting of ballots.

Turner regularly carried a measuring tape with him in order to harangue his favorite targets. According to a story in the *Chattanooga Times*, he often used the tape measure with great fanfare; measuring people to determine their height in case they should ever need his casket burial services. Turner could be crass at times and had a reputation for "scuffling" with competing ambulance services over victims at accident scenes. However, in sharp contrast to what many considered as character flaws, he also had a softer side. He was known for his skill at consoling widows and for providing funeral services for families with no money. Despite the personal drawbacks with Turner, Don discovered many parallels with the funeral home business and the ministry; they both involve helping and caring for people. He realized he was in a perfect position to help those who were in need.

Don remembered the hard work he performed for Turner during that first year:

> I drove the ambulance to the site of accidents, even though I still did not have my driver's license. In those days, funeral homes provided ambulance services until the cities assumed responsibility for this job. We and several other funeral homes, handled all of the emergency calls for the Chattanooga area. Even though I received a place to live for my work, if I had a call for a car wreck, a shooting or a suicide in the middle of the night, I had to get up and go.

Don recalled a rather unusual story about his experience driving the ambulance, "I remember one time I was attending a large man who had been in a gunfight, He began to fight me while we were in the ambulance. The only thing I could think of to stop his aggressiveness was to stick my index finger in his gunshot wound. That sure settled him down."

In the 1940s and 1950s, funeral directors in the South had a wide political influence in the local community, and Turner was not afraid to use his influence. On one occasion, he had Don attach signs on the sides of an ambulance that stated, "Help Get Rid of a Sick Government-Vote Hugh Abercrombie for County Judge." Memories of that experience have not faded from Don's mind:

> For days, I drove that ambulance around Chattanooga, the siren sounding wherever I went. This was not the only political tactic used at the time; other more nefarious activities included the common practice of distributing liquor on the day of an election. We would go into parts of town where people oftentimes did not know who to vote for, give them a half pint of liquor and suggest the name of our candidate. The practice was nothing to be proud of, but that was county politics back in those times.

Regardless of the undesirable side of the job, Don was prepared to continue with the funeral business. Don received his funeral director's license when he was only 17 years of age. Afterwards he could embalm as well as any in the industry, thanks to Bill Johnson who taught him so well. "Turner encouraged me in the business and even offered Bill Johnson and me a vested interest in the funeral home when he retired, IF we performed exactly as he wanted," Don recalled. However, Don began to realize that his education was of the utmost importance and working toward his college degree would conflict with Turner's grand plan for him.

Don was not, in his own words, a "swift" student, but he knew that he needed to complete his high school education. Don remembered how time consuming and difficult funeral home work could be. "This work was very demanding. I was not only on-call for ambulance runs, but I also had to prepare the cars and the funeral home for services. Because of this hectic schedule, it was difficult to devote the time and attention to my studies." Despite the challenges, Don successfully completed his high school years. However, working at the business and attending college would prove to be an even greater challenge.

CHAPTER TWO

Setting The Course For Life: College
And Seminary Years

After completing high school, Don had his sights set on college. In 1949, immediately after graduating from The Baylor School, most of his high school classmates were going to attend prominent colleges, but Don did not have a clear plan for his future. He could not afford to attend any of the major universities, but his cousin, Bill Evatt, had received a basketball scholarship to Tennessee Tech in Cookeville. Don decided to follow him there and enrolled in the fall of 1949.

Don's major was pre-medical studies during his first year in college. He also made two important discoveries; that life in Cookeville was less exciting than he had expected and that he needed more income to survive. Making ends meet was always a challenge for Don as he pondered his options for living quarters:

He remembered the Spartan living arrangements in those days:

> Few dorms were available on campus, so I shared a room for a brief time in a private house in Cookeville with three other students. The off-campus house only had one bath, which was not an ideal housing arrangement. Fortunately, I discovered Carver Funeral home up the street from where I was staying. I arranged to meet with the owner, Jack Carver, and told him of my funeral home experience in Chattanooga. We made a work agreement, which included arrangements for me to sleep in a spare room next to the casket display. The Carver family lived upstairs at the funeral home, and we hit it off very well. I used a single hot plate to cook my meals, and worked for

Carver in exchange for the room, but received no pay for my work during my first year of college.

Don's college life had become relatively stable, but it was suddenly interrupted one day in the most jarring manner imaginable. He described the tragic day with great clarity:

> At the end of my first year of school at Tennessee Tech in Cookeville, one of my best friends, J.M. Malone and I were driving the 200 miles to Chattanooga when we had a terrible automobile accident. He had just bought a new Nash convertible and was driving us home early one morning through the mountains. The weather and conditions were good, but the two-lane road was treacherous. He wanted to show me how his new car handled and he began driving fast. He lost control of the car as we came out of a narrow curve and the Nash skidded sideways and flipped over several times. The impact threw both of us through the canvas top and on the highway just before the car rolled on all four wheels straight down a steep mountain cliff. When I came to my senses, I realized what had happened. Though I was injured, I mustered enough energy to flag down a motorist who stopped to help. When I looked at my friend, I knew he was seriously hurt. His head was bleeding and blood was coming from his mouth and nose. With the assistance of the motorist, we placed J.M. in the back of his pickup truck, and the man drove him to the nearest hospital in Pikeville, TN. J.M. was carrying some cash on him at the time of the accident, but somehow, it was not on his person when he arrived at the hospital. Later, I determined that the 'Good Samaritan' apparently robbed him before he arrived at the hospital because the police could not find the money that I knew he was carrying at the time.

Due to the seriousness of his injuries, J.M. was taken from the small hospital in Pikeville to the Veterans Hospital in Nashville. Don called Bill Johnson, the Turner Funeral Home manager, who drove an ambulance from Chattanooga to pick up him and take him to the dorm at the funeral home. Don was lucky. He was not seriously injured, but suffered many scrapes and bruises. Sadly, his friend J.M. died at the Veterans Hospital.

The accident caused Don to experience an awakening, and ask why his life had been spared. He reflected on the occurrence many times over the succeeding years.

A funeral was underway when the ambulance arrived at the Turner Funeral Home with Don inside. He was carried on the stretcher from the ambulance, through the morgue and to his dorm room. At one point, Don gave the attendees quite a scare when he suddenly sat up on the stretcher, surprising a number of unsuspecting people who initially thought the ambulance was delivering a corpse.

By his second year at Tennessee Tech, Don located the Whitson Funeral Home, a competitor of Carver's in Cookeville and negotiated a deal to work there for a room with modest pay. He then bid farewell to the Carvers.

Also at this time, Don became involved with St. Michael's Episcopal Church in Cookeville and joined the Canterbury Club, a small organization of young, faithful students that attended the college. This experience would later prove to be very meaningful to Don as he relied on their support and encouragement when he began to pursue the ministry.

Don worked hard to pay for college expenses and spending money. He could not afford a car while in Cookeville, so he had to walk wherever he went, often long distances. He stayed busy balancing his college classes with his work at the funeral home, though the work came natural to him.

Overall, Don was like most young people in college in 1950, high-spirited and self-assured. However, the car crash took some of the spirit out of him. He finished his second year at Tennessee Tech and began to consider a transfer to The University of Tennessee at Chattanooga the following fall semester of 1951. Don wanted to be nearer to his home and friends. Eugene Turner actually wanted Don to help Bill Johnson operate the funeral home if Don would return to the business. He was able to convince Don that he would be better off in familiar surroundings.

After some soul-searching and coaxing from Turner, Don decided to return to Chattanooga following his sophomore year at Tennessee Tech. As an enticement, Turner offered to pay Don's college tuition at UT Chattanooga (UTC) and to let him live in the dorm at the funeral home. Of course, Don realized what this offer meant. He would have to be on-call 24 hours a day and work whenever Turner wanted. Still, it was an offer Don could not turn down.

Don now faced more obstacles because of his extremely busy schedule. UTC was much more challenging academically than Tennessee Tech and Don was responsible for working more hours at the funeral home. As a result, his grades during his junior year suffered. Don was involved in almost every aspect of the funeral business. He learned to play the organ for funeral services, but knew only four hymns. "If you attended two funerals in a row, you would hear the same music each time. I didn't get any extra money, but it did add to my job security," Don shared with a measure of amusement.

In spite of the many distractions in Don's life, he began to sense a call to become more involved with his church in Chattanooga. He had been attending St. Paul's Church in high school and became good friends with The Reverend Joseph Urban, who was an assistant clergyman there. Don stated, "It was because of Joe's interest in me and his encouragement that I pursued the ministry." Don had little time for social events due to his commitment at Turner Funeral Home; however, he did find time to continue his participation in the Canterbury Club at UTC, which is a student organization supported by St. Paul's and other Episcopal Churches in the area. He also joined the Pi Kappa Alpha social fraternity, also known as "Pike," and was elected treasurer during his senior year, a position he took very seriously.

Don's friends and classmates held him in high regard. Don recalled a few zany things he did with some of them during his college days:

> My fraternity at UTC required me to take a 'goat trip,' which is similar to a scavenger hunt. We traveled to Atlanta to search for and bring back of a number of crazy items on our list. Two other pledges and I were required to hitchhike to obtain Atlanta Mayor William Hartsfield's signature on a raw egg at midnight. Fortunately, Eugene Turner understood our plight and placed an automobile at the Chattanooga city limits for us to use to make our trip. We also had to take back a city limit sign and painted the lions bright red on the front lawn of the SAE house at Emory University at midnight, which required a photograph to prove it.

Don remembered another episode where he and two other pledges were blindfolded, driven about 50 miles out of Chattanooga near Benton, TN and left on a dirt road at 1 a.m. to find their way back home. Don was aware that bootlegging still was rife in that area of the country and was afraid of running into some unsavory moonshiners.

To avoid a possibly dangerous situation, the pledges decided to stop by the police station in Benton and inquire as to the location of Higgins Funeral Home. Don knew Helen Higgins as a fellow student at the university, and her father owned the local funeral home in Benton. The idea was to stay overnight at their funeral home. Don recalled:

> When we arrived, and after hearing our story, Mr. Higgins was happy to put us up for the rest of the night. He even participated in our little college adventure by calling our fraternity the next morning and making up a story that we had fallen off a mountain in East Tennessee. He did not tell our fraternity brothers we were killed, exactly, but his convincing story led them to believe we were dead or seriously injured. The news of our demise traveled quickly around the campus.

Due to Mr. Higgins' call, the Pikes immediately called an emergency fraternity meeting, dismissed classes for the day and began to ponder their fate. In the meantime, Mr. Higgins kindly drove Don and his two pledge brothers from Benton to the Pike House in Chattanooga. When their fraternity brothers witnessed their arrival on the campus, they beat them severely with fraternity paddles for posing such a stunt.

Nearing the end of his senior year at UTC, Don recalled Turner's promise to give him a part interest in the funeral business. While the offer was tempting, Don had his doubts. Turner's dubious reputation in the political arena was a concern. For example, he demanded that Don register to vote in the state Congressional election in 1950, though he still had not reached legal voting age. Regardless of this legal obstacle, Turner made arrangements for Don to register and vote. Turner's overly zealous appetite for politics put a negative cast on their partnership. Though Don enjoyed working in the funeral business, he could not envision himself becoming increasingly involved in the politics and questionable deals, which had become such an integral part of Eugene Turner's life. The funeral director position began to lose much of its appeal, consequently Don decided that it was time to consider other options as he planned for his future. The lessons he learned from Turner opened his eyes to the world around him as Don began his journey to become a positive influence on the lives of others.

From an early age, Don enjoyed helping people. While working at the funeral homes, he saw the need to minister to those in mourning. He learned from Father Urban that people had a need for ministry throughout their lives, not just during a family member's death. Don began to learn more about becoming a priest from Father Urban and discovered he would have to devote three additional years of graduate study. The thought of three more years in a seminary plus an internship was not what he had in mind. However, Don's visits with fellow members of the Canterbury Club at UTC, had a major effect in his decision to follow a spiritual calling. His friends in this club of Episcopal students listened and encouraged his early aspirations.

Don's final decision to enter the ministry came after a sensitive meeting about his future with Eugene Turner. Don discovered Turner's callousness during the meeting when he said to Don, "You're not going anywhere. You prepared for this funeral business and you can't change your mind now." Don was ordered to get his clothes and leave if he would not accept Turner's offer of the funeral business. Given this ultimatum, Don left Turner and his aggressive tactics and returned to Father Urban – his course set for the ministry.

SEMINARY YEARS: HEARING THE CALL

After Don's graduation from UTC, Joe Urban and the people at St. Paul's Church elected to shepherd Don in his priestly journey. Their support helped him in his decision to become a priest. The recent graduate always enjoyed investing himself in others' lives and refined an early ability to connect with people. Meanwhile, his interest in matters and service of the faith unfolded in greater intensity.

Almost everyone Don knew who entered the Episcopal priesthood had attended The University of the South at Sewanee, near Chattanooga. However, The Reverend John Vander Horst, who was then Rector at St. Paul's Church, advised him against attending Sewanee. Vander Horst instead directed Don to attend the Berkeley Divinity School at Yale. Berkeley Divinity School at Yale is an Episcopal seminary and often confused with Yale Divinity School, a non-denominational institution. Though students from both seminaries often attend services and certain classes together, they remain two distinct institutions.

After a measure of hesitation and contemplation, Don made the necessary application. The application process involved five or six intensive interviews followed by a great deal of paperwork and a psychological exam. Don was concerned whether he could make the grades at Berkeley, but Father Urban insisted that he try since Urban's uncle, The Very Reverend Percy Linwood Urban, served as dean at the college. After obtaining The Rev. Vander Horst's blessing, and with the support of Bishop Barth and Father Urban, Don was accepted to Berkeley and began perhaps the most important journey of his life. In September 1953,

Don became the first Tennessean to study for the Episcopal priesthood at Berkeley Divinity School at Yale.

Don remembered how the experience at Yale changed his life:

> I learned a lot about people in my seminary studies. I also examined and began to understand why I believed in certain things. In some cases, they tear down your preconceived notions and perspectives, and you are left to reconstruct your thoughts. It is pretty rough on some people who come in with definite ideas and soon find themselves changed, but I thoroughly enjoyed seminary. I liked the people of New Haven, CT. and even the cold winters. I would not take anything for my days in the seminary.

Don came to know most of the faculty members very well since they attended small seminary classes. Professor Howard Dunn taught homiletics (the art of preaching), which made a lasting impression on Don throughout his ministry. His most difficult subject was Greek, which was required of every divinity student, so he could read and understand original text of the New Testament.

The first year in the community of New Haven was a revelation for Don, who was not fully accustomed to northern culture. Typical of most college students, Don was always trying to find extra jobs to pay for school expenses. He waited on tables at the school refectory to make ends meet and worked part-time for Thelma and Morris Widder. They often invited Don into their home where he learned many of their Jewish customs.

The Widders were in the new and used clothing business. Thelma was from Atlanta, so her familiarity with the South provided them with common ground. Don often coordinated the sale of used clothing belonging to Yale students, which the Widders bought for resale, so the "Yalies" could have extra spending money. Often, Yale students would purchase expensive clothing from Brooks Brothers or other upscale clothiers in New York City and charge the clothes to their parents. If they needed money for a date or the weekend, the students would then sell their clothes to the Widders for cash. The couple also made and sold cassocks and vestments (religious robes) to the seminary students. "I became their clothing representative and sold tailor-made vestments to the Berkeley students. In return, I received my own vestments when I needed them at no cost."

The Widders regularly undersold their competitors, thereby cornering a good share of the business from the seminary. Additionally, Morris was an accomplished musician and former concertmaster for the Boston Symphony. He encouraged the love of fine music in Don and took him to several classical concerts in New York City. Morris Widder's son, a paratrooper, was killed in France during World War II, so his absence made the Widders' relationship with Don more special. They took Don in as a member of their own family. This "family" relationship was important to Don during the second and third years in seminary.

During the summers, Don returned home to work at St. Paul's Church in Chattanooga. There, he found interest in the outreach program, "*In As Much Mission*," that served a neglected Chattanooga neighborhood. The complex that housed the mission contained a chapel for services, a library, a room to study and exercise and a clinic for neighborhood people to receive medical help. The mission of St. Paul's was his first taste of ministry in an urban setting. There, he first participated in developing programs for youth, including overnight camping experiences on Lake Ocoee near Cleveland, TN. He even worked two summer vacations for the registrar of the courthouse recording deeds. It was just another way to earn money for school. Don worked one last time for Eugene Turner selling burial insurance, but as that summer ended so did the relationship with Turner because he failed to pay Don the commissions he had earned.

In 1954, his second year at Berkeley, Art Archer, who was a friend and was one year ahead of Don in school, was working as a student assistant at St. Peter's Episcopal Church in Milford, CT., which was just south of New Haven. When Art graduated, he asked Don to take his old job at the church.

Don recalled the experience:

> I took the job and was excited about the opportunity because I liked the people, and they became fascinated with 'the kid from Tennessee.' The people at St. Peter's Church were very good to me and liked my Southern accent. So much so that when I finished seminary, they asked if I would assume a position as a full-time assistant. As it turned out, Rev. Vander Horst had other ideas for me.

Transportation was a problem for Don in the early years at seminary. When he began working at St. Peter's in Milford, he needed a vehicle for the 40-mile round-trip to New Haven. He remembered acquiring his first car:

I did not have much money and had to make it stretch a
long way. I had saved a little money and spotted an ad in
the local newspaper. A professor at Yale had a four-door,
1941 Dodge, which had been resting on blocks for the
duration of World War II. It was in good shape with very
few miles and was a "fluid-drive" automobile – one of the
first of its kind that did not require manual shifting.

Don bought the old car for $150 and drove it back and forth to St.
Peter's in Milford. His parents, knowing his plight and wanting to help
with his transportation, surprised Don with a sporty 1956 Dodge when
they came to New Haven for his graduation. However, Don felt very self-
conscious about the new car and did not accept it. He had grown close to
his old '41 Dodge and wanted to keep it. His parents were a bit dismayed,
but respected their son's wishes.

Don wondered where he would eventually be placed after seminary
and John Vander Horst played a key role in that decision. He had been
Don's minister when he attended Yale Seminary and was named Bishop
Coadjutor of Tennessee in 1955. He and Don had developed a special
relationship, exchanging letters often about more specific directions to
take regarding ministerial work. When Don graduated from Berkeley in
1956, he made a request to Bishop Vander Horst that he would like to
be sent to a larger town instead of a small rural Tennessee community.
Don recalled, "I felt that due to my experience with *In As Much Mission* in
Chattanooga, that he would certainly grant this request." Much to Don's
surprise the bishop's written response was brief and to the point:

> Dear Mowery,
> You will be placed where the Lord and I see fit.
> Sincerely,
> + John Tennessee

Don reflected on the bishop's response:

> When I read that note, I knew right away that I had little
> choice in the matter and realized that I may not have as
> much 'pull' as I thought. When I mentioned I was offered
> the assistant position at St. Peter's Church to Bishop
> Vander Horst, he made another all too familiar response,
> 'Absolutely not! You've been trained to work in the vine-
> yard of Tennessee, not in Connecticut, so that's where

you're going.' As a result, Bishop Vander Horst gave me my first assignment – St. Andrew's Episcopal Church in Nashville, TN.

After graduation from Berkeley at Yale, Don was ordained as a deacon at St. Paul's Church in Chattanooga on Sunday, July 1, 1956. This was another step on his path to the priesthood. The dean of Berkeley Divinity School, the Very Reverend Percy Linwood Urban, delivered the ordination sermon. Bishop Vander Horst, The Reverend Joseph Urban of St. Timothy's Church, Signal Mountain and The Reverend John Bonner, rector of St. Paul's Church all made stirring presentations that. The Reverend George Andrews Fox, rector of Christ Church, was master of ceremonies for the ordination. The ceremony included a full choir and was broadcast on the radio. The following Wednesday, Don was on his way to Nashville to greet the members St. Andrew's, his first congregation. Don was ordained as a deacon along with James Holt Newsom, who was assigned to Trinity Episcopal Church in Winchester, TN. After serving as a deacon for a year and completing other assignments, Don could then be ordained as a priest.

DON, AGE 5   DON, AGE 17 AT
                                  BAYLOR

DON AND PARENTS, MYRTLE AND CLARENCE, AT BAYLOR
GRADUATION, 1949

CHAPTER THREE

St. Andrew's: The Church With The Red Doors

On July 4th, 1956, Don arrived in Nashville to lead his new church. As a Mission Church, St. Andrew's had never attained full financial self-sufficiency. Interestingly, it had remained in a type of dependent status for about 75 years. As Bishop Vander Horst wrote in a letter to Don, "It is a small mission church with a very nice edifice in a neighborhood that has never been given a fair shake. However, it must become self-sufficient right away, so you have to get in there and work hard." The objective for Don was then set.

St. Andrew's Church had only about 30 active members when Don arrived and had never had a full-time minister in its entire 75-year history. Bishop Vander Horst's challenge resonated with Don, "You wanted a city church; well, you have it. You must bring St. Andrew's to Parish Church status; fully self-supporting in one year, or it will have to be closed." Upon his arrival, Don rose to the challenge and provided the small congregation with exactly what it needed. He began by establishing close relationships with all of the members and remained at St. Andrew's Church for the next seven years.

St. Andrew's Church was founded in 1889 as a mission of Christ Episcopal Church in Nashville. Services were held in the railroad depot on Charlotte Pike until a more permanent church was built at the corner of 47th and Georgia Avenues in 1892. That building was demolished by a tornado and its replacement was subsequently destroyed by lightning. A new building was consecrated in 1902, on the corner of 49th and Michigan Avenues. In 1908, The Reverend J. F. McCloud became the first vicar and served until 1918, succeeded by various clergy from Christ Church until he returned in 1924. Three years later, he once again moved the congregation to 46th and Park Avenues with the chapel itself transported on rollers. In 1933, a new church building made of stone was begun and the old church became the parish house. When Father McCloud died in 1946, Christ Church presented St. Andrew's with a used pipe organ in his memory. The Reverend Frank E. Walker, who became vicar of St. Andrew's in 1949, was responsible for converting the old frame of a church annex into a modern parish house.

St. Andrew's was situated in a modest neighborhood and was constructed with beautiful decorative stone. The building was in good shape structurally, but needed substantial improvements. Several devoted supporters such as Mr. and Mrs. Tom Joy, who owned Joy's Flower Shop in Nashville, began to lend their time, energy and money to assist in beautifying the property. Though they were not members, the Joys graciously donated plants and volunteered their services. Their efforts improved the appearance of the small urban church tremendously. The Horton and Wendell Smith families refurbished the inside of the building with a deep cleaning and fresh paint. It was decided at that time to paint the front doors red. By tradition, a church that is named for a martyr may have red doors, symbolizing martyrdom. "We purposely painted the front doors fire engine red, so people would immediately recognize our church," Don recalled. The "church with the red doors" soon became known as a place where people could find assistance in many forms.

Don not only helped build the inner workings of St. Andrew's, but found himself working with youth on a large scale. As Don spent time getting to know the people in the area, he helped with coaching duties for two high school football teams and created a boxing club. Don was remarkable at creating new marketing ideas. First, he decided to keep the church doors unlocked 24 hours a day. He recalled other ideas to promote the church, "I had pencils made to distribute, which helped market the church. I handed them out at schools, hospitals and other places I visited. The inscription read, '*St. Andrew's Episcopal Church — The Church with the red doors — that are never locked.*' You couldn't leave the doors of a city church open today though." The promotion was a big hit and helped spread the word about the little church with the big message.

Father Don recalled a story about the unlocked doors of the church:

> We were located near a main highway and began to have a couple of break-ins because people could just walk in the front door. I thought the best way to monitor this was to have a microphone installed in the church with a speaker in my office. When I was there, I could turn on the system and hear anyone who might be in the sanctuary.

One day, I was in my office when I heard the front door open and someone entered the sanctuary. I then heard coins hitting the floor and realized that the offering box had been opened. When I went to investigate, a man was running out of the front door. I immediately chased him down Park Avenue, caught him – literally – by the seat of his pants and took him back to the church. I took him into my office, called the police and awaited their arrival. The man told me he had just gotten out of prison the day before and just wanted money. This somewhat humorous and yet sad story represents only one of many such accounts of the troubled souls with whom I came into contact.

Don has never forgotten the generosity of the members of his first church, including Eddie Horton, Bill and his sister Pam Hickman, the Elmer Allen family, Clyde and Jim Wyatt, the Rochelle family, the Harry Pavey family, the Bishop and Smith families, the Storey family and the "matriarch" of the church Ms. Blanche Graves, among others. Their mutual efforts helped substantially in shaping the future of St. Andrew's.

Ministering to youth came naturally to Don. He was always finding new ways to reach the younger generation. One Sunday, in September 1956, he opted to include some pearls of wisdom, sharing his philosophy of young people in the St. Andrew's church bulletin:

Thinking that three hours at a movie are harmless for the child, but two hours of church and church school is too much for his nervous system, is irrational thinking. Letting them listen to several hours of radio and television thrillers with no time for a short prayer and a few Bible verses is unbalanced.

Don recalled, "Since I had no assistant, I was basically on my own. We depended on the bishop for financial support. To become an independent parish, you have to educate people how to manage their money, so they will give to support the church. That is one thing I was ordained to do, and I enjoyed it very much."

There was no rectory (clergy residence) at the church, so Don lived in a small apartment nearby for which he paid $75 per month from his modest $300 per month stipend. He kept busy renovating the church and creating a network of future members, while changing the hearts of all with whom he came in contact. Don remembered vividly:

> We had very few resources to build this congregation – not even a typewriter. One day, a man appeared at the church door from the Good Luck Margarine Company with an offer. If my congregation used Good Luck Margarine and sent in the labels from the packages, the company would donate something to the church. From this campaign, we received a new typewriter. I felt fortunate to be blessed with these and many other opportunities that helped in giving St. Andrew's new life.

On January 18, 1957, six months after Don arrived to lead St. Andrew's Church, he was ordained as an Episcopal priest. This was the first ordination within the small mission church. A hometown delegation of 20 came from Chattanooga for the occasion, and the choir that sang for the ordination was composed of members from Don's fraternity, Pi Kappa Alpha at Vanderbilt.

Each day began at 7 a.m. with the celebration of Spiritual Communion at St. Andrew's and ended with evening prayer. Bishop Vander Horst's wish that the church would become Anglo-Catholic in orientation was being realized. Upon Father Don's priesthood ordination, Bishop Theodore N. Barth, the Bishop of Tennessee, remarked that Don exhibited "great spiritual perception and depth," and that he was "one who will be exceedingly able to lead this next generation spiritually." The Reverend Raymond T. Ferris, rector of Christ Church in Nashville, preached the ordination sermon. He challenged Don to "live in that other world where your priesthood has its most prominent part, in order that, through you, God may bless His people." Don's mentor, Bishop Vander Horst, presented Don for ordination. Because of Father Don's creative and natural networking ability, the congregation at St. Andrew's grew rapidly during his first year as priest.

The church facility was not the only thing in need of an upgrade. Don's 1941 Dodge was showing obvious signs of wear. Don recalled, "I liked my old car and continued to drive it until I realized some of my parishioners were embarrassed for me to arrive for a visit at their house in the old car. One of them told me it was time to buy another car." Motivated by this comment, Don obtained a no-interest loan and purchased his first new car. He then gave his beloved old Dodge to a church family who had no personal means of transportation.

Father Don quickly became involved with many of the key people in the Nashville community. He became friends with the warden of the state penitentiary, who was a member of the Episcopal Church. Since St. Andrew's Church was in the general vicinity of the state penitentiary, the warden asked Father Don to work with a group of older prisoners who needed someone with whom to talk and confide. Don agreed and counseled the inmates who spent most of their days tending flower gardens and were not a flight risk. In another very different program, Don began to visit teenagers at the State Training School for Boys at Jordonia, just north of Nashville. These boys were very difficult to control, and many were placed in "dark" isolation cells; however, they too needed someone with whom to communicate.

The late 1950s was a racially tense time in the South, and Nashville experienced its share of unrest. One of the neighborhoods near St. Andrew's was a considerably rough area. "Eddie," one of the "tough guys" in the neighborhood, had a reputation at Cohen High School for being under the influence of drugs or alcohol at school, so his friends took care of him as he changed classes throughout the day. Interestingly, Don and Eddie had become friends through Don's ministry. One afternoon, Eddie was hanging around the front of a local drug store near St. Andrew's Church when he saw an African-American woman approach the front door. After making an inappropriate remark to the woman, she went to her nearby housing project, returned with a gun and shot Eddie between the eyes in front of the drugstore. He was immediately rushed to Baptist Hospital by ambulance.

Don recalled seeing a crowd gathering at the drug store and realized something was wrong. After hearing about the tragedy, he rushed to the hospital and found hundreds of kids from Cohn High School standing around the building. Don remembered telling the doctor at the hospital, "We were probably going to have a racial outbreak because an African-American woman just killed a white boy."

After Nashville radio and television broadcast the news of Eddie's death, a large crowd of white kids began to gather at the hospital. Don saw the need for ministry and asked if the hospital could open its chapel to accommodate the kids, but surprisingly his request was denied because the floors had just been cleaned. If there was ever a time people needed the chapel, it was now. Because of the hospital's lack of cooperation, Don opened St. Andrew's to these distraught students and called some of his church members to prepare food for them. Don kept the church open for them to meet and grieve for the next three days.

This became a very tense situation, as many of the white kids went to the African-American neighborhood to seek revenge.

Father Don recalled after the incident:

> FBI agents interviewed me because I knew what was going on in the neighborhood. They commended us and said that we probably prevented a race riot by opening the church to these young people. There may have been serious trouble if the kids were left in the streets. We kept the kids together and continued ministering to them during Eddie's funeral. It was very tense for a long time afterward.

Don soon had little difficulty gathering volunteers to help the church. The congregation of St. Andrew's was invaluable, raising much-needed money from various events and volunteering for sponsored functions. With the help of these core members, many new people were baptized and confirmed within a short period of time after Father Don's arrival, ultimately growing to scores of new members within a couple of years. Additionally, several members of St. Andrew's would take children who had no family into their homes during Thanksgiving and Christmas holidays. Many of them came from Tennessee Preparatory School, the state's largest school for neglected and dependent children. They also reached out to the kids in Vanderbilt Hospital's Polio Ward. Don arranged for the members to pick them up and spend time in their homes during the holidays.

Don and members of his congregation planned various events in order to promote the church within the Nashville community:

> In order to boost St. Andrew's image in the area, several of the church members agreed to have a bazaar. We blocked off the street in front of the church for the visitors to have pony rides, cakewalks and other activities. I had an idea of marking the event in a rather unconventional way by printing brightly colored paper fliers and distributing them prior to the event from an airplane owned by a friend of mine who was a pilot. Hundreds of the announcements were tossed out of the plane over Nashville, while people chased them as they fluttered to the ground. We sure attracted a lot of attention.

Fortunately, there were no complaints about the aerial stunt and the church event was a huge success. Interestingly, Don began flying lessons while in Nashville, but quit the program after two of his instructors were killed in separate flying accidents.

The bazaar gave Don a great opportunity to meet many new people and network within the city. He began to expand his reach into the community by the work he started at two local high schools. Cohn High School was close to the church, and Don began to know the young people by attending their football games. He emphasized getting kids involved in sports and keeping them active and off of the streets. Don also started softball and boxing teams at St. Andrew's, and some of his kids did very well in the Golden Gloves competition, advancing to the national finals in Chicago. The softball team consisted of church and neighborhood high school youths and was coached by a member of St. Andrew's, Bill McCarthy. Bill also served as general manager and coach of the Nashville professional baseball team known as the Nashville Volunteers.

Don also became friends with Frank Mueller, the chief of the Nashville Police Department and created a program that developed a better relationship between the police and the young people in the streets. Teens were encouraged to meet police officers at designated points in the neighborhoods. Soon the officers began to know many of the teenagers by name. Don recalled his experience with the city's youth:

> Mayor Ben West asked me to be the police chaplain on a part-time basis, so we could help expand our efforts with young people and provide spiritual support for the police officers. Prior to this program, the chaplain position was only part-time and not an active position. They gave me a chaplain's badge and I rode with the officers, talking with them about their concerns. I thought it would be a positive thing for the community if the police officers and the young people knew each other better.

Chief Mueller also asked Don to conduct devotionals and discuss important issues with the police officers on Saturday nights before each shift change. Other ministers attended and represented police officers of different faiths. There was an initial concern of whether the officers would attend, but it turned out to be a very popular and beneficial program. They appreciated the devotionals because they allowed police officers to attend them between duty shifts. Moreover, many police officers found themselves on duty Sundays, which prevented them from being able to attend church services.

Mayor West then offered Father Don the police chaplain position on a full-time basis, thinking it would be of great value to the police officers and their families. "I was keenly interested in the job, but had to discuss this with Bishop Vander Horst." Though the bishop liked the idea of having one of his clergy doing this work full-time in the city of Nashville, other plans were in store for Father Don.

Meanwhile, Don's work with youth continued in earnest. Some of the families did not have automobiles at that time, keeping many of them from attending ballgames. Don recollected how they found a solution to this problem:

> Some church members and close friends of mine, Bill and Frances Hickman along with many other supporters, helped us acquire a new 54-passenger bus. To advertise our youth outreach program, we painted, *St. Andrew's Episcopal Church – 46th and Park Ave., The Church With the Red Doors That Are Never Locked'* on the side with our address and phone number.

On the rear door, Don had painted "Drive Carefully, You Might Hit an Episcopalian." The bus drew a lot of attention, but it was also great to have a means to transport people to and from various events. Church members installed a loudspeaker system under the hood of the bus, so that the driver could talk to people or the cheerleaders could cheer to crowds as they rode along. They also used the bus in the Christmas parade and played Christmas carols along the route.

Cohn High often played Hume-Fogg High School, which was a vocational school primarily for inner-city kids who had no particular affinity for college. Hume-Fogg lacked many of the amenities other schools enjoyed. The team practiced at Centennial Park downtown because they had no football field of their own and traveled to their games in a big truck that their coach, Hank Miller, drove. Don revealed, "I became good friends with Coach Miller. He told me of his experiences with some of the boys on the team who did not have much and knew very little about the rules of football. Seeing their need, I told the coach he could use our bus to transport his team to Centennial Park."

Father Don was so successful in his youth work in Nashville that he soon outgrew the facilities at St.Andrew's. Eventually, the church had to purchase an adjacent house that was situated behind the parish house in order to expand their youth programs. Don described his overall experiences at St. Andrew's as "phenomenal." The membership grew to a size that required four services on Sunday (7:30 a.m., 9:00 a.m., 11:00 a.m. and 7:30 p.m.), along with other activities. The additional Sunday church services left only 45 minutes for Sunday school, so we added a Saturday bible school in order to provide young people with sufficient training. Don believed that Christian education was very important and the Saturday class became popular with the congregation.

As the church grew, it began to receive donations from many people who saw what Don and his congregation was doing and wanted to help. One such example was when a non-member donated Eucharistic vestments for the church. They were expensive and would have been beyond the reach of the small church had it not been for the benevolence of this person. Don grew personally and spiritually from the efforts of his parishioners, while he built his youth program:

> Parishioners often donated to our church youth programs. We took the young people on trips to places such as Old Hickory Lake just outside of Nashville. A couple, who were members of Christ Church, generously offered the use of their cabin and boat located on the lake for our program. We began using it regularly as an outdoor religious retreat for the young people at St. Andrew's Church.

During this time, Don met Tony Castile, an eighth grader who played football at Hume-Fogg High School. Tony lived at the Monroe-Harding Children's Home, an established orphanage associated with the Presbyterian Church. Tony was taken away from his mother at an early age and was 14 when he and Don met. Don remembered, "Tony was very likable, but very few people wanted to adopt an older boy. He had great potential, and I wanted to make sure he stayed on the right path in life." Tony considered Don as a father figure, a relationship that would soon prove to be a reality in the months ahead. Even though Don was not married, officials at the Monroe-Harding Children's Home arranged for Don to be his legal guardian.

Don ministered to people of all ages and occupations in order to grow his church, but continued to focus on young people because of their special needs. He received credit for bringing many new young people to St. Andrew's and with starting several essential Christian youth development programs. He felt compelled to help the youth of Nashville whenever and in whatever manner possible. This initiative would prove true wherever Don went.

When Bishop Vander Horst discovered what Don and the people at St. Andrew's had accomplished, he wrote to Don saying, "I'd like for you to do the same thing in Memphis and serve on the staff of St. Mary's Cathedral." In response to the Bishop's request, Don traveled to Memphis in December 1962 and met with the board of Youth Service, a youth agency that had been operating in the city since the 1920s. He instantly liked St. Mary's, what he saw of the community and the Youth Service agency. Don was also pleased that the bishop had such faith in his abilities and that he wanted him to be on the staff of St. Mary's Cathedral. After some deliberation, Don accepted the challenge and began plans to relocate to Memphis.

Don was interested in the Youth Service position in Memphis, but had to consider Tony in his decision. After meetings with officials at Monroe-Harding Children's Home, Don officially adopted Tony and brought him to Memphis. Tony graduated from Central High School and joined the Army immediately after his high school graduation. He served two tours of duty in Vietnam and was awarded a Bronze Star with "V" for heroism. While on a search and destroy mission as a radio -telephone operator, his unit encountered hostile fire. Tony quickly moved to a position and called for a barrage of artillery fire which quickly neutralized the Viet Cong. He then participated in a sweep of the camp to ensure the enemy's total withdrawl. After military service, Tony moved to Houston and began working for Holiday Inns. He and his wife Margaret have one daughter, Heather Mowery Ashford and a grand daughter, Holland Mae.

Don's accomplishments at St. Andrew's were far reaching. The church achieved full parish status in January 1960 due to his ability to raise the membership and make the church financially sound. Father Don left St. Andrew's in good hands in 1963, along with a great legacy of helping others. The Reverend Edwin L. Connelly, formerly of Dallas, took over in 1964, and on the Feast of the Ascension of that year, celebrated his first service as Rector. Due to their growth and success, the parish left its West Nashville home of 75 years and relocated to the former Robert Cheek Mansion in the Green Hills area. On August 27, 1965, with "The Litany of Saints" being sung in procession, the congregation held their first service under Reverend Connelly's leadership in their new church building.

Upon his departure from Nashville, Don praised St. Andrew's members by thanking them for joining in helping him in his work with young people. Just prior to his departure, St. Andrew's senior warden, Hugh L. Johnson, described Father Mowery as a "virtual genius" in youth work and said, "We hate to lose him, but we're happy to see an opportunity develop for him to devote full-time to working with youngsters."

ST. ANDREWS CHURCH, 46TH AND PARK, NASHVILLE, TN, 1958

DON ORDAINED AS DEACON AT ST. PAUL'S CHURCH
IN CHATTANOOGA, TN. (L TO R), REVEREND DONALD
MOWERY, THE RIGHT REVEREND PERCY URBAN,
REVEREND JAMES HOLT NEWSOM, BISHOP JOHN
VANDER HORST, 1956

DON RECEIVING ORDINATION, JAN. 18, 1957

THE REV. DONALD MOWERY ORDINATION AS PRIEST,
ST. ANDREW'S CHURCH, NASHVILLE, TN,
JAN. 18, 1957

FATHER MOWERY AND HIS MOTHER, MYRTLE
AT ST. ANDREWS

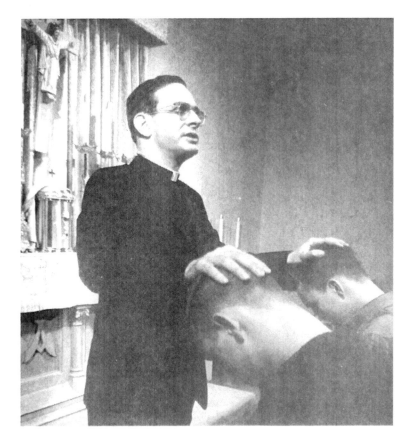

FATHER MOWERY IN PRAYER AT THE ALTAR AT ST. ANDREWS

SUNDAY SERVICE AT ST. ANDREWS CHURCH,
NASHVILLE, TN

FATHER MOWERY COUNSELING YOUNG PEOPLE IN HIS
OFFICE AT ST. ANDREWS

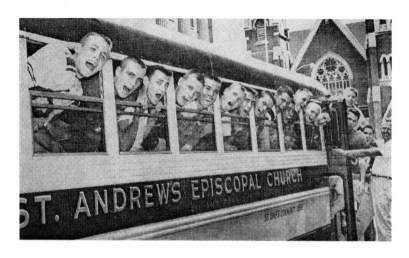

ST. ANDREWS CHURCH BUS TRANSPORTING HUME-FOGG
FOOTBALL TEAM TO A GAME
(PHOTO BY THE NASHVILLE TENNESSEAN)

HUME-FOGG FOOTBALL PLAYERS RALPH LANGFORD AND
DAVID GILL PRESENTING AWARD TO FATHER MOWERY

ST. ANDREWS BASEBALL TEAM WITH
COACH BILL McCARTHY, 1959

TONY MOWERY, FATHER DON'S ADOPTED SON

CHAPTER FOUR

Youth Service, Memphis: A Brief History

During the early part of the 20th century, the Episcopal Church was shaped in part by the Social Gospel Movement and by a revived sense of being a national church in the Anglican tradition. A determined force formed the backbone of the church's urban outreach programs by providing health care, education and economic assistance to the disabled and disadvantaged. These activities made the Episcopal Church a major leader in the movement. Through its missionary work, the church saw it as its responsibility to spread not only the riches of American society, but also the well-esteemed Anglican tradition.

Highly prominent Episcopalians, such as industrialist Henry Ford and banker J.P. Morgan, played vital roles in shaping a distinctive upper-class culture, especially with emerging social issues arising from industrialism. They also had an interest in preserving the arts and history for future generations. These wealthy philanthropists propelled the Episcopal Church into a position of national importance and played a major role in the country's cultural transformation. Another mark of their influence is the fact that historically, 25 percent of all presidents of the United States have been Episcopalians.

One particular youth assistance organization was established in New York City in 1909 by Trinity Episcopal Church, Wall Street to assist needy families and unwed mothers. Operating as the Church Mission of Help (CMH), this urban outreach mission formed branches in other parts of the country including Nashville, Knoxville, Chattanooga and Memphis. The Women of Calvary Episcopal Church and St. Mary's Cathedral formed the Memphis branch of the CMH in 1922. Official records reveal that the Tennessee branches of the CMH were part of the larger National Council of the Church Mission of Help in New York City. This organization had

financial ties with the Memphis Community Chest, a charitable organization, which is now known as United Way. Its principal initial work
was to help young, unmarried mothers find pre- and post-natal care for
their babies, as well as to assist them in finding jobs and housing. Ms.
Agnes Grabau, a social worker from Trinity Church Wall Street, served
as the executive secretary of the Memphis agency for the lengthy time
extending from 1925 to 1961. She was born in Connecticut and was a
formally trained social worker before coming to Tennessee. The program
in Memphis was the only one of the four CME Branches in Tennessee that
survived long-term in the state.

The executive committee of the CMH believed that Christian social
services should not be confined to organizations of the Episcopal Church,
but that the church should foster, through spiritual influence, the work of
other welfare agencies. The committee believed the CMH was not merely
an Episcopal Church mission, but a provider of vital social services to all,
regardless of creed.

During the first years of the CMH in Memphis, five Episcopal Churches
contributed to its growth. They included Calvary Church, Grace Church,
Holy Trinity Church, St. Mary's Cathedral, St. Luke's Church and St.
John's Church. Other Episcopal churches in Shelby County joined the
work of the CMH during the period of the 1930s through the 1960s:
Good Shepherd Church, St. George's Church, St. Andrew's Church, All
Saints Church, St. Anne's Church, Emmanuel Church, Holy Communion
Church, St. Elisabeth's Church, Christ Church, St. Paul's Church, St.
James' Church, Otey Chapel and Grace St. Luke's Church.

The Church Mission of Help normally held its meetings in the crypt
of St. Mary's Cathedral on Poplar Ave., but also convened meetings at the
YWCA Building on Monroe Ave. A rotating system composed of board
members serving three-year terms, included not only clergymen, but also
lay people of the church.

The organization regularly sponsored conferences and educational programs in Memphis for the promotion of Christian social work. Organizers
and staff were confident that the vital work with youth performed by
this organization would demonstrate the value of the program and serve
as an example of social service work throughout the diocese. According
to the bylaws of the organization, members of the CMH had to be com-
municants of the Episcopal Church, though funds were accepted from
contributors regardless of their religious affiliation. Incorporation allowed
the organization to operate county-wide under a more formal structure.
A variety of charitable organizations became associated with the CMH,
including Church Home, Bethany Training Home for Girls, St. Mary's

Daughters of the King, Ella Oliver Refuge Home and the Hoffman Youth Home for African-American children.

Volunteer workers from the churches seemed to be plentiful and were praised for the progress they made to address the problems facing young girls in the Memphis community. The CMH also accepted girls from other social and charitable agencies offering them help according to their available resources. Services provided by the CMH included temporary housing for girls and unwed mothers, guardianship of babies, care for and prevention of illegitimate children, recreational activities and facilities, referral services and transportation. CMH referred many children to the local Children's Bureau. Branch organizations that supported the CMH included the Mother Goose Club and the Women's Auxiliary of the Episcopal Church.

The social philosophies that formed the basis of these organizations have been described in numerous ways. However, Memphis Juvenile Court Judge Camille Kelly, the first female Juvenile Court Judge in the South, shared her belief that impressions made upon a child's mind were lasting and that personality was most important in dealing with children. Presently, the Urban Child Institute in Memphis, headed by Gene Cashman, with which Father Don Mowery has been associated since his retirement from Youth Service, delves into these very trenchant issues.

As the success of CMH increased, so did the amount of interest in the agency from other groups in various Episcopal parishes and among the general public. Auxiliary clubs within the Episcopal Church began to volunteer more of their time and services to join the cause of helping female youths in Memphis. The CMH began to assume greater responsibility for the growing problems affecting Memphis youth, often stepping in to handle situations otherwise ignored. The members of CMH were relentlessly engaged in fundraising efforts. Unfortunately, these efforts proved to be difficult during the austere years of the Depression. With reduced funding, the CMH faced the risk of not being able to pay staff members or provide services to the community. When a deficit occurred, the agency made the decision to appeal to the Community Fund, for additional funding. The Community Fund eventually provided up to three-fourths of the CMH annual budget, but had no control over its internal affairs or any of the other agencies it supported.

After the end of World War II, the CMH began working closely with other youth agencies, such as the Boy Scouts, Girl Scouts, YWCA and the Youth Service League. The organization reached out to public and private schools for financial help and volunteer support. In November 1946, the board considered a name change for the CMH; the purpose was to promote more publicity for the organization. The board of the CMH officially changed its name to Youth Service in Memphis, Inc. in December 1947. With the name change, the board of Youth Service chartered a new course and expanded its program to assume a greater role in the lives of young people in the Memphis community.

The value of these extended programs was evident after the first year and the Community Chest agreed to supplement funding to the agency. The program proved to be invaluable to those whom it served and won the full support and additional funding from the Community Chest for the following year. Youth Service had the opportunity to expand its social services at a modest increase in expenses if it offered a vocational counseling program. Over the years, the new vocational counseling initiative matured into a dynamic and formal youth assistance program.

Led by The Rev. (Dean) William Sanders of St. Mary's Cathedral, the Board of Directors of Youth Service decided in 1956 to expand beyond the confines of a few local neighborhoods to serve the entire Memphis community. Until then, Youth Service had primarily handled cases involving unmarried white mothers, but developed a new initiative to include troubled boys (in addition to girls) and African-Americans (in addition to whites) by the late 1950s.

Public relations efforts were an ongoing challenge for Youth Service. Many people within the Episcopal Church, as well as the general citizenry, were not aware of its beneficial youth social work. Therefore, an advisory committee specifically designated to increase publicity was formed to promote the activities of Youth Service.

Members of the Episcopal Church in Memphis believed that important areas of life were becoming too secularized, particularly in the field of education. They believed they had a responsibility to educate people to the message of Christ. Dean Sanders commented:

> Too often, the field of social work has tended to be divorced from the religious motivations and convictions that were its original source and power. At Youth Service, we not only serve and guide boys and girls in times of deep need, but we also bring the insights and attitudes of Christ into the entire social work field. At least, this is our high challenge and responsibility.

Spreading the word was of paramount importance for the organization in the late 1950s, and as a result, devoted volunteers tripled the amount of money and members coming into Youth Service from the parishes.

As the program expanded, some members of the Episcopal Church struggled with the question of whether they should be in the business of acting as a social agency. The efforts of a social-serving institution took a great deal of time and resources, and many believed that government agencies should be supplying more assistance in this area.

The church responded, stating their official position on the matter, as recorded in the Youth Service record:

> All social work began in the church, and the church has always been the background of social work. As true church people, we believe we have two responsibilities that kept us in the social work field: First, to reflect the love of Christ by ministering to those who are in need. Love cannot be possessed until given. Secondly, to bring the impact of the Christian Gospel upon the whole social work field by witness and example.

Despite a few detractors, a new set of values and goals proposed by the agency had removed most of the doubts by 1961, a time during which Youth Service was gaining strength as a valuable resource to the Memphis community.

CHAPTER FIVE

Youth Service, Memphis: 1960 – 1962

As the decade of the 1960s dawned, Youth Service maintained its head-quarters in the McCall Building, located between Main and Second streets and adjacent to what is now the Orpheum Theater. The agency faced some of its most challenging times. Russell Perry, a Memphis insurance executive, led the board with its 255 supporting members. Shelby United Neighbors (SUN) replaced the organization known as the Community Chest and was at the forefront of support for many non-profit agencies at the time.

While continuing to grow as a social service agency, Youth Service wanted to create its own charter and bylaws. In 1960, the members of the board for Youth Service began to disassociate themselves from their parent organization, Youth Service of Tennessee, led by The Reverend John Bull of Knoxville.

Two exciting developments occurred at Youth Service during this time. The first was introducing a new "Hard to Reach Program" for young people in Memphis. The second was to secure a new executive director to lead the organization. Ms. Agnes Grabau had decided to retire and Carl Obenauf, a social worker who previously worked at Grace Hill House in St. Louis, became the executive director in November 1960. Obenauf was selected to run a program built on the concepts conceived at the Hull House Training Center in Chicago. Obenauf was an experienced social worker, but had spent most of his time in positions of management. He plied his professional life working in the welfare field in Pittsburgh, Chicago and New Orleans.

By long-standing tradition, February was Youth Service Month in the Diocese of Tennessee. Episcopalians enrolled as members of either the Knoxville or Memphis branches of Youth Service in Tennessee. However, the Knoxville branch had merged with several other welfare services in that city and no longer participated in this annual enrollment drive. Youth Service in Memphis was the only remaining service that was sponsored by the Episcopal Church across the diocese focusing on youths 13 years of age and older. Youth Service obtained memberships from anyone willing to donate five dollars toward this important mission.

Coinciding with the retirement of Ms. Grabau, its executive secretary for more than 35 years of service, the board of Youth Service in Memphis began to explore the possibility of changing the manner in which the agency served the public. Board members believed the organization should continue to concentrate its work on young people that were generally outside of the influence of the usual social services, churches, schools and community centers. These young people were described as delinquents, truants, petty criminals, and those who had quit school, thus making them a higher crime risk. However, some members felt that these "hard-to-reach" youths did not constitute an immediate threat to whole-some community life. Others soon convinced them that if this segment remained under-served, they would eventually increase the social ills of many families and ultimately the entire community. In July 1960, the board of the Memphis branch of Youth Service in Tennessee made a com-mitment to begin serving these "hard to reach" individuals with a youth intervention program designed to combat these increasingly important issues.

The Youth Service intervention program included one part-time youth worker, placed into carefully selected neighborhoods in order to make contacts with youngsters having the greatest need. The agency was con-stantly searching for ways to engage young people and provide them with enriching activities. With only one group worker and a family caseworker, resources necessary to serve an ever-growing population were lacking.

Plans for local field trips began late in 1961. In May 1962, Gary Duvall was hired by Carl Obenauf to work with some of the more troubled youth in the city. That summer, Duvall took a small group of youngsters to Shelby Forest for Youth Service's first camping trip. However, these field trips did not become a full-fledged component of Youth Service until Father Don headed the program in 1963. Don's idea to expand the camping program eventually became a critical part of the organization's success. Summer camping was considered an inexpensive and wholesome option for the boys because it gave inner-city young people a chance to live, learn, work and play together outdoors. Officials believed that the youths would benefit from the teamwork and leadership skills they gained through participating in such activities.

Youth Service took advantage of modern approaches to social work. It borrowed some leading-edge methods to enable the troubled youth of the community to understand that most adults are interested and willing to listen to teenagers with problems. Social caseworkers provided critical assistance for young people, families, teachers, clergy, and others inside their neighborhoods and homes, where they felt more at ease. Members of the agency were convinced that they must work with the family as a whole, and with the peers of these troubled youngsters, in order to be fully effective. The initial plan included vocational, educational, and psychological testing to help youth understand their needs and potential. In some special instances, the counselor would conduct a limited job-finding program. This plan later materialized when Father Don became the director in 1963. The staff engaged a broad network of community organizations, working together to stimulate interest in addressing problems faced by youth and to help coordinate available efforts and resources to address them.

The problems with troubled and disadvantaged youngsters extended far beyond issues exclusive to adolescent males. Errant behavior increased for many teenaged girls within the local community during the early 1960s. Unfortunately, there was not enough available funding to hire a female group worker to serve "hard-to-reach" girls. Additionally, the new Hard to Reach Program did not include African-American children at that time; however, plans were discussed as early as 1961 for Youth Service to open its doors to all troubled kids; white and black, girls and boys. Parents often received aid and professional counseling as well when a severe family problem arose.

The task of the group worker was different from that of the caseworker. For instance, as a group worker, Gary Duvall would go into targeted areas in the neighborhood to make friends and assist local young people. If he could gain their confidence, he would try to help them discover a new direction in life. They were often nonconforming kids; teenagers with a big "chip" on their shoulder, who lacked family structure in their early lives. Many had trouble in every aspect of their lives, at school, at home and sometimes with the authorities. Duvall wasted no time in making himself known to the "gangs" as he attempted to gain acceptance as a friend. He formed a club of sorts, which met informally each week. Duvall provided spiritual advice to the young people and discussed subjects including truancy, staying out of trouble, good grooming, personal problems, being around the right kinds of friends, setting goals, school issues and strategies for seeking jobs. Duvall was easygoing and a rather unassuming person, but nonetheless effective with the teens. Many of the young people he worked with had a great deal of respect for him and for what he was trying to do. The majority of the casework was performed during the day, but some night hours were required as Gary became better acquainted with the group.

Duvall made detailed reports of the activities of the individuals he worked with, many of whom lived in or near St. Mary's Cathedral, Hurt Village and Lauderdale Courts, where Elvis Presley and his family once lived. There were several one-parent families, with troubled boys from 13 to 17 years of age, who were in need of help. At first, many of the boys were resentful and they would test Duvall, attempting to find out if he was truly a friend or if he was someone who would take advantage of them. His open, forthright approach worked, and most of the young people realized that he was trying to help them.

Later, as youth programs matured, volunteers and college students began assisting Youth Service to help young people find a new direction in life. These valuable workers made an impact on the lives of the kids, brought in primarily through juvenile court referrals, and helped them avoid court action by agreeing to live under Youth Service supervision for a specified time.

Increasingly, Duvall gained the respect of some of the boys with whom he worked, as many of them began to turn to him for help and guidance. One of the football coaches at Humes High School said upon first meeting Duvall, "I have my doubts about this chap. He will never be able to get anywhere with these rough, big boys out here." A few months later, his opinion had shifted dramatically. "That young man sure surprised me. What he has done is just short of a miracle," the coach exclaimed.

Many of the boys the agency served had received "social promotions" throughout their school years. Social promotion was a term used for a child who was passed to the next grade if he had been in a grade more than once and the child's size and age would create embarrassment. Most of these boys had been expelled or were awaiting the time when they could quit school legally. Almost all of the young people were seeking respect and recognition of some sort. Many of them were ashamed of their families, embarrassed by their home life, and wanted something more to satisfy their sense of belonging. Some of them had additional, more severe problems at home, such as alcoholic parents or parents with criminal records. About 30 to 40 percent of the boys contacted by Youth Service either had either quit school or were expelled. Thus, these situations portrayed youngsters who were truly hard to reach.

Occasionally, caseworkers would share the stories of their young clients. Mental illness, emotional problems, deviant behavior, truancy, and family problems were often cited as major issues that confronted the youth. Juvenile Court and Youth Service worked together closely to help these young people find a new path in life. Some young men were encouraged to enter the armed forces as an alternative to their wayward lifestyle, but the armed forces were becoming more selective in choosing their recruits.

The state organization, Youth Service of Tennessee, officially dissolved its charter in May 1962, allowing Youth Service in Memphis to operate independently of a parent organization. Youth Service was now poised to move forward with a new sense of purpose, but not without resistance. The diocese briefly considered dropping Youth Service from its budget due to competition for funding from other churches. To keep the agency intact, Youth Service solicited various local Episcopal Churches to support it directly as a kind of financial hedging. The board established a special committee to create better relations with the diocese and to provide an enhanced insight of the goals and objectives of Youth Service. In an effort to save the agency, the committee contacted Don's former rector, friend and mentor, Bishop Vander Horst. The committee members acquainted him with the goals and objectives of Youth Service and specifically the Hard to Reach Program. The bishop not only supported the agency's initiatives, but also improved the organization's leadership. He accomplished this by bringing forth the man who soon would end all doubt as to whether Youth Service could be self-sustaining and successful.

The Hard to Reach Program for the youth of Memphis began with the assistance of the Planning Council committee and Dr. Jameson Jones, president of Southwestern at Memphis (now Rhodes College). Since Southwestern was within the scope of the targeted communities, Dr. Jones helped provide guidance and advice for the program. Teachers and guidance counselors at Humes High School worked closely with Youth Service and with troubled youth they encountered on a daily basis. Shelby United Neighbors also endorsed the new direction Youth Service was taking with the new Hard to Reach Program. Their efforts and support led to substantial progress, and many young people received these critical services. Another initiative proposed to move the Hard to Reach Program to the all-white Lamar Terrace housing project, but no funding existed for such an expansion.

Youth Service continued to search for ways to extend services to African-American youths – a group in the greatest need base among the hard to reach. Obtaining funding was the most trying aspect of this initiative. A large number of organizations became concerned about a growing problem with a set of unruly boys in the Booker T. Washington High

School community. Reports illustrated that some of the students were "out of hand," and the situation was only getting worse. Manassas High School in North Memphis became another growing problem area that required attention.

By 1962, Youth Service began to include another important underlying problem – the difficulty faced by its constituents in finding jobs. Gainful employment among the youth was a growing challenge throughout the intervening years.

The Youth Service Board wanted to secure funding from the Federal Delinquency Control Program because it was determined that the agency alone could not handle the problem. The workers utilized good net-working to bring together the Memphis Housing Authority, the Juvenile Court, the Juvenile Bureau of the Police Department, the Urban League, Public Recreation, the YMCA, the YWCA, the Boy Scouts, Family Service, LeMoyne College, and school and church personnel in assisting with this effort. A five-point program for Youth Service was developed to address these emerging issues:

1. More adequate policing of problem areas

2. Parental counseling

3. Securing tenant relations personnel for the housing projects

4. Improving job opportunities

5. Securing group workers

In response to this ever-growing need, the Special Committee of the Health and Welfare Planning Council made a special request to add an African American social worker to the Youth Service field staff in the fall of 1962. This social worker would devote his energies to "hard-to-reach" African-American teens. The efforts of this individual would be concentrated first in the LeMoyne Gardens area of the city. The director of Shelby United Neighbors agreed to hire the worker, with the estimated $6,700 per year added to the Youth Service annual budget. However, Youth Service began its own campaign to raise the funds since any additions to the budget were often contested.

In the fall of 1962, Gary Duvall attended a six-week course on delinquent and "hard-to-reach" youth at the National Federation of Settlements and Neighborhood Centers at Hull House in Chicago. The

president's Committee on Juvenile Delinquency and Youth Crime provided the funding for the course. The driving force behind this grant was
the recently enacted Juvenile Delinquency and Youth Offenses Control
Act. Upon Duvall's return from Chicago, he shared with his peers what
he learned from the conference, which included the use of volunteers to
supplement the Youth Service caseworkers. Youth Service staff expertise
was maturing, both by experience and by formal tutelage.

After serving just over a year as executive director, Obenauf surprised
the staff of Youth Service when he submitted his resignation in December
1962. Obenauf had accepted a position as an assistant director with the
charitable organization Shelby United Neighbors (SUN), later named
United Way. The Executive Committee of Youth Service immediately
began discussions about hiring a new director. This time, they tried to
find a member of the clergy to take the position. Father Don Mowery of
St. Andrew's Church in Nashville became a natural candidate. His work
was well known throughout Tennessee due to his many successes in
working with youth, handling delinquencies and working with the local
police and fire departments.

The Youth Service Board invited Father Don to come to Memphis to
interview for the job in mid-December 1962. After arriving in Memphis
from Nashville, Don attended several meetings at their offices in the
McCall Building next to Goldsmith's department store downtown. After
one of the morning meetings, the executive committee and Father Don
had lunch at Goldsmith's restaurant. After lunch, Don and the Youth
Service board members were going down the escalator when they saw two
men fighting on the main floor of the store. The store detective had caught
a shoplifter trying to steal some leather coats. The two were running into
counters and knocking over racks of clothing. Father Don immediately
ran over and joined in the fray. He helped the store detective handcuff the
offender and escorted him upstairs to the security office. Officials had just
released the man from prison only three days before.

A woman who said, "I want to thank you for what you did," stopped
Father Don as he left the store. "This sort of thing upsets my husband."
The woman was Mrs. Goldsmith, the wife of the storeowner. She offered
to return the favor if Father Don ever needed anything. The newspaper
caught wind of the incident and later printed a brief story headlined,
"Hoodlum Priest Gets Memphis Post." Because of this incident, Father
Don made a lasting impression on his first day in Memphis.

The representatives of SUN voiced their enthusiastic support of the
prospect of a priest running the agency. Stephen Nelson, director of SUN,
stated that the addition of Father Mowery as executive director was "just

what we need." Bishop Vander Horst gave his blessings regarding the decision and declared, "They are getting the top man in this field." The board of Youth Service and SUN approved Don's appointment unanimously and he arrived in January 1963 to begin his work with the agency.

CHAPTER SIX

New Leadership For Youth Service,
Memphis: 1963

Youth Service operated alongside several other organizations working with troubled youngsters in Memphis during the early 1960s. In this locale, as was the case across the nation, many cities were experiencing similar problems. In 1962, *The Cross and the Switchblade* was published, written as a real-life account by urban street preacher David Wilkerson, who later founded Teen Challenge. It depicted the growing problem of youth crime and delinquency around the country, as well as grassroots religious solutions to the problem. A film adaptation of the book was released in 1970. The movie starred Pat Boone as Wilkerson and Eric Estrada as Nicky Cruz, the teen gang member in New York City whose life was transformed by Wilkerson's influence. Like Wilkerson, Father Mowery often found himself in the midst of juvenile crime and delinquency through his extensive work with youth. Relocating to Memphis only heightened this experience.

Don would say, in describing his own vision of his work, "I am a priest of the church first and a social worker second; primarily, attempting to teach young people and bring them to Christ through the church." Father Don began his work in January 1963 during a time of national societal unrest. Lunch counter sit-ins and boycotts in America provoked racial tension just months before President Kennedy's fateful day in Dallas. Don left St. Andrew's Church in Nashville, so he could continue his ongoing passion of working with young people in Memphis.

A Nashville newspaper branded Father Don as the "Hoodlum Priest," shortly before his arrival in Memphis. The unexpected designation was drawn from a movie of the same name starring Don Murray, which depicted a true story of Father Charles Clark, who helped ex-convicts return to society. Nevertheless, the appellation was one with which Father Don felt uncomfortable. At the same time, that he was designated the "Hoodlum Priest," he was recognized as a person who was capable of reconciliation in tense situations, and law enforcement increasingly valued his role. Father Don was quoted in the article as saying, "We don't dwell on their past, we just help these young people make it through tough times."

Don had a reliable administrative director, Mrs. Francis Myrick, who worked for the agency as one of only three full-time staff persons when Don arrived. Francis began her work with Youth Service in the 1950s and was hired by Ms. Agnes Grabau, who ran Youth Service until her retirement in 1961. She taught Francis the principles of social work and helping young people. "We received referrals from churches of all denominations, juvenile court and the public school system, and had a wonderful working relationship with social agencies in Memphis," Mrs. Myrick said. "We also worked with work-study students from LeMoyne College, Memphis State University (now The University of Memphis) and Christian Brothers College." Mrs. Myrick remembered that Father Don worked very well with members of the church and they were very fond of him. "I thank the Lord for putting me in the path of Youth Service," she exclaimed. Francis would counsel people referred to Youth Service about their specific problems, but also discussed the proper principles of family living. She created a pamphlet as a guide for the youth counselors after noticing a trend of counseling the children and not the whole family. The guide included the key concepts of independence, honesty and taking advantage of opportunities.

Youth Service remained a long way from garnering interest from celebrities and top military officials at that juncture of its history, but one notable entertainer was reaching out to assist his local community. Elvis Presley, who grew up in Lauderdale Courts public housing, learned of Youth Service through Memphis Mayor Henry Loeb. Elvis had been donating money to charities in Memphis since he gained celebrity status. After hearing about the work of Youth Service in 1964, Elvis graciously added the agency to his list of recipients. The association between Youth Service and Elvis was engendered when Mayor Henry Loeb called Don to meet Elvis. After an introduction by the Mayor in his office, Elvis presented his first donation to Don for Youth Service.

Each year thereafter, between Thanksgiving and Christmas, Don received a call from Graceland. Either Elvis, or his father Vernon Presley, would meet with Don and present Youth Service with his annual contribution. This practice continued for many years. As requested by Elvis, the Youth Service board banked the money for a "special project" to help young people near the Lauderdale Courts community.

Elvis also later became a listener of Father Don's *Talk It Out* radio program on WHBQ, according to his longtime friend and WHBQ disc jockey George Klein. "To my knowledge, every year that Youth Service received a check, it came directly from Elvis. The envelope containing the donation always featured Elvis' autograph on the front," Don recounted.

After his death in 1977, the Presley estate continued to support Youth Service with an annual donation. Graceland celebrated Elvis' 50th birthday in 1985 with a dinner party for the biggest Youth Service donors and offered them dinner and tour of the mansion. Don and his wife Julie attended this special event, at which Don was the featured speaker. This gathering provided Graceland an opportunity to create more interest in the historic home, since many people still did not know that Elvis' home had become a museum and a showplace for his accomplishments. The tour allowed the donors to take pictures and to have access to special areas that were off-limits to the public.

Several days before the Graceland dinner, a large snowstorm hit Memphis, which caused Don to question the attendance. He recalled, "I expected very few to attend, but I was surprised to find the house packed with people, most of them from out of town. When I completed my talk, a well-dressed lady approached me and spoke of her commitment to Elvis and the charitable organizations he supported." The woman was Victoria Fontana of San Antonio, Texas. She had become one of the faithful individuals, who came to Memphis religiously for anniversaries of Elvis' death and birthday.

Ms. Fontana became an avid supporter and, in later years, was instrumental in helping start a Youth Service job training program through World Vision in San Antonio. Don recalled his experience with Victoria Fontana:

> Several board members and I flew down there to set up the program. When we landed at the airport, we were asked to stay onboard the plane. When the door finally opened, we were welcomed with a red carpet by representatives of the San Antonio Chamber of Commerce. Victoria was very generous and, in addition to her support of Youth Service, she later presented a large donation to the Elvis Presley Memorial Trauma Center at the Regional Medical Center in Memphis.

By all standards, operating income was scarce for Youth Service in 1963. According to Francis Myrick, Youth Service was on a "shoestring" budget the year Don came to lead the agency. That year, after expenses, the agency showed a balance of only $11.48. Despite challenges with funding, the agency was able to serve 160 clients with 302 total client contacts and 220 family conferences.

Part of Father Don's initial job was to be on the staff and to assist with the services at St. Mary's Cathedral. Being ordained, he could preach about Youth Service from the pulpit, inform, and recruit volunteers for their efforts, which was a nice bonus for his dual mission. Naturally, he began immediately to build a business and social network of key contacts in the Memphis community. He knew the importance of getting to know city officials, most notably Memphis Police Captain Kenneth Turner, who at the time was running for the office of Juvenile Court Judge. The Memphis Juvenile Court had gained a national reputation for being a leader in juvenile justice, but that image had declined over the past few years. Don liked Turner's philosophy of dealing with youth and supported his campaign for the judgeship. The people of Memphis elected Turner to the office in November 1963. Don and Judge Turner soon forged a close partnership for the good of the youth of Memphis. They attended many speaking engagements – together with many diverse groups and organizations around the city composed of both African-American and white audiences, which was considered reaching "across the aisle" in that day.

One of the greatest needs of Youth Service early in 1963 was to help train and locate jobs for the young people whom it served. Therefore, Youth Service participated in the new National Jobs for Youth program initiated by President Kennedy. Father Don hoped that Youth Service could benefit from some of the money appropriated for this jobs program. He met with the staff members of the Tennessee Department of Employment Security in the search for employment opportunities for the young people in his programs. Additionally, the agency solicited more men's organizations in order to gain their interest and contributions. Calvary Church's Loyalty League was among these notable support groups.

When Father Don began to lead the agency, he had just two outreach workers; one white male, Gary Duvall, who worked with troubled kids from two housing projects and one white female worker, Nell Bell, who dealt with the families, primarily the mothers. They continued to stay busy with referrals received from the Board of Education, various churches and of course, Juvenile Court.

Don recalled separate meetings with two important individuals. "Male role models were desperately needed to work with boys who chose to live their lives on the street. Jack Hurt was one such role model and was one of the first adult men supporters I met upon my arrival." Hurt served in the Marine Corps Reserve and was the manager of Western Union office in downtown Memphis. The other important figure in this story was Brinson Paul, one of the 18-year-old men who frequented the Teen Center at St. Mary's Cathedral.

During Don's first day on the job, Gary Duvall was giving him a tour of the Hurt Village housing project when they saw Brinson Paul walking down the street. He was the first youth Don met after he arrived in Memphis. Brinson dropped out of school after the seventh grade and was then 17 and without a father. Brinson's family was poor and his mother washed and ironed clothes for people in the community to support her six children. Brinson needed a job to get him off the streets, so Don made Jack Hurt his mentor. As a result, Jack gave Brinson his first real job delivering messages for Western Union.

Back then, boys delivered telegrams and messages on bicycles and Jack helped obtain one for him to use. Brinson began making a little money and soon bought some clothes. By his third paycheck, he bought an old car for $25, but within a few days, the car needed a battery. Unfortunately, the only way Brinson knew how to acquire a new battery was to steal one from another car. A police officer saw Brinson in the act and arrested him. As a result, Jack had to terminate the young man because he could only have employees he could trust. Nevertheless, Don and Jack knew that Brinson needed to be in a more structured environment, so Jack arranged for him to join the Marine Corps. Don remembered, "I received several letters from Brinson after he joined the Marines, thanking me for helping him during those tough times." Sadly, he was killed in the Vietnam War, but the letters from Brinson Paul proved to be instrumental in launching Youth Service programs into the national spotlight.

While Youth Service worked with boys and girls from some of the toughest parts of town, the programs were not yet racially integrated. Father Don related, "It seemed every church in town had a project in Hurt Village, which was all-white then. There was great poverty in the inner city, but the white kids in the projects were still better off in many ways than some of the African-American kids across town."

Louis Haglund became president of the Youth Service board after Polly Lemmon resigned in March 1963. Haglund was a local architect and political insider and became a tremendous help to Youth Service because he had political connections for networking. He also provided fresh thoughts and ideas. Haglund suggested that Don visit the Memphis Police Juvenile Squad immediately after taking over at Youth Service. "Upon my visit, police inspector Tony Lawo informed me that his squad had been advised by the Nashville Police Department that I was coming to Memphis and that I was a friend. That was welcomed news for me," Don remembered.

Don wanted to know how the juvenile justice system operated in Memphis so visited the Memphis Juvenile Court, headed by Juvenile Court Judge Elizabeth McCain in 1963, prior to her defeat by Kenneth Turner in the November election. He vividly remembered the conditions at the Court:

> I could not believe the filth and the stench of the living quarters when I first saw the youth detention facilities in Memphis. I realized how bad the conditions were when I witnessed the old worn mattresses without sheets. By comparison, the Juvenile Court in Nashville was clean and well run. After seeing these conditions, I decided that this situation had to be improved, and I was willing to do anything to help.

The agency continuously sought donations for expanding and improving programs to help youth. Youth Service officials increased their efforts to gain new members in order to fund activities during Don's first year as director. As was the case with most charities, raising funds was competitive and a continual challenge. A concerted effort was underway to encourage additional memberships among the local parishes, as well as non-Episcopalian members. These new members helped to spread the word to the public. Additionally, the Youth Service Board of Directors expanded to include one clergyman and one layperson from each Episcopal Church in Shelby County. The agency was successful in securing the cooperation of the Memphis Police Department, Youth Guidance Commission, public welfare workers and other social organizations.

The Reverend Paul Walker, as Clergy Advisor to the Young Churchmen of the Diocese, felt young people of the Episcopal churches responded most readily to the call to action. He believed that young people could raise funds for the work of Youth Service and create an appreciation among the younger set for their less fortunate teenage counterparts. Many people believed that if the young people of the church became involved, their parents would become interested in helping as well. Meanwhile, SUN continued to be engaged in all decisions regarding the budget and spending. However, in the spring of 1963, SUN could not increase the budget of Youth Service, causing a sobering wake-up call and forcing

Youth Service to double memberships in order to raise money to fund existing programs.

JOBS FOR YOUTH AND NEW DROP-OUT PROGRAMS

Because Youth Service needed additional funding, the agency's Program and Service Committee proposed to expand the current programs to include taking care of school drop-outs. It was hoped that money could be raised to support the new Jobs for Youth Program in Memphis, which was modeled after a similar program that originated in Chicago.

Gary Duvall learned of the Jobs for Youth Program a year earlier while attending the workshop at Hull House in Chicago. Duvall put this concept into practice immediately after his return to Memphis and recalled how the program began in a 1962 *Memphis Commercial Appeal* newspaper article:

> The first thing we did was take a selected group of boys to get haircuts at Jim's Barbershop, which was located next to the Malco Theater on Main Street. We also obtained clothing and assisted them in obtaining social security cards. They came to our office on a regular basis to receive instruction from church volunteers on how to wear a shirt and tie and to understand employer expectations. We would send two or three young men out to the same job opportunity to submit an application and give them some sense of competition for these jobs. We also had business executives serve as mentors for them, providing them with tips on obtaining and keeping a job.

The plan expanded after Father Don's arrival in Memphis. The Jobs for Youth Program added a formal training component and included a series of classes conducted for young people on proper behavior. Training classes included how to apply for a job, how to improve people skills and how to fulfill job responsibilities. The four-week training program began with six participants chosen by the group worker who dealt directly with street kids, and each young person received a sponsor. However, there existed the ever-present problem of finding understanding employers who were willing to place these young people in part-time jobs after they completed the program. African-American teenagers were included in the school drop-out program after Youth Service hired a part-time African-American group worker later in 1963. The at-risk teens met with business executives, who helped support the teens' interest in school and advised them on the value of education.

Delinquency issues were evident in the inner city, but were cropping up with youth in the eastern sections of the city as well, and not just boys, but girls as well. Because there were members of other Episcopal churches living in the East Memphis area, a move to fund a program to cover the East High School neighborhood began.

A large map of the city showing delinquency rates in each police district helped to plan future expansions of services. Some of the growing hot spots for trouble were in the Colonial School and Gregg School neighborhoods; however, Youth Service did not yet provide services in these areas. The most prevalent crimes among delinquents in the Colonial Acres area were larceny and car theft. The Colonial area was unique because some of these middle-class parents often used their influence with the authorities and were able to shield their children from punishment. As a result, much of the trouble was "hushed up" that the severity of the delinquency problem was not fully known by the public. A better relationship with the Memphis Police Department helped to bridge the gaps with delinquents. The Reverend Don Henning, Rector of Calvary Episcopal Church, volunteered to help and had discussions with Police Commissioner Claude Armour about improving relations. Father Mowery soon acquired a slide projector and a police radio with money donated by people who attended Father Don's speaking engagements, so he could hear and respond to police calls as they related to teens.

By September of Don's first year, the Youth Service Board included 27 board members making decisions regarding the Hard to Reach Program. Because of the number of non-Episcopalians receiving services, SUN and the Memphis Shelby County Welfare Council recommended that Youth Service consider making non-Episcopalians board members. The board approved the idea and a special nominating committee began the process.

During that first year of transition, Father Don observed that many kids were getting in trouble during the summer months and quickly determined that an innovative program to help young people was needed. According to Don:

> Many kids would regularly hang out on the street corners at night. Most of them had low motivation and self-esteem, and were just getting together to go do crazy things. Many young people were being arrested and jailed at Juvenile Court. Once released, they would continue

their criminal behaviors with little support or guidance. I thought maybe if we could teach them how to use their leisure time in the summer, it would help them be more productive. I happened to enjoy outdoors and camping, so we began a new and improved camping program.

THE FIRST CAMPING PROGRAM

Father Don was never one to stand still and believed a new approach could break the shackles of these disadvantaged young people. He had the idea to organize a formal camping program that would provide more than simple recreation, but include teaching young people how to enjoy life. Don believed that camping would give urban boys a chance to experience nature and the outdoors along with valuable life lessons. Compared with other youth group activities, camping was a relatively inexpensive activity. Father Don conducted his first camping trips at Fuller State Park during the summer of 1963. This was a substantial step up from the pilot program Gary Duvall attempted the year prior. Father Don recalled, "We started there because they didn't charge us and it was convenient, but we still needed funding for transportation, food, water, tents and supplies."

The first night at camp proved to be memorable. Father Don had to break up several fights. One boy was cut with a knife and another injured an arm in the ensuing mêlées. It became obvious that weapons were going to be a problem. As a result, one of the camp counselors purchased a footlocker and padlock at a nearby store. The campers were required to deposit their weapons prior to camp with the assurance they would be returned. Interestingly, no other serious injuries occurred from fights after Father Don "laid down the law" to the boys.

Don could see the immediate benefits of getting these teenage boys away from their neighborhood turfs. In the beginning, there were only one or two adult counselors to work with the campers. As the program grew and funding was made available, one counselor to every 10 boys was the desired ratio. The boys would hike, explore and learn how to prepare their own meals, clean up after themselves and have the opportunity to meet other kids from different parts of town.

Ken Clark, a Memphis attorney and Calvary Church member, provided Father Don with his first financial support for the camping program during a lunch at the Calvary Waffle Shop. Ken was a trustee and head of the Theodora Trezevant Neely Foundation and supported the camping idea for inner-city kids who lived in Hurt Village and Lauderdale Courts.

He immediately approved funding for the program's equipment and supplies, believing that the benefactor, the late Ms. Neely, would have enthusiastically given to helping kids in programs such as this one. She was an avid adventurer herself and had asked as a testamentary directive that her estate provide challenging experiences for inner-city boys and girls, both white and black. It was a very forward-thinking concept in its establishment.

Ms. Neely never married and was an independent spirit, often taking adventure trips on tramp steamers. She instructed the administrator of her estate to provide for kids who did not have a chance to do what she had done – to mirror some of her experiences in hiking and backpacking. Therefore, a gift of $500 was donated by the Neely fund for Father Don's first camping program.

Ken remembered the impact Father Don had on him personally at the time. "I was very active at Calvary Church, and we were fully vested in Don's idea with Youth Service." The funding from Ms. Neely's trust gave Father Don early confidence prior to the program moving to the naval base just outside Memphis. Ken's support for Father Don and the work he was doing for the kids of Memphis is evident in his remark, "Don is the real deal when it comes to the priesthood. As a member of the cloth, he wears it with great sincerity." The gift from the Neely Trust Fund significantly increased the next year (for the 1964 summer camping program) to $1,350 and continued for several years.

Once Father Don secured the camp funding, he immediately went to visit Lester Gingold, who managed the mail order catalog department at Sears Crosstown. After telling Lester that they needed some camping equipment for the Youth Service program, the fellow Episcopalian gladly helped by providing the necessary gear at wholesale prices. Lester's son, Paul, became an ardent supporter of Youth Service. He served as a group counselor and was one of the most well-liked and popular workers in the agency.

According to Father Don, the kids were not initially excited about camping. Most did not like to haul the equipment and sleep outdoors with snakes and other "creepy critters," but Don wanted them to have the experience. The program began slowly because the inner-city teenagers were unfamiliar with the outdoors and had wild imaginations. The young people felt much more comfortable standing on the street corner in their housing project than spending the night at Fuller Park under the stars.

Youth Service recruited community leaders to help teach the kids how to enjoy camping in order to make the program work. At first, there was only Father Don, a camp counselor and the kids who all slept in tents on the ground. Many of the inner-city youths had never had an opportunity to be outdoors overnight. Interestingly, the difficult job of digging a grease pit was dirty work for the boys, but it soon became a competitive job (and even a privilege) for those who were not used to being in that kind of environment. Don remembered, "Our camping program finally caught on and eventually became what the kids referred to as the, 'thing to do.'" When the campers returned home, they told their friends about the positive experiences they had. We were teaching these kids two very important things; how to enjoy the outdoors and how to work and live together in harmony."

Don was able to raise additional funding, beyond the financial support of the Neely Foundation and the SUN organization. Bert Ferguson, general manager at WDIA, used their Goodwill Fund to purchase a horse trailer to transport the camping equipment and Shelby County Sheriff Bill Morris provided a bus to transport kids to the camps. In addition to Ferguson's support, Father Mowery received funding from other groups and private donors that enabled the boys to participate in both day outings and overnight camping trips. The camping program quickly became popular among kids of all ages.

Notably, the Neely Foundation supported improvements in the program over the next several years, which resulted in over 4,000 boys and girls attending camp at other parks outside of Memphis.

GUILD OF ST. AUGUSTINE

In May of Father Don's first year, he spoke to a group of women at the Church of The Holy Communion who wanted to know how they could help. They quickly responded to his request for volunteers and within a few months, organized the Guild of St. Augustine. The group of volunteers soon expanded to include women from other Episcopal churches in Shelby County. Their sole purpose was to assist the efforts of Youth Service. The women raised money from garage sales, book sales, and art shows. They also served as role models and helped in some cases to secure jobs for young people.

The women of the Guild met monthly for fellowship and for planning various fund-raising events. They also provided Youth Service with much-needed volunteer office assistants and occasionally assisted the counselors with group activities. Additionally, they hosted parties, gathered clothing for needy families and even waited tables at the Calvary Waffle Shop to earn money for Youth Service. St. Augustine's Guild offered the women a real opportunity to be the "Church in Action" and to be of service to the young people of Memphis. The organization utilized its many talented and highly organized women as it coordinated activities for Youth Service. Father Don and the board were always grateful for the role the Guild played in the success of the agency.

Another important Youth Service supporter was Mrs. J.B. Cook. Shortly after Father Don became executive director of Youth Service, Mrs. Cook, a prominent member of Grace St. Luke's Episcopal Church, became a valuable resource to the agency. For years, she opened her large estate and swimming pool in Memphis to a variety of Youth Service activities. During Father Don's years at Youth Service, Mrs. Cook's estate served as a carefree gathering point for many of the recipients of services in Father Don's care. Interestingly, Mrs. Cook and the young Elvis Presley became good friends in the late 1950s. Elvis often visited her and enjoyed fishing and hunting snakes in the large lake on her property.

THE TEEN CENTER AT ST. MARY'S CATHEDRAL

Church members had long used the basement gym and adjacent club-rooms of St. Mary's Cathedral on Poplar Ave. for events and activities, but during the early 1960s, the facility was renamed the Teen Center and became a gathering place for neighborhood youth. The group of young people who attended the Teen Center dances at St. Mary's Cathedral was primarily 13 to 17 years of age and typified the participants of other Youth Service programs. All were white youths who lived predominantly in public housing areas near the cathedral. Father Duff Green, one of the priests at St. Mary's at the time, coordinated the activities at the center, but had the difficult task of working with the sometimes rough neighborhood kids.

Young people called the center "The Green Door," possibly because the doors leading to the clubroom in the basement of the Cathedral were painted green. However, according to some people, the club picked up the name because of a popular song at the time called, "Behind the Green Door" and possibly because of Father Green.

In July 1963, St. Mary's renovated the clubroom and added classes in good grooming habits, manners, and deportment prior to the Friday evening gathering. Organized activities were part of the evening's program. The attraction in those days was that the "Green Door" was one of the few places for kids to get together. Boys came to find girls and girls came to meet new people and to dance. They generally did not have any money, and the Teen Center was available to them at no charge.

Youth Service volunteers prepared snacks for the young people at the Teen Center and tried to relate to them as best they could, but it was hard work for the adult volunteers who served as chaperones. The women of the Guild, with their husbands and volunteers from other Episcopal churches in the city, worked at the Teen Center on Friday nights. In spite of the adult assistance, Father Green had difficulty handling some of the rougher boys. Most of the volunteers had not received training to supervise such programs at the church. Because of the risk of violence, this was truly the "longest night" of the week for many of the volunteer chaperones.

One evening, a group of rowdy boys attacked Father Green who sustained serious injuries. This act promptly sent two of the guilty boys to Juvenile Court. After the altercation, Father Don and the Youth Service staff assumed responsibility for the operation of St. Mary's Teen Center on Friday nights. Don soon organized a council of six youths from the teen members, so they could share the responsibility of running of the club and assist in planning activities. After Father Mowery's tough restrictions were imposed, those who wanted to fight were directed to settle their disputes across the street from the church in what is now Morris Park. However, brief skirmishes developed constantly. Father Don would later state, "Some of our volunteers gave the kids a ride home after the dance because it was easier to take them home than to have to return later to get them out of jail."

Through his unpublished historical sketch of Youth Service, former Youth Service board member Jay Eberle, related the story of a youth named "Lem," who was the youngest of 10 children and had recently moved to Memphis from Arkansas. Lem recalled having to fight his way through the housing projects to the Teen Center on Friday night and being anxious at the end of the dance when he had to go outside and face the "tough guys" who were not admitted because they refused to give up their weapons. Once, Lem was taken to jail because of his involvement in a fight. Father Don posted Lem's bail and started a friendship, which later led Lem to become the president of the Teen Center Council. Lem said of his position, "The most difficult part of being on the council was enforcing a dress code and searching for knives and brass knuckles. If it hadn't been for Father Don's encouragement not to get in trouble, I don't think I'd be here now."

The young people received ID cards for membership and were searched before being admitted. Knives, brass knuckles, and other contraband were often confiscated. Liquor was often smuggled into the dances, but was easily discovered in creative hideaways such as the water tank of the toilet. Because of Father Don's experience and strict rules, the violence eventually subsided, and the Center ran more smoothly as Youth Service began to build a positive image in the Memphis community.

Father Don remembered other teens that frequented the Teen Center dances. Tina, one of the tough girls who attended the center, would tattoo herself with the initials of her latest boyfriend on her arms and legs with a long needle. She dipped the needle into India ink and pricked her skin to form the initials. If the relationship with the boyfriend ended, she would take a lighted cigarette and burn the tattoo to form scar tissue and obliterate the letters of her lost beau. Fortunately, Tina settled down in later years, married and had two boys. Unfortunately, her husband died in prison in Nashville, but the boys did well for themselves in school. Tina credits the efforts of Youth Service with helping her have a family and for keeping it together. Years later, she visited Father Don to locate a picture of her husband, who also had been a member of the "The Green Door." She wanted her boys to know what their father looked like during those days.

More young people began to receive individual attention in an effort to improve their attitude and behavior. They received concerned counsel for personal problems, school-related issues and social adjustment, as well as job placement. The immediate families of teenagers also received counseling in an effort to strengthen their home situations. Youth Service also strengthened its working relationship with law enforcement officials. The Teen Center continued successfully for several years through the patience and understanding of the Youth Service workers, who eventually generated a mutual trust and respect with these youngsters.

Father Don was also concerned about their spiritual condition and wondered why young people who attended the Friday night activities could not attend church on Sunday mornings. He also knew that many of the kids had made St. Mary's Teen Center a part of their lives, but were not attending church services. Don was successful in having them attend regular services, but recalled how some of the church members reacted to the visitors:

> We had a small chapel above the center, so I decided to conduct an informal service before the Friday night dance. The voluntary devotion service provided them an opportunity to have a church experience. The young people liked the idea, and some of the kids began to

come to Sunday church services at St. Mary's Cathedral. Unfortunately, many of the regular church members, who thought the cathedral belonged to them, did not care for their children being around the rough neighborhood kids.

The cathedral played a central role in the early growth and development of Youth Service. The staff at St. Mary's has influenced the Memphis community beyond measure, as thousands of people worshiped and participated in its activities through the years. It would be hard to imagine the Memphis community without St. Mary's Cathedral.

That possibility almost became a reality on August 24, 2000, when a fire, sparked by workers removing paint, almost destroyed the Diocesan House of West TN and the adjacent cathedral buildings. Ninety fire fighters and 20 pieces of equipment were required to bring the three-alarm fire under control. The bishop and cathedral clergy lost valuable books, research data and notes, but due to the efforts of the firefighters, many historical documents relating to the story of Youth Service survived and are contained in this account. Memphis Fire Department Chief, Larry McKissick was committed to the task when he stated, "We are going the extra mile today to help preserve historic items in the damaged building."

The fire department immediately blocked off Poplar Avenue so they could position their equipment. Church workers placed food, reserved for a catered event later that day, on tables in the middle of the street for the benefit of the fire fighters. Many of the homeless people who slept at the nearby Union Mission down the street graciously helped to carry damaged articles from the church. Seeing that food was being provided for the workers, one of the men said in jest, "Episcopalians really know how to put on a good fire."

Repairs began immediately and St. Mary's was restored with the assistance of its local leaders and people throughout the community. Followers of the Episcopal faith, white and black, other local churches, Jews and Christians and several private and nonprofit organizations, all helped bring back the historic church. Rabbi Micah Greenstein of Temple Israel was one of the first religious leaders to respond to assist with the restoration process. The Very Reverend C. B. Baker, St. Mary's Dean (pastor) remarked, "They have all rallied around a place that has been not only a sanctuary for people in need, but also a central institution in justice and peace issues in our city through the years. The people have boldly stated what is important to them, God and God's work."

Along with the indoor activities provided by St. Mary's, the outdoor activities of Youth Service provided the best route to help young people channel their teen energy and promote learning. Father Mowery headed the committee that selected boys for the Youth Conservation Corps in 1963, which was under the direction of the Youth Guidance Commission. Memphis Police Captain Kenneth Turner headed this agency prior to his election as Juvenile Court Judge. Both African-American and white boys made applications and were eligible to participate. The program started with 25 boys who had court records, were high school dropouts, or were at a high risk of dropping out. Their first project was to help develop a recreational area southwest of the airport known as McKellar Park. The Variety Club and the Film Transit Company provided busses to transport the kids.

Don attended a two-week study course in November 1963 at the National Federation of Settlements and Neighborhood Centers in Chicago. A government grant under President Kennedy's Committee on Juvenile Delinquency financed the invitation-only seminar for program administrators around the country. Quite sadly, Don's session was cut short when news reached Chicago that President Kennedy had been assassinated in Dallas.

In order to promote Youth Service, Father Don became a frequent speaker at local clubs and organizations in Memphis. The Memphis Social Workers Club held one such meeting in December 1963 regarding the newly launched Hard-to-Reach Program. Don assisted with a comedy skit performed by The Reverend Paul S. Walker, Rector of Holy Trinity Church, who played the role of "Switch Blade Sam" the delinquent. Father Mowery opened the presentation with slides of Youth Service programs and called on members of his staff for remarks. The real fun began when he told the group he had brought along a real live delinquent for them to see and talk with firsthand. In came Father Walker, disguised as the "punk of all punks;" shirttail out, face dirtied, dark glasses, a cigarette dangling from his mouth, and in one pocket, a knife, some 10 inches long, which he promptly drew and brandished at Father Mowery. Then, "Sam" strolled over, began to play the piano and sang a few song parodies about being a juvenile delinquent much to the delight of the audience. The performance was very effective and enthusiastically received by all. Because of events such as these, Youth Service was fast becoming well-known in Memphis for its successes with troubled youth and an agency with a reputation for getting a good "bang for the buck" for those who invested in its work.

YOUTH SERVICE CAMPERS CLEARING A SITE AT FULLER
PARK, 1963

FATHER DON, SHORTLY AFTER HIS ARRIVAL IN
MEMPHIS, JAN., 1963

MEMPHIS MAYOR HENRY LOEB AND FATHER MOWERY,
1964

CHAPTER SEVEN

Youth Service In The Mid – 1960s

The period of 1964-1967 encompassed many watershed events, including the continuing social and cultural struggles, such as the civil rights movement and the intensifying Vietnam War, all of which made an indelible impact upon the youth of Memphis and elsewhere.

Meanwhile, Youth Service had begun to turn its focus on schools and the needs of young people who lacked educational and social guidance. Humes High School, situated in a segment of Memphis known for having a sizeable population of hard-to-reach young people, was a primary focus for Youth Service. Humes also served as the school district for the all-white public housing projects, Hurt Village, and Lauderdale Courts. Elvis Presley attended Humes High School while living in Lauderdale Courts.

The mostly African-American LeMoyne Gardens community was also in need of help with growing juvenile delinquency and had a high rate of school dropouts. To address this situation, in 1964 the Youth Service board enlisted help from leaders of the LeMoyne Gardens area and welcomed George Holmes as a new African-American social worker. Paralleling this effort, the African-American radio station WDIA continued to support the work of Youth Service in a variety of ways.

In a *Commercial Appeal* article in March 1982, journalist and television executive Ron Walter remembered how effectively Youth Service helped to bridge friendships between African-American and white youths 13 to 21 years of age. Walter explained that Youth Service was one of the first social service organizations to break away from assisting only white children and to include African-American youth. The agency fought local pressure to segregate services in the 1960s, and constantly worked to obtain a truly integrated mix of youth according to need and not color. According to Walter, it took true fortitude and leadership on the part of

Father Don to make that happen. Walter also served as executive assistant to Tennessee Congressman Harold Ford in the 1970s and has been an ardent supporter of the Youth Service program for years.

The never-ending financial need of the program is why, at the end of his first year with Youth Service, Father Mowery averaged one speaking engagement for every working day of the month. His slide presentations proved effective in spreading the word about the agency and helped gain funding for the programs. Early in 1964, with very limited funding, Gary Duvall and George Holmes were handling more than 500 casework contacts with young people across the city of Memphis. However, they would not allow their meager budget to stymie the work they had begun. The board had ultimate responsibility for fundraising efforts and began to promote interest in Youth Service programs to local organizations.

In the summer of 1964, representatives of the Memphis and Shelby County Health and Welfare Planning Council, along with Ezra Young of the South Central Region of the American Friends (Quaker) Society, approached Father Mowery with the idea of sponsoring the American Friends Service Committee (AFSC) to work with Youth Service's Hard To Reach Program in Memphis. Young spoke to the agency and won the approval of the board to begin the program. AFSC had gained extensive experience working with African-American children in projects throughout the country, teaching crafts, leading them in construction projects and taking them on field trips and to day camps. Youth Service had recently acquired an African-American group worker and the Neely Foundation had donated extra money for the camps, so the African-American youth could be a part of this new summer project.

The AFSC furnished a husband and wife leadership team and brought in six college students from around the country to assist with the program. Similar summer programs had been a part of the Quaker program, and they involved college students from around the world. Youth screened its workers carefully before selecting workers for these projects, which engaged college students in meaningful service to others. Owen College volunteered its housing facilities for the workers and Youth Service provided funding from a special account. The program also received approval from the SUN agency. According to the agreement with AFSC, Youth Service would supervise the program and have the final say in the areas worked and the placement of all college students involved.

Plans progressed for the project until questions arose regarding how student workers were to be deployed in the surrounding neighborhoods. Youth Service planned to have white students work in Lauderdale Court and Hurt Village, both white housing projects, and the black students were to work in the mostly African-American LeMoyne Gardens, Foote Homes, and Claiborne Homes housing projects. Young had other ideas and suggested that the AFSC officials supervise the placement of social workers. He then surprised the Youth Service program planners with his request that all of the Youth Service programs, not just the summer project, be entirely integrated. This meant that all group workers would work together in all areas of the city regardless of race. However, the "separate but equal" rule still governed social services across the South. The idea of full integration in 1964, even for youth programs, was a radical idea for Memphis at that time. City officials and Walter Simmons, Director of the Memphis Housing Authority, strongly suggested that Youth Service not participate in the program for fear of social unrest. As a result, AFSC withdrew from the project in June of that year when Youth Service was unable to comply with Young's request of full integration.

The outdoor camping in nearby state parks continued to grow due to the support of Theodore Trezevant Neely Foundation. Others supporters included representatives from the wholesale grocery firm of Malone & Hyde, who gave enough good food from damaged cartons to feed hundreds of youngsters on these camping trips. Automobile dealer and business executive Milton Schaffer, WDIA radio, and the Variety Club, all provided transportation for the kids to various activities. Local insurance executive and board member John Collier provided a car for use by group workers and offered Youth Service complete insurance coverage for only $0.05 per camper per day. These examples of support were the direct result of Father Don's "spiritual networking," which helped to build an effective group of valued contributors during his years as executive director.

Eighteen weeks of camps were planned for the summer of 1964. Camping equipment was generously shared with the Girls Club, which worked with girls in the same areas of the city as Youth Service did with boys. Summer activities such as crafts, swimming, and sports were an integral part of the camping experience, but Youth Service always provided important counseling and mentoring sessions as well. Few people realized the potential impact of the camping program in the mid-1960s. Soon; however, Father Mowery's groundbreaking idea of involving a series of miniature summer boot-style camps for boys would become a recommended community action plan for selected military bases across the country.

Aside from camping programs, work in the Memphis housing projects continued as George Holmes formed two youth groups in the LeMoyne Gardens area. George was highly regarded for his work with the young people. The Youth Service board once proclaimed, "Thank God for people like George." WDIA radio praised his valuable work with African-American youths in the city.

Youth Service hired two additional group workers in September, one African-American worker, Foster Adams and one white worker, James McKinley. Additionally, the agency hired a third group worker, James Hicks, to work in the predominantly white Lamar Terrace and Colonial School areas. Foster Adams quickly secured the confidence of the board, as he found unique ways to raise money for the program. Adams eventually secured the cooperation of the City Recreation Department to stage basketball games with his club members in the Gaston Community Center located in the Raleigh community. David Finley replaced James McKinley who resigned in March 1966 when he accepted a position with the State Probation Board. Additional funds from non-Episcopal churches helped support this effort.

Interestingly, the Gailor Home for Boys, named for Episcopal Bishop Thomas F. Gailor, began in March 1939 in the Rectory of the Episcopal Church of the Good Shepherd in Memphis. The organization later moved to Summer Avenue in 1943 and in 1952 changed their name to Memphis Boys Town. This organization is now part of the vast Youth Villages organization.

The agency helped provide for homeless children and those who were in troubled homes. During a September board meeting, Father Don told of an interesting case in which Youth Service was attempting to find a foster home for Ray Pittman, a 14-year-old boy with no place to live except for Juvenile Court. Ray had not seen his parents in several years. His father was in jail in California and his mother was serving time in a Mississippi prison. Ray had run away from Tennessee Preparatory School (TPS) in Nashville, the largest school for dependent and neglected children in the country and from St. Michael's Farm for Boys in Picayune, Mississippi. Youth Service intervened with a plan to find Ray a foster home when the Juvenile Court attempted to send him back to TPS. After a great deal of searching, an Episcopal family in Collierville, TN gave the boy a home. There he was enrolled in school and was accepted by the family as one of their own. Ray was very happy with his new family, especially to "have a mother and father." He commented, "It sure is nice to sleep on a real bed with springs and a mattress; it has been years since I did that." Father Mowery and his staff assisted many young people like Ray who had no family and no place to stay.

Ray was a pleasant boy and related well with his new circumstances, but was plagued with the temptations of many of the delinquents with whom Don worked. One Sunday morning, while walking to church, he noticed the keys in the ignition of a car. He quickly decided to take the car and began a journey into Mississippi in an attempt to locate his mother. The Mississippi Highway Patrol apprehended him later the same day. A Youth Service supporter flew a Youth Service worker to Mississippi to obtain Ray's release and bring him back to Memphis. The Highway Patrol released Ray and the car to the Youth Service representatives, but failed to communicate to all districts of the Highway Patrol that the stolen car situation had been resolved. On their way back to Memphis in the "stolen" car, the Highway Patrol stopped the Youth Service representatives again, forcing Father Don to be on the phone the remainder of the day with the Mississippi authorities, working to resolve the matter.

Ray and Youth Service continued to cross paths as he searched for direction in life. One day, Ray stopped by the Youth Service office for a visit. Francis Myrick noticed that his face was green from eating wild greens, commonly known as "Polk Salad," that he found growing near the railroad tracks where he traveled. Apparently, tough times had returned for Ray. He landed in Cookeville, TN, a short time later sleeping under the steps of a church. A female church member noticed Ray and began to feed and care for him. Strangely, the two began a relationship and later married. Ray's new wife began communicating with Francis Myrick and Father Don to keep them abreast of his physical condition and progress.

One day, Don received a call from Ray's wife who explained that Ray's teeth were falling out because he had not had dental work for many years. Father Don used his "spiritual network" and located a dentist in Cookeville, through the Dean of the UT Dental College in Memphis. Memphians Tommy and Liz Farnsworth provided the funding for this worthwhile cause and Ray was able to receive a new set of dentures. Don stayed in touch with Ray for many years until he received word that Ray was struck and killed by a car in Chattanooga while riding a bicycle, delivering used clothing to a needy family.

An important person, who had a lasting impact on Youth Service for decades, was board President J. Lester Crain, Jr. His early involvement with Youth Service began around 1964, shortly after Father Don arrived in Memphis to head the agency. He served on Youth Service, Memphis and Youth Service, USA boards and was a member of the Finance and Executive Committees. The former naval officer and pilot was a Harvard-educated attorney and served in many capacities over the years, lending his creative ideas and assisting the agency in a multitude of ways. He also interceded with advice on legal matters and played a significant role in creating the framework for Youth Service, USA in February 1970, which expanded the programs nationally.

Lester Crain's wife Brenda was also instrumental as a staunch supporter of Father Don and the Youth Service programs. Shortly after arriving in Memphis, she invited Don to speak to a group of church members at her home. After the luncheon, Brenda introduced Don to her husband, Lester. This important meeting started a relationship that later provided the foundation for the national Youth Service, USA Program.

In November 1964, the City of Memphis, through the Youth Guidance Commission, initiated a proposal to the U.S. Department of Labor for funding from President Johnson's Anti-Poverty Bill. Memphis Mayor William Ingram and representatives of the Shelby County Health and Welfare Planning Council worked primarily to continue the Youth Conservation Corps through this 1964 Economic Opportunity Act. Father Mowery advised the board that Youth Service had an opportunity to participate for a share of $250,000 from the Office of Economic Opportunity (OEO). The mayor's War on Poverty Committee had asked for help in spending part of this government grant.

Youth Service immediately went to work to promote the initiative and played an important role in obtaining this federal funding through the help of SUN. Agency officials hoped that some of the OEO money would assist the programs of Youth Service. These efforts came to fruition the next year, as funds were finally made available. Hundreds of delinquent teenagers were now eligible for rehabilitation due to this money. This unique program was successful through the combined efforts of a church organization, the community, and the federal government.

Initially, Father Mowery was apprehensive about forming a partnership with the federal government, knowing all of the potential "strings and red tape" involved. However, in 1965, Don launched the government partnership with Youth Service with what he referred to as "fear and trembling." His efforts quickly drew the unwavering praise of the public for taking this bold step with his groundbreaking youth programs.

At the same time, Dr. Hollis Price, president of Memphis' LeMoyne College, was working toward obtaining federal funding for a work-study grant for his students at the historically African-American college. Many of the LeMoyne students came from homes where the total family income was under $3,000 annually, and most had few opportunities for jobs during and after college. Father Mowery shared, "I became good friends with Dr. Price and realized the area surrounding the college was in great need of church social services."

When Dr. Price discovered that funds were available through the Poverty Act, he appealed to the local Health and Welfare Planning Council for an agency to supervise a work-study program to enable some of his more impoverished students to remain in college. Youth Service was the agency selected to facilitate this program. The additional student workers increased the staff tremendously. Youth Service professionals supervised the students, and LeMoyne paid for their services with the money received from the federal government. This allowed Youth Service to work with youth in the LeMoyne Gardens, Lamar Terrace and to expand across Memphis in both black and white communities. Clearly, Youth Service was a forerunner for outreach and racial reconciliation for bridge building in the community.

The Episcopal publication, *Tennessee Churchman*, reported that the work-study program began with 15 LeMoyne College students who worked full-time with Youth Service. The students received $1.25 to $1.50 per hour, worked 15 hours a week during the school year and up to 40 hours a week during the summer periods. Funds for 90 percent of the salaries came from the federal government. By 1965, Memphis State University began to participate in the work-study program. Later, Youth Service added students from Christian Brothers College to the program.

Along with the growing problem of delinquent youth, gang activity began to grow in the troubled areas surrounding the housing projects. The Memphis Police Department soon began to rely heavily on Father Mowery and his group workers, as well as the LeMoyne student workers for information that would help quell potential crime and violence. The majority of the student workers counseled young people in the streets under the close supervision of professional group workers. The students spending time with troubled youth helped them to develop a stronger principle of assisting people in a way that they could never learn from books.

The program began with five female college students working with caseworker Nell Bell and 13 male students, working under the supervision of group worker Foster Adams. Youth Service assigned the college juniors and seniors to work in different housing projects. Since the student workers were familiar with the neighborhoods in which the youths lived, they could cross barriers quickly and establish a positive identity in the area. A major focus of these students was to help reduce the dropout rate among local high school students.

Other student workers served as home visitors, who assisted the caseworkers, while several helped with clerical work at the Youth Service office. The social workers discussed issues with young people in their homes, as well as on the streets. At the time, this was a relatively new concept for youth programs. Father Don stated, "One can learn a lot by seeing how the family interacts in the overall environment of the home, whether rich or poor."

Dr. Price spoke highly of the Youth Service project, "Over the years I developed faith in the Health and Welfare Planning Council, and when they said Youth Service was the agency to handle the program — that was good enough for me."

Racial integration, especially in the South, was not easy to achieve in the mid-1960s. However, in 1964 the Memphis Juvenile Court had begun integrating its services under Judge Kenneth Turner. By 1968, Youth Service had become the first non-governmental agency in Memphis to integrate its social outreach services. "Of course, there were people who traditionally did not support this type of learning experience, but we did it and it worked very well," recalled Father Mowery.

Father Don's positive relationship with Judge Turner developed from the style Turner chose to manage Juvenile Court. Turner was a former Marine and believed strongly in organization and discipline. He also reached out to the community for participation in dealing with family problems. Youth in conflict at home needed more supervision; someone to give the kids direction.

Judge Turner's Juvenile Summons program proved successful because of the strong support of agencies like Youth Service, which was the first organization in Memphis to work with the court in this capacity. Youngsters whose offenses were not of a serious nature had an opportunity to work with the counselors of Youth Service. In this way, many young people avoided formal court proceedings and possibly a criminal record. This program served as a model for juvenile courts across the country, and eventually federal support developed through the Law Enforcement Assistance Administration (LEAA).

By 1966, there were hundreds of troubled youths participating in Youth Service programs in the Memphis area, though the professional full-time staff remained at five people. Upon seeing the ever-growing value to the community, many businesses, civic groups, churches, and individuals in the community began to increase their efforts to contribute supplies, equipment, and facilities for the Youth Service initiative. The Memphis City Beautiful Commission provided materials, supervision, and space for planting projects for the kids. Soon, in-kind contributions came from many different organizations and individuals. A local department store provided clothes in addition to the services of a fashion coordinator to instruct girls in proper grooming.

To promote the programs of Youth Service, Father Mowery participated as a panelist on the Ed Goetz television show in the mid-1960s. Guests included Judge Turner and other local officials. Goetz helped to promote the activities of Youth Service by showcasing club activities and scenes from camping trips. Additionally, Don was a regular guest of Peggy Rolfe's popular talk show on WMC-TV called "High Noon." His participation would later prove to be a good foundational "rehearsal" for a soon-to-be-created radio show featuring Father Mowery called *Talk It Out with Father Don,* which would debut years later in 1970.

The close ties between Juvenile Court and Youth Service became evident when, in April 1965, Youth Service held a monthly board meeting in Juvenile Court's auditorium. Nancy Ratcliff, Judge Turner's valued assistant and special activities director, led the group on a tour of the facilities. Afterward, Claude Pearson, Chief Probation Officer, told of the excellent working relationship between the Court and Youth Service.

In October 1965, Father Don was on a regular speaking circuit, selling Youth Service to local community organizations. At the Optimist Club, he met Shelby County Sheriff Bill Morris, who immediately became a supporter of the agency. Morris would later prove to be a valuable ally, serving as a conduit for the successful Bridge Builders program years later in 1988.

By the mid-1960s, Judge Kenneth Turner and his staff, the Shelby County Sheriff's Department, housing development officials, local school and college administrators, civic leaders, and churchmen, were praising Youth Service workers for providing an effective means of deterring juvenile delinquency in the Memphis area.

Nell Bell worked with Youth Service for 18 years and concentrated her efforts working with families. She worked with the First Methodist Church to establish and run the Mother's Club in Lauderdale Courts. All of the housing projects had a mother's club and Bell would organize the mothers as she worked with the families. Other workers often ventured into high-crime neighborhoods to work with wayward teenagers. It took time to cultivate the trust of these young people, as the Youth Service workers often hung out with them on street corners, alleys, and in pool halls. The process to gain a young person's confidence was slow, yet visible progress was being made one step at a time.

Often, group workers would accompany a recently arrested youth to Juvenile Court to provide guidance and encouragement. The caseworkers also visited the homes of teenagers to discuss their problems with parents or guardians. There, the caseworkers could witness and report the home environment conditions. They often referred these young people and their families to other health and welfare agencies if they needed further assistance.

The group workers organized clubs when gang activity seemed imminent and utilized existing educational, recreational and community social programs to combat delinquency. The road to recovery was slow for a boy whose rehabilitation was interrupted by serving a sentence in the state reformatory for car theft or spending time in the charity ward of a hospital for injuries received from a street stabbing. To some of the kids, the male group workers became loving and understanding father figures, enabling new attitudes and positive behaviors to develop.

One important resource allowed Father Don to stay abreast of the most recent happenings in the housing projects. The Memphis Police Department approved the installation of police radios in Father Mowery and Foster Adams' cars. The Juvenile Court dispatcher routed the incoming calls to Youth Service; therefore, communication and response time in the field were greatly improved. Father Mowery, in a parallel manner, was involved with the Law Enforcement Committee, a division of the Optimist Club, which promoted respect for law enforcement. He also worked with Judge Turner, Dr. Jack Sparrow, and Dr. Fredrick Green, director of the National Children's Bureau. Dr. Green, who was interested in the work of Youth Service, had a representative with his Washington, D.C. office come to Memphis to conduct a complete evaluation of the Youth Service program in order to benchmark the benefits, methods, and experiences.

Father Mowery wrapped up the interesting summer of 1966 with an array of activities for young people in the Youth Service program; however, activities such as camping and swimming at Shelby and Fuller State Parks had become standard. Other special events were added, such as an outing on the Mississippi River with the Marine Rescue Squad headed by Commander Barney Butler, head of attendance for Memphis City Schools, and the Art Tea event at LeMoyne College.

Early in 1967, Youth Service received funding from the Anti-Poverty Bill to expand services into several more trouble spots. This allowed for an additional 16 workers for the coming summer. These additional staff members were primarily schoolteachers who worked for Youth Service during the summer, men and women, black and white. Because of the expanded staff, five more troubled areas were able to receive additional services from the agency, including the neighborhoods of Orange Mound, Hollywood, Whitehaven, Gregg School, and Lamar Terrace. Youth Service reached out to over 11,000 young people in Memphis and Shelby County with much-needed services that summer.

Father Don recalled a humorous story, which occurred in March of that year. Group worker Foster Adams called late one night to advise him that one of the boys in his charge had won a Shetland pony during a hockey game giveaway at the Mid-South Coliseum. However, moving the pony from the fairgrounds became a problem. Fortunately, Youth Service supporter Mrs. J.B. Cook was contacted and graciously agreed to keep the pony at her estate until other arrangements could be made for the animal. Adams removed the seats from a Volkswagen bus in order to transport the pony to Mrs. Cook's residence. The pony was too small for the teenagers to ride, so it stayed with her as a pasture pet until it was sold about a year later. There are many interesting stories, some happy, some sad, involving the countless young people Father Don counseled.

CHAPTER EIGHT

Rapidly Changing Times: 1968

The work of Youth Service continued to expand across neighborhoods that needed assistance in addressing growing problems with youth within the city. Father Mowery began to ride with city police officers on their beats and with deputy sheriffs on their nightly rounds in the county. In doing so, Father Don and the Youth Service staff were not simply passive members on the sidelines during these turbulent times.

Unfortunately, crime and delinquency in Memphis was growing at a greater rate than the services available to support delinquent youth. For example, *The Commercial Appeal* reported that approximately 60 young people were arrested each month in the Whitehaven area alone during the first 10 months of 1966. Whitehaven residents, disturbed over the high rate of delinquency and crime, organized a committee in 1967 that raised $7,000 for programs to curb juvenile problems. David Finley was one of the committee-paid Youth Service workers and began a counseling program with about 40 Whitehaven youngsters facing juvenile court action. Mrs. Harry Baddour served as chair of the Youth Service committee in charge of raising funds to combat this delinquency problem. Other members were trying to get Whitehaven churches to sponsor or expand year-round youth programs. One participant encouraged delinquent kids to attend church-related activities, but at the same time, mentioned that some of the churches were reluctant to open their doors to troubled youths.

The Whitehaven committee reached an agreement with the Sheriff's office and the Juvenile Court, which allowed Finley to counsel first offenders. This action prevented many of them from acquiring police records. The counseling agreement carried with it certain restrictions. Under the agreement, young offenders were required to obey their parents, attend church and school regularly and refrain from unlawful acts and offensive behavior. The participating youth, the parents, a juvenile squad officer, and Finley had to sign the agreement. Any violation of its terms by the young offender could send them to juvenile court for action. In the first year of the program, none of the youngsters Finley counseled under the agreement were sent to Juvenile Court, a testament to the effectiveness of the program.

Despite the efforts of the juvenile squad and Youth Service, delinquency continued to grow in the Whitehaven area. In October 1967, for instance, there were 50 more juvenile arrests than a year earlier, which was largely the result of the expansion of the Sheriff's Department Juvenile Squad from one man to four. The youngsters, who ranged in age from nine to 17, were being arrested for various offenses such as minor thefts, siphoning gasoline, public drunkenness, and disturbing the peace. Interestingly, most of the youngsters came from families with average or above-average incomes. People who knew of troubled teens began to call Finley directly rather than the Sheriff's office. He was glad to report, "I'm finally getting a chance to work directly with disturbed young people before they come to the attention of the Sheriff's office."

Public awareness of the Youth Service program was always critical. By January 1968, churches began to offer space for counseling, while parents, teachers and ministers were asking for Finley's help. He and police Lt. Tony Sanson urged families, churches and civic organizations to take an increasing role in providing outlets for youth and group counseling programs to help solve the entrenched problems of wayward youngsters. The committee hoped to organize panel discussions with youths at various Whitehaven churches in hopes that they would take responsibility for helping other young people in the community.

The time had come for Youth Service to take a serious look at beginning a program of instructional help with the young people, so the agency began to pattern its work after a new innovative project. A discussion ensued of how Youth Service might adopt an effective school dropout program, originally used in the ghettos of New York City. The program recruited 100 young people in the Memphis community who were dropping out of school with high IQs, but had performed poorly in school. The project helped them to overcome the failure syndrome cycles and to better prepare them in English and math, which provided them with a greater sense of self-confidence and self-respect. The agency also provided psychiatric help for selected adolescents and teenagers.

Another prominent community service agency, the Junior League of Memphis, proposed a public forum on delinquency in 1968. A panel consisting of Sheriff Bill Morris, Memphis Police Director Frank Holloman, Juvenile Court Judge Kenneth Turner, and Father Mowery addressed the issues of teenage delinquency in Memphis. The purpose of their meeting, which took place at Christ United Methodist Church, was to create interest among the various churches and civic clubs in recognizing and promoting assistance programs for young people in the central and eastern parts of Memphis.

Interventions with wayward youth began to reach every area of the city, but these interventions did not always result in jail time. In one instance, two boys stole a car in Memphis, drove it 200 miles into Mississippi, then returned the car. The authorities apprehended the boys, but the owner failed to press charges because she did not want the boys to have a police record. After meeting with the boys, their parents, and Juvenile Court authorities, they were paroled to the supervision of Youth Service.

Youth Service continued to work closely with Juvenile Court and created a supervised program that helped reclassify many young people to a probationary status rather than have a docketed arrest record against them. Father Don also supported preventive measures that would steer youths away from crime and bad behavior. Youth Service group workers invited 150 young people to see the inspirational movie, *The Restless Ones*. Concerned business people who wanted to help bring a "scared straight" perspective to young people tempted by a violent life brought this film to Memphis.

In yet another illustration of effective networking with law enforcement officials, Father Mowery and Youth Service supporter Jack Stepherson of the Optimist Club discussed options with Police Commissioner Claude Armour. The agency workers and the police officers in their areas worked with the young people to instill a greater respect for the law and build a better relationship with teenagers and the police. Relations between Youth Service and the Police Department were very good. Father Mowery became a permanent lecturer at the Memphis Police Academy and was appointed by the Memphis and Shelby County Juvenile Court as an auxiliary probation officer. Youth Service also played an active role in a testimonial dinner for Judge Turner and the Court in March 1968, displaying another example of close support and solidarity with law enforcement officials and members of city and county government.

Juvenile crime had spread graphically throughout Memphis and Shelby County during the late sixties. The delinquency rate, which continued to rise in affluent East Memphis, caused concern among all law-abiding citizens. The threat was widespread, which prompted Calvary Episcopal Church to raise enough money to fund another full-time caseworker in East Memphis. The issues concerning youth in the South Memphis community of Whitehaven became serious enough to start an ecumenical movement that involved seven denominations and numerous men's and women's clubs donating money for a full-time caseworker there. The surge in juvenile crime prompted Judge Kenneth Turner to reveal a report that found children under the age of 18 committed 62 percent of major crimes in the city. It became more and more evident to the residents that there was a critical need for the work of agencies such as Youth Service.

Youth Service officials also tried to interest Memphis boys in scouting. They had hoped that Boy Scouts could begin working with the boys after they graduated from the Youth Service experience. However, in the late 1960s, the scouts had little funding for youth work outside of the specific Boy Scout mission, and most urban kids did not have the money for uniforms or equipment. Regardless, some of the inner city boys took advantage of the opportunity to become scouts as the Boy Scouts began to increase their involvement with inner-city youths.

Countless other examples exemplify Father Don's work with troubled teens. One interesting case arose when a 14-year-old boy was arrested and taken to Juvenile Court for a minor offense. When questioned, the boy revealed that he and his mother had burglarized numerous homes during the past year. The duo's modus operandi was as follows: The mother would check the newspaper for wedding announcements to locate the houses where bridal gifts would be sent prior to the wedding ceremony. She and her son would arrive when the family was away for the wedding. She then placed their own house cat through an opening to check for dogs that might be in the home. If there were no occupants, the two entered the house and left with all of the wedding gifts they could carry. After receiving this statement from the boy, he was immediately taken from his mother and sent to French Camp Academy, a rural home and school for wayward youths located in north-central Mississippi.

Judge Turner sent many young people to French Camp. Their staff had an excellent reputation for counseling youths far away from the enticements and complications of the city and because of their faith-based approach.

Since early childhood, many inner-city children were taught to hate and fear the police. To counter this image, the Community Relations Bureau, a then-new division of the Memphis Police Department, went into action. Police officers attended the club meetings sponsored by Youth Service group workers and tried to change the negative image of police officers. The meetings provided an opportunity for the young people to get to know the police officers under better circumstances.

Father Mowery realized that many of these young people were destructive in various ways. No one wanted them, so they turned to each other. Youth Service allowed and often encouraged the young people with whom they came into contact to form social clubs. The biggest problem for the development of these clubs was finding a safe place to meet. The agency helped to form two boys clubs; one met at St. Mary's Cathedral and the other at Emmanuel Church. Each club elected their own officers and conducted their own meetings. Additionally, Robert Walker, director of the Memphis Fire Department, offered selected fire stations around the city as meeting places for the groups.

The Youth Service boys clubs continued the camping trips to Fuller and Shelby Forest state parks. The target population for this program came primarily from the housing projects that served needy children. Camping expanded to include out-of-town trips to Natchez Trace State Park with a full-time camp director. Activities included not only camping, but also boating, swimming, leather crafts, ball teams and competitive tournaments. Counseling was a very important part of this process of working with kids who ranged from age 9 to 19. Often, many of these boys had managed to get kicked out of school by age 16, and most of their parents were not concerned as much with formal education as they were with having another wage earner in the house.

Don realized the value of the camping program from how the experience taught urban youth the valuable lessons of self-reliance and teamwork. Unfortunately, the Neely Foundation informed Father Don in January 1968, that funding for upcoming camping programs would be reduced. A new source of support was needed if the program were to continue. Tents and camping equipment were worn from several years of hard use and needed to be replaced. Where could he find the facilities and support he needed? Would all these years of hard work go down the drain? It was an anguishing period for Don, but using his well-established "spiritual network," he always found a way to make it happen.

THE ASSASSINATION OF DR. MARTIN LUTHER KING, JR.

The spring of 1968 found Memphis in the throes of the citywide sanitation workers strike. The setting was one of a racial divide because most of the striking workers were African-American. Street marchers began protesting poor pay and working conditions, which brought eruptions of periodic violence to the downtown area. By the end of March, the strike drew Dr. Martin Luther King, Jr. to Memphis to mediate the situation.

Father Mowery knew the strike would have a considerable impact on the city and Youth Service and cause ripple effects farther afield. Since they worked with young people in the streets, the agency's staff worked closely with the police department and juvenile court authorities to help check any rumors or information that could prevent an outbreak of crime and violence. They cautioned the students not to participate or excite any disturbance, rather, to concentrate on positive, constructive work with teenagers. With this new threat, there was a growing concern for the safety and welfare of the young people of Memphis. Because of this volatile situation, Father Mowery requested additional two-way radios for the staff members, so they could monitor the events from their cars.

Any historical account will properly put into perspective the tragic assassination of Dr. King who was shot and killed on April 4, 1968 at the Lorraine Motel in downtown Memphis. The fact that this sad event occurred near Ground Zero of Youth Service operations placed the event in the heart of everyone associated with the organization. Nevertheless, it was in the aftermath of this tragedy that Youth Service went to work once again with creativity, understanding and tenacity.

The day Dr. King was killed was a very traumatic time for Father Don, Youth Service and the city of Memphis. Father Mowery recalled the tense the situation and the events from that day:

> Earlier in the day I had been on the roof of the McCall Building where the Youth Service offices were located, watching the march of sanitation workers with signs bearing the humble inscription: 'I Am a Man.' The police helicopter spotted me on the roof of the building and thought I might potentially be a sniper. After receiving a call from a friend, I made a quick descent from the roof before they closed in on me.

> At 6:01 p.m., the exact time Dr. King was shot, I was inside Jim's Barber Shop on South Main Street, which was adjacent to the Malco Theater (now the Orpheum Theatre). The shop, which was only a few blocks from the scene of the shooting, was an African-American-staffed barbershop, and since my office was in the McCall Building next door, I would always have my haircut there. Our Youth Service workers began to obtain valuable information from the inner-city kids that the authorities needed. We immediately funneled that information to the

police department to help prevent violence and property damage. We were very much involved because the Main Street and Beale Street protest marches were virtually around the corner from our office. I knew that many white people did not accept Dr. King's presence, and he had some problems with his own marchers, so trouble seemed imminent.

Suddenly, I heard a loud siren. I was on Main Street, which is now the South Main Historic District and I knew something was wrong. At the same time, a fire department ambulance rushed by Jim's Barbershop. I told the barber something serious must have happened because it was coming from the area of the Lorraine Motel, where Dr. King was staying. We turned on the radio and heard that he had been shot. The barbershop closed immediately and we vacated the building because of the dangerous situation. I knew that there would be trouble in the city that night and onward for some time. I hurried to my car and heard on my police radio the dispatcher mention the chase of a white Ford Mustang - and sheer confusion. As I passed Main and Beale streets, I saw several police cars and Sheriff Bill Morris racing down the street to the scene of the crime.

As soon as the news spread of Dr. King's death, chaos ensued. Don called the Youth Service staff and told them to suspend work with the kids in the streets until they could determine a plan of action. The city issued a citywide curfew and Memphis entered into a virtual lockdown for the next several days.

Shortly after Dr. King's death, Memphis clergy representing all denominations met at St. Mary's Cathedral. In an impromptu move, Dean William Dimmick of St. Mary's (later Bishop of Northern Michigan) took up the Cathedral's processional cross and led many of the assembled ministers of various denominations down Poplar Avenue to City Hall. They petitioned Mayor Henry Loeb to end the sanitation worker strike, which King was helping to negotiate. That action represented a bold move, since some church members disagreed with Dimmick's reputation for supporting the strikers and promoting racial unity.

A command post was established at Idlewild Presbyterian Church to coordinate the efforts of the social service agencies that worked with youth of the city during this troubled time. A planning room was set up to develop strategies to coalesce a fractured and hurting community.

The overwhelming emotions of fear and rage existed in the Memphis community after the assassination. Father Don realized the explosive potential of the situation and with a small group of Youth Service street workers, went into the troubled neighborhoods to try to maintain peace. They tried to channel angry young people into constructive rather than destructive paths.

The Tennessee National Guard was quickly deployed in an effort to stem potential violence and property damage. Army tanks and personnel carriers lined the streets, and troops carrying loaded weapons instilled fear and dread on every corner of downtown Memphis. Random fires were set in the area and property damage from break-ins and looting added to the danger and confusion. The curfew helped to quiet a violent city as night approached.

The local social service agencies realized early on that they needed to begin to work together for the benefit of the youth of Memphis. Father Don recalled how the leaders began to ban together to address the situation:

> They realized the critical nature and potential destruction, which could be unleashed because of this incident. The leaders of Shelby United Neighbors (SUN) told me and the Youth Service team that if we could develop a good, innovative program to keep kids off the streets, they would help pay for it. With the SUN funding, we immediately set to work to raise money to begin programs that would assist inner-city youths living in recently damaged areas of the city.

> Donations received from this effort were combined with emergency surplus funds that had been earmarked for times when money either was short or was needed for a special program. Interestingly, the money donated by Elvis Presley provided funding for many of these special programs and expanded our services during that turbulent time and for several years.

To further compound the already tense situation, Father Don received a call from the FBI shortly after the assassination. They informed him of a man that was believed to be coming through Memphis with a mission to kill priests. Because of his high profile as a community leader, Don was considered a prime target and was warned to be careful traveling in the city, especially at night. The FBI assigned an agent to shadow Don until the threat passed. Fortunately, the killer was arrested about three weeks later in another city.

In the aftermath of Dr. King's assassination in April, some doubted if there would be any youth activities in Memphis for the summer of 1968. Father Don's camping program, which had both black and white campers, became problematic and could not continue in its present format. Therefore, a new strategy had to be developed in the wake of this tragedy.

CAMPING AND VOCATIONAL EXPOSURE PROGRAM

As Father Mowery tried to launch the summer camp in 1968, Youth Service had to tackle the racial problem head on. Obviously, race relations had taken a step backwards with the civil rights leader's death. Those who were not in Memphis in the spring of 1968 following the death of Martin Luther King, Jr. may find it difficult to understand the climate of the city during this critical time. As fear and confusion gripped the city, the goal for Youth Service was to find a safe place for the youngsters that would take them away from the day-to-day stress of street life.

Father Don's good friend Shelby County Sheriff Bill Morris called him shortly after Dr. King's assassination, warning Don that camping in Fuller Park with his group of interracial Youth Service kids would not be safe. Morris was afraid that someone would take a shot at the group, which would create more havoc throughout the city. He urged Don to discontinue the camping program in the public parks and to make other arrangements.

Sheriff Morris was right. Don began searching for an alternative location for the integrated camping program:

> The sheriff suggested that we discontinue the camping program. SUN on the other hand, said they would pay for it if we could conduct a program. I believe it was board President Lester Crain, former Navy pilot, who suggested that we contact the Naval Air Station (NAS), just outside of Memphis near Millington, as an alternative location.

At that time, NAS Memphis was the world's largest inland Navy base. Father Don thought it would be perfect for camping and began to envision a plan to use some of the vacant government land to pitch tents and have some of the same activities they enjoyed in the state parks. Concern that the upcoming long, hot summer would see a renewal of disturbances was the driving force behind the move. Father Don approached officials at the Naval Base to determine if the idea was viable. Not surprisingly, the base executive officer, who imagined too many military regulations to over-come, rejected Don's plan. The executive officer cited three reasons for rejecting the request: First, civilians were not authorized to reside on or use a military facility for any non-military purpose, secondly, this type of program had never been done before, thirdly, the Navy would be respon-sible if someone in the program was injured.

Father Don remembered his disappointment after the meeting, but still pursued the matter:

> With the tense climate in the Memphis community after the assassination, still the idea seemed like a good one. The more I thought about it, the more I was motivated to make it work. I began to think how the young Navy personnel could influence our teenage boys in a positive way and how they could share their stories and give them hope of a different kind of life.

However, in order to initiate such a program, more groundwork and a major influence was needed. Because of Father Don's community work, he often visited the United Service Organization (USO) where Executive Director, Ella Turner, hosted sailors and marines from the Memphis Naval Air Station. She invited Al Whitman, a Memphis stockbroker and Military Affairs Council member of the Chamber of Commerce, to discuss the issue over lunch with Father Mowery. From his meeting, it became obvious to Whitman that Don had much to learn about military protocol if he were to find a way to use the base facilities. Fortunately, Whitman knew how to be creative in connecting the commanding officers and their wives with the community and often invited them to lunch at Calvary Church Waffle Shop.

As if by divine providence, Ella Turner invited Father Don to a tea a few days later. Attending the gathering was RADM Ernest E. Christensen, Chief of Naval Technical Training, and his wife Marge. ADM Christensen had several bases under his command, one of which was NAS Memphis, which also served as his headquarters.

While at the Saturday event, Don made the most of the opportunity to bring up the camp idea again and recalled:

We were all sitting at a table together and the admiral left to speak with some other people, leaving his wife Marge and me to talk. I pulled out a letter I had just received from Brinson Paul, the first youngster I had met and counseled on my first day on the job in the Memphis Hurt Village housing project. The letter said at length how much his experience with Youth Service had helped and influenced him in a positive way. Brinson said how proud he was to be a part of the Marine Corps and felt that he was doing something that was truly worthwhile.

When the admiral's wife heard that the executive officer rejected Father Don, Marge said, "That is ridiculous. I want you to come back to the base on Monday and ask again." Don returned on Monday morning as she requested and was pleasantly surprised with a much different attitude. The executive officer walked up to Don and said, "I don't know what happened over the weekend, but I received a rare call from the admiral at my quarters yesterday." The admiral had heard about Father Don's request to use the base for a youth camping program and decided to allow Youth Service base privileges, but under certain conditions. The admiral realized that he could not legally authorize the use of the base, but agreed to support the program in a somewhat clandestine fashion. Father Mowery accepted the offer on the spot. As fate would have it, Don's brief conversation with the admiral's wife proved to be decidedly influential, and the beginnings of a camp at the military base became a quiet reality, yet a reality all the same.

Sadly, two weeks later, Father Mowery received word that Brinson Paul had been killed in action serving in Vietnam. The news of Brinson's death hit Don like a bolt of lightning. Father Don had helped many young people over the years at Youth Service and most were doing well, but Brinson, well, he was special. Brinson's experience with Youth Service acted as the catalyst, which helped transform a fledgling camping program into what would later become a national model.

There were strict conditions to such a planned arrangement for the first year. For example, Father Don had to be present any time the young participants were on the base. As a result, Father Mowery spent the entire summer of 1968 on the base, with only an occasional trip to Memphis for a staff meeting. On his birthday that year, longtime Youth Service supporter Mrs. J. B. Cook brought Don a cake. They celebrated the occasion sitting on the sidewalk at the base because Don did not want to leave the camping area.

Another stipulation was that the program had to be entirely a Youth Service program and not a Navy program – in other words, the agency had to provide the supervision and funding for the counselors. No civilian program of this kind had ever been tried on a military base, so Don had to accept responsibility for the program and all of the participants. This initiative quickly gained additional support from the President's Youth Opportunity Program, United Way, the Memphis Chamber of Commerce, community leaders, the Youth Service board, and a host of volunteers. With this humble beginning, Don initiated what became the first civilian program of its type to operate on a U.S. military base.

After seeing the progress of the camping program, the admiral surprised Don by offering him access to several activities available on the base. However, he added a third condition with this statement, "Our mission here is to be a technical school for navy personnel. Our students are in class during the day, so you may use our facilities until 3:30 p.m. At that time, the premises must be vacated for use of our Navy and Marine students." As a result, the campers enjoyed recreational amenities such as bowling, hiking, basketball, volleyball, and softball.

In the evenings, the campers and counselors gathered to discuss what they had accomplished and learned on that day. Counselors provided spiritual guidance during these meetings and gave credit to naval personnel who assisted with the program. This evening activity proved to be one of the most important times of the day.

ADM Christensen and Marge became very interested in the program and wanted to know more about the campers. Father Don described the kids as inner-city teenagers who had entered the program with criminal records, delinquency problems, or family issues. Others were on probation or wards of Juvenile Court. Many of them were in trouble at school and did not understand the value of education. "We were just trying to keep them in school and out of trouble during the summer, while at the same time trying to teach them how to enjoy a totally new experience," Father Don explained.

The admiral later added, "Instead of sleeping in tents, I have an old barracks you are welcome to use. That would give the kids hot and cold water for showers. Also, instead of cooking your food outside, you can eat in our galley." Don was elated with the use of the barracks and the food, but was concerned because Youth Service could not afford to pay for these amenities. The admiral's response was almost unbelievable. He replied, "It will cost you almost nothing, because we want to support your program." However, the Navy will have to charge for the food, which was only $1.50 for three meals a day, and it was all one could eat. Don could not refuse and enthusiastically accepted the admiral's offer.

The Navy base provided training for service members who were about to begin their work in any of the 170 jobs within the naval system. The admiral suggested organized tours for the Youth Service participants in hopes that some of them might be inspired to be a mechanic or an air traffic controller. This initiative prompted the vocational (job) exposure part of the program, to be added to the camping experience.

The base was very well organized and disciplined, something that these kids had never seen. The Navy provided scheduling for the many recreational activities provided. ADM Christensen later authorized the full use of the base gym, baseball fields, swimming pools, as well as fishing and boating on the lake. The campers also enjoyed horseback riding and organized track meets, which gave them an opportunity to display their athletic skills.

Finally, ADM Christensen insisted on yet one more caveat: He did not want the program publicized until it was fully tested. The admiral needed time to gauge its success and shortcomings since they were operating the camp without proper authorization.

NAS Memphis had many capable officers such as Chuck Novak, who was assigned the task of scheduling visits of campers to the different areas of the base. His coordination was a prime factor in the success of the first camp. Additionally, the military personnel benefited from working with a positive and meaningful Youth Service program. Novak later became a key individual when the program expanded nationally. CDR Joe Duggar, who had responsibility for recreation on the base, was also invaluable to the success of the program. Don recalled, "Joe loved kids and would leave no stone unturned to get what we needed."

Don remembered, "We had kids of both races together at the base, so they could learn about each other. There were usually more African-American kids because there was more need in that community. We began to notice that many of these kids acquired leg cramps and had to be pulled from the swimming pool. As a result, we changed the routine of when we ate." That discovery led to the base doctors giving physical exams to every Youth Service camper within the first hour of their visit. This was another first for the program and provided protection for both the Navy and the campers. The Navy doctors were very interested in this discovery and wanted every child examined to determine the cause. They quickly discovered that the leg cramps were caused by an inadequate diet.

Health problems discovered among the kids led to referrals and subsequent medical treatment for many of them when they returned home.

As a result, the doctors corrected some of these issues at no expense to the teenagers or their families. The agency contacted the parents in cases where their children needed serious medical attention. Additionally, Youth Service asked the doctors in Memphis to help. "We had a large number of professional men and women; doctors, dentists, lawyers and others, who volunteered their help whenever we called on them," Father Don said.

Once the Naval personnel became aware of the purpose of the program, they were committed to making this a positive experience for the participants. The kids arose at the sound of reveille each day and retired with taps along with the base personnel. They marched, ate food in an orderly fashion from the galley, and stood inspections. They even took the standard Navy physical fitness test during their visit. By the time they left the station, many of the youngsters had adopted many of the accepted military behaviors.

The Youth Service camping program also placed a big emphasis on character building. The combined civilian-military leadership model had paid off. The guidance and attention also inspired examples of latent determination in many of the youngsters. The boys began to gain a respect for authority they had never experienced before. They also knew that Father Don was a priest of the Episcopal Church, which instilled trust and was a moving force behind the new, enriching life to which they were being introduced.

As the program matured that first summer on base, the nature of its mission as a training facility became an added benefit. The classroom and teaching facilities offered an opportunity for the youngsters to view the technical training firsthand and learn about the different jobs taught on the base. These were the seeds of what would later become the formalized Vocational Exposure Program. This fostered competition among the participants and allowed them to make new friends.

Finally, the admiral agreed to share the success of the program with the public. The *Blue Jacket*, a publication of the Memphis Naval Air Station, reported in October 1968 that more than 3,500 Youth Service campers and counselors passed through their gates that summer on tours and for related activities. Among that large, youthful contingent were hundreds of previously forgotten young people, most subjects of poverty, many of whom had never been outside their impoverished neighborhoods, let alone inside a Naval Air Station. The Youth Service staff worked diligently to free these young people, at least briefly, from their impoverished environments and to channel their talents and energies into more constructive activities.

Father Don recalled with enthusiasm:

We had the full support of the commanding officer who wanted it done right. They did everything they could to help us. The Navy and Marine personnel began to assist in the program with some friendly competition with the naval personnel. It provided the base personnel an opportunity to help others. It was great for our program because it helped the kids learn about teamwork.

During the turbulent summer of 1968, Youth Service ran the camping program seven days a week with no weekends or days off. There were as many as 50 teens in each group, depending on the resources available, with at least one Youth Service counselor for every seven campers. The experience became increasingly popular, consequently each time the Sheriff's department bus picked a group of kids from St. Mary's Cathedral parking lot, a "standby" group would wait patiently with their paper sacks and tennis shoes or whatever they were wearing, hoping that someone would drop out, so they could take their place.

The Youth Service counselors were heavily involved in selecting participants for the camping program, assisted by Juvenile Court officers and teachers with the Memphis City School system. Youth Service counselors provided needs-based criteria, and together these groups made the final decisions. Youth Service staff worked closely with the schools on a regular basis and knew most of the teachers. Many of schoolteachers, who knew some of the boys, became paid counselors for the summer.

Groups of about 50 young men formed competitive squads upon their arrival to the base. In the background, jets were taking off and landing, and sailors were marching back and forth to the barking orders of their instructors. The counselors paired the campers with someone they did not know in order to promote diversity awareness. Once inside the first building, they would see Father Don's "magic words," "Yes, sir," "No, sir," "Thank you, Sir," and "Please" posted at the camp." The campers used these words during their entire stay at the base, especially in the mess hall, in order to teach them proper manners and to show their appreciation to those who served them food.

At the camp, the group lined up according to height from the tallest to the shortest boy in one single line. After counting off, the boys were divided into equal squads for parity. Each camper wore either a yellow, green, blue, or maroon colored T-shirts immediately upon their arrival. Squads were formed and room assignments were made according to the color of their shirt. A sense of competitiveness filled the ranks as the young men began their camping experience. Father Don recalled how the camp affected the lives of these young people:

> I witnessed many benefits from the camps. Most of the young people changed their self-centered ways because of the program and began to work together as a team. The young military personnel who assisted as counselors also benefited from the experience. The military volunteers were excellent role models and were able to contribute to the growth and development of the campers. Everyone stopped in the morning when the flag was raised so the kids could see firsthand the respect and discipline shown for their country. These things were new to the campers, but they soon became part of our routine as well.

Many of the first Youth Service campers recalled fond memories of the experience. "Deadrick," a 16-year-old African-American youth was recruited to attend the first summer camp at NAS Memphis. He had heard about the camping experience from a younger brother who was in the first week of camp there. He had always wanted to go to a summer camp, but being the oldest of five brothers, this was not possible. His father worked for the Illinois Central Railroad and provided only a modest income for his family. Deadrick was accepted with the fourth group that summer and related his feelings:

> All of a sudden, I became rich. You know, like Santa Claus pouring gifts on you. There was not enough time in a day to do all that was available at camp. From sun-up to sun-down, we were in activities designed to show us the inside of the base and to educate us in the jobs they had there. I could not believe all the facilities they had.

The next summer, Deadrick became a Junior Counselor at the newly formed Youth Service program at Blytheville Air Force Base in Arkansas. He was paid $30 a week for organizing the campers, cleaning up the barracks at the end of each camp, and standing fire watch. At the end of the summer, he flew with 60 specially selected campers to Pensacola, Fla. for a six-day stay at the Pensacola Naval Air Station. The boy recalled, "I lived with kids from all backgrounds – black, white, poor minority kids, middle-class, and even rich kids. I still correspond with some of them.

This experience has given me faith that this country is a lot better than the media says it is."

Another success story from those first years of the Camping and Vocational Exposure Program was Air Force Major Willie C. Register, who worked for Youth Service as a college student. Because of his performance and desire to excel, he became a counselor in the Youth Service program. Register eventually joined the Air Force and later became an assistant professor of aerospace studies at Memphis State University. He later became one of the Jaycee's "10 Outstanding Young Men of America for 1981."

Don recalled how nutrition was an important part of the experience for the young campers:

> They learned about new foods that had never seen before. The base furnished the food menu from the galley each week, so the staff knew what they would eat each day. We would have macaroni and cheese or slaw, but many of the inner-city kids had never had these foods. We encouraged them to try something new and as a result most were pleasantly surprised. This became an important learning experience for them," They were getting all the good food at the Naval Air Station that they could eat, but so many of them were used to eating whatever they could scrounge up around the house. Because their digestive systems were not used to a diet of fresh meat, vegetables and milk, many became sick from the rich foods.

The staff also discovered that some of them had been eating a particular kind of dirt they dug up from the ground in their neighborhoods, a kind of sweet clay. Though rich in minerals, it was hardly the wholesome food they needed for proper growth and development.

More than 4,000 naval personnel ate in that galley each day, so the campers had to be on their best behavior. Don and his staff taught the young people to use the "magic words" whenever they addressed others. They learned that any kindness shown to others is always appreciated. These simple lessons were seldom taught at home, but made a lasting impression on the campers. They also took turns offering a prayer before the meals. One time, the lieutenant in charge of the galley admonished Don for arriving with a group five minutes late. Don never forgot the discussion with the officer:

He reminded me about the thousands of people he had to feed each day and how he needed to stay on a strict schedule. It only took one time for him to tell me that. From that point forward, we took extra special care to be on time and to be on our best behavior while in the galley. At the end of the camping season, the lieutenant praised the well-behaved kids and welcomed them anytime.

The Navy base also had a very large hospital that treated hundreds of wounded service personnel who had returned from Vietnam. During their convalescence, the service members visited the Youth Service campers, and many helped the program in various ways; telling stories about where they were from and offering words of encouragement to the young people.

Racial reconciliation was a long-standing, behind-the-scenes objective. Robert Jones, one of the African-American Youth Service counselors, once stated, "The greatest thing we achieved with the camping program was that there were no racial problems." Other counselors, Youth Service employees, and Navy and Marine volunteers assigned to the camp for this first summer session, shared that opinion. One of the volunteers, a Navy Airman, had a degree in psychology and had worked previously in a youth program, was asked if he had observed any difficulties between African-American and white youths. "No, I didn't, which surprised me. I thought I would, but I actually thought the African-American and white boys behaved better with each other than they did in their own racial groups."

Harrell Morgan, the Youth Service camp director, was a little more reserved in estimating the change:

Over the week, if any specific change had taken place, it was in the boy's attitude toward people different from him. They were not quite as prejudiced once they started to know the other boys. However, it is still hard to say for sure what is simply superficial. Nevertheless, I did see quite a bit of togetherness and pride between the boys and their teams.

Father Don recalled how the boys tried to emulate the actions of the military personnel on the base:

The most orderly way to get from our barracks to the galley was to march in formation. Since the sailors and marines marched, the campers wanted to try to outdo the military personnel. It was truly an unfamiliar world to them, but they responded well to the discipline. They learned to be orderly and act appropriately when around others in public.

Youth Service counselors worked hard to instill in the campers the qualities of good citizenship, staying in school, developing their social skills, and planning for a career and a better way of life. Youth Service counselors reinforced these lessons when they visited the homes and assisted the campers and their transition after the camping season. In the evenings, Father Don or one of the camp counselors would debrief the campers about the day's activities in the barracks. Navy chaplains also came in to give informative talks or maybe to discuss an educational film they saw that day. The result was a very comprehensive educational and counseling program for the young people. On the last day of camp, Father Don always urged Youth Service campers to write letters to ADM Christensen to advise him of what they had experienced. Those letters helped reinforce the positive impact of the program among the top brass.

The first camping program on the Navy base began as a three-day event, but quickly grew to a weeklong activity. The growing popularity of the program prompted officials to begin planning for the summer of 1969 almost immediately. No one was more aware of the success or failures than Father Mowery. As he recalled:

> In the early days, Navy officials required me to stay at the camp almost all of the time. If anything went wrong, I wanted to be the first one to know about it. I knew that the camping program could grow into something big and meaningful, and realized it provided a rare opportunity to help these boys understand that they could look forward to more than just their day-to-day existence.

The camp's higher purpose was to let the campers see, for at least five days outside of their own limited worlds, new horizons and to have hope. The formula was simple and included well-trained, dedicated counselors working with youngsters from varied racial, ethnic and economic backgrounds on an informal, "man-to-man" basis, in order to grow self-esteem and to broaden their horizons

In a more intensive experiential sense, the instructors exposed participants to various aspects of engine and airframe mechanics, fire-fighting, air traffic control, and many other jobs that the Navy and Marine personnel learned while in the service. However, these demonstrations were never meant to be a recruiting effort. Youth Service counselors talked with the teens at night and advised them that they could have these opportunities if they would stay in school and get an education. The Navy men and women served as good examples for the kids and told them that they could not join the Navy without a high school diploma. Oddly, many of the campers had never seen anyone get up and go to work in the morning. Many of them hardly knew what work was.

Marine Pvt. Jules King, a camp counselor in the summer of 1968, taught his group that they could do anything they wanted because that was what he learned at Marine boot camp. King said he enjoyed working with the group because he, too, came from a poor family and wanted to pass on lessons he learned to kids less fortunate, so that they could have a better future.

Boys from all backgrounds attended the camps, even those from wealthy families. A board member, who was a doctor at Le Bonheur Children's Hospital in Memphis, explained to Don, "My son, Jim, has attended private schools all of his life and thinks that everyone has a nice house and clothes, good food, and a car. I will pay his way if you will take him to your camp, so he can see how other kids live." Father Don agreed, and when the day came for this young man to go to camp, he arrived at the Youth Service office dressed in a starched shirt and pressed pants. Jim soon saw the other teenagers coming in with their belongings in meager grocery sacks and with their old jeans and tennis shoes that did not fit properly.

Young Jim began to have second thoughts upon seeing the other boys. Jim told Father Don, "I don't think I want to go this week. I will wait and go another time." He did not think he could relate to the other kids. However, Don reassured him and the week-long experience began. By the end of the week, Jim had experienced a life-changing moment. He had made friends with all of the boys and had even given all of his nice shirts to those who did not have much. Jim returned home feeling confident about himself and standing virtually 10 feet tall in his own estimation. He reported to Don, "This has been one of the greatest weeks I've ever had! I love it! Can I go back next week?" Don agreed and made Jim a Junior Counselor, so he could help train the groups during the remainder of the summer. Jim loved the camping experience with the diverse groups and served several times as a counselor, becoming sort of an ambassador for the camping experience. When Jim returned, he told the teenagers at his church, "Every one of you should be required to go through this program.

I learned more about different people in that week at camp than I learned in all of my years in school." Incidentally, this program was the forerunner of Youth Service's successful Bridge Builders program, which began many years later and will be discussed in a later chapter.

Youth Service counselors, hired for the summer to provide both supervision and direction for the boys, were one of the critical links in the program. Like the campers, officials attempted to balance the number of white and African-American counselors, but, according to Father Mowery, it was very hard to find qualified counselors who knew about camping, fishing, and other outdoor recreational activities and could be away from home for an extended time.

Father Don remembered the importance of providing counseling to the campers:

> We tried to keep the ratio of campers to counselors as low as possible. That way, the counselors could spend more time with each boy in order to know him better. Probably, one of the most important parts of the camp was the 'rap' sessions between the counselors and their boys, either individually or together. Sometimes, these boys were deeply moved by a counselor who understood them and could make them see that they could have a happy, productive future.

Youth Service's funding continued to rise by 1968, but the agency needed more money to provide services for an ever-growing youth population. The cost to Youth Service for each camper on the base was surprisingly affordable, about $5.60 per day. A breakdown of the costs for one Youth Service camper included:

Food	$1.50 per day
Insurance	$0.05 per day
T-shirt	$2.00
Counselors	$2.00
Total	$5.60

Most of the funds for the first summer program came from SUN through its Project Extend and from the special project fund donated by Elvis Presley. Youth Service paid for meals, transportation, and counseling for the boys as a part of the project, while the Navy provided the facilities and volunteers donated their valuable time. Since transportation was provided by the Shelby County Sheriff's Department, basic program costs were limited to food, insurance, T-shirts and counselors. This network of resources and the cooperative effort of many others helped Father Don begin the most successful Youth Service program in Memphis.

At the conclusion of each session, Father Don insisted on a formal graduation ceremony at the base chapel for those who successfully completed the camp. Graduation ceremonies were significant events because for most of the participants it was the first program from which they (both boys and girls) had ever graduated. Graduates would invite family members, and dressed up for the special occasion. Father Mowery highlighted the importance of each graduation, which created excitement for the participants and their families:

> Graduation ceremonies clearly were some of the best showcases for the program. The graduates were very excited because many of them invited their families and guests. We also invited company sponsors and representatives from United Way, Juvenile Court, the police department, and officials from the War on Poverty. The graduates would take their guests on a tour to show them the facilities. They had lunch with their guests and shared the special memories of their camping experience. We hoped that the youngsters went home with a better understanding of themselves and a better relationship with their neighbors. We had a guest speaker who conveyed the purpose and importance of the program to the campers and the audience.
>
> Near the end of the ceremony, the graduates removed their colored T-shirts and donned their white Youth Service T-shirt with a cross on the front as a symbol of their accomplishment. Invited speakers told them the story of the cross and that they must wear it with dignity and honor whenever they put on the shirt. The young people realized the value of what we were doing. We wanted them to have a place where they could bring

their personal problems for solutions and receive help in planning their school and job ventures. They usually responded with adult behavior because we treated them as adults.

The military always played a large part in the success of Youth Service. Graduates of these camping programs gained self-respect and discipline, which was a direct result of the military setting. The USO was a United Way agency as well, and the programs of the two organizations had a kindred goal, spirit and methodology. Ella Turner with the USO in Memphis became very involved with Youth Service as an affiliate organization. Father Don and Ms. Turner became good friends, and both directors searched for opportunities that service members could be more involved with young people and community activities. This initiative, originally called Project Extend, was conceived in June 1968 at a thank you party in the home of dedicated Youth Service board member Lester Crain. Later, the name of the program was changed to Big Brother.

SUN sponsored the Big Brother group with the cooperation of the Youth Service and USO. A sailor or Marine from the Navy base was paired with two Youth Service boys and the result was a "Big Brother Team." Every Saturday morning, 30 youngsters selected by Youth Service arrived at the USO Center to team up with 15 military volunteers for a day of activities around the Memphis area. The boys ranged in age from 12 to 16 and usually came from the low-income sections of Memphis. Most of the military personnel looked forward to these weekend activities, and the youngsters enjoyed a full day of activities with their "Big Brothers." The Navy provided buses for transportation, and members of the St. Augustine Guild prepared lunches for the Big Brother groups every week. It was a win-win situation, where the service members could enjoy a weekend activity, while the Youth Service boys had a volunteer mentor to share personal experiences. "This partnership worked out very well for both groups." Don recalled.

The weekly groups visited local sites, such as Shelby Forest, Fuller State Park, the Fairgrounds, the Memphis Zoo, Chucalissa Indian Village, and Lakeland Amusement Park. Eager servicemen interested in the program signed up at the USO center at the beginning of the week, always providing plenty of participants in the program.

Youth Service staff worker Foster Adams briefed the military personnel about the boys before the trips because many of the campers had been in trouble or others came from broken homes. Interestingly, many of the Navy and Marine personnel had similar backgrounds. The Big Brother groups offered a chance for the boys to spend time with someone older who might understand their problems. Adams reflected, "The boys needed an image of authority, which was a hard thing for some of them to accept. It was hard to get these boys to talk about their personal problems, but the servicemen gave them someone to look up to."

Dale Cheek, instructor at the Avionic Fundamental School, served as president of the USO Armed Forces Council. He once said that the service personnel benefited greatly from the Big Brother group. "It gave them a sense of personal responsibility and let them get away from some of their own problems." The Big Brother program was very successful and many of the military personnel returned week after week to participate.

J. D. Carruth, who was United Way Campaign director in 1968, reflected years later that the only way the program worked was from the commitment of Father Mowery. "It was the most successful program that came out of that original investment we made in the youth program and it was the only program to come out of Memphis to have a national impact as a result of Dr. King's death."

There is no doubt that the military connection was a life-changing jump-start for Youth Service and its larger mission. It was central to everything it worked to accomplish from the late 1960s onward. Soon, other vast changes would act as a continuum for future programs. Father Mowery recollected, "Had it not been for the camping program, we would not have developed an association with the military at the Navy base. And, if we had not chosen camping as an activity for these kids, Youth Service in Memphis would have been severely limited and the national Youth Service, USA program would not have existed."

MEMPHIS JUVENILE COURT JUDGE KENNETH TURNER,
1965

MRS. J.B. COOK AND ELVIS PRESLEY AT HER ESTATE,
AROUND 1957

MEMPHIS MAYOR HENRY LOEB IMMEDIATELY AFTER
THE ASSASSINATION OF DR. MARTIN LUTHER KING,
JR., APR., 1968 (PHOTO COURTESY UNIVERSITY OF
MEMPHIS SPECIAL COLLECTIONS, DEPT.)

REAR ADMIRAL ERNEST E. CHRISTENSEN

CHAPTER NINE

Job Training, The Birth Of Youth Service, USA
And Talk It Out With Father Don

The year 1969 was pivotal for Youth Service. Father Don increased his travel ten-fold around the country, promoting the Camping and Vocational Exposure initiatives to military bases. Every day, Don would fly with military officers such as USN CAPT Hap Chandler to a distant military base or would return from a city whose citizens wanted to hear about this unique youth program. The stress of travel was evident as Don stretched every minute of every day to accommodate anyone interested in supporting Youth Service.

The Camping and Vocational Exposure Program launched a significant addition, namely the formative stages of a job-training component. The campers gained valuable information from the vocational exposure they received as they toured the bases and military classrooms. "The average age of the campers was 16 and the average age of the military trainees on the base was 18.5, so there was not much difference," Father Don said. "We would take a 16-year-old boy and turn him loose with the 18-year-old Marine or Navy person and let them tell our camper what he was learning in the military service." In this typical scenario, the military man would reveal his experience as a jet engine mechanic and his plans to work for an airline when he left the Navy.

The Camping and Vocational Exposure Program grew over the years with refinements and vital expansions. Don saw the opportunity to initiate vocational counseling work because he saw career opportunities for the boys as they were touring the bases. ADM Christensen wanted the youngsters to see the types of work performed at the base as well. The summer camping experience that year added a formal job-training program as part of the activities. As camp participants toured classrooms on the base, the young people witnessed firsthand how they could accomplish their goals and prepare to obtain a civilian job.

The young adult military personnel were encouraged to verbalize their Navy experience, as well as their home life with the camper, and the campers listened to them, more than the Youth Service staffers. Many of the young naval personnel had similar backgrounds as the kids in the Youth Service program, therefore they could identify with them. These positive connections and effective networking were what Father Don wanted for the program.

Don had another unique concept and returned to ADM Christensen's wife Marge, who had been so helpful from the beginning. Don wanted to provide formal training as well as vocational exposure to the older 18 to 24-year-olds. The base instructors would provide the training and Youth Service would guarantee jobs for their participants. After some consultation, the admiral agreed to try the idea.

Father Mowery quickly advanced to the next logical step:

> I called on several car dealers in Memphis and asked them if they would hire a person trained by the military as a basic mechanic. Every car dealer I spoke with agreed that their best-trained mechanics were trained by the military. As a result, we chose young men who were unemployed, but were able to successfully complete the classroom training. The trainees could learn this skill in the military way. If the military instructors lacked a few people for a full class, they would fill those chairs with Youth Service people. It did not cost the military anything to fill a few extra seats and the added participants would constitute a full class.

The foundation for the job-training program began in part at the Memphis Defense Depot, which operated as a major supply terminal for the Department of Defense since 1942. Led by USA Col. Bill Freeman, this became a valuable training site for future Youth Service programs. Hundreds of people, both men and women, were provided training classes at the Depot and moved on to well-paying jobs. The program went beyond job training and included coaching assistance on job interviews.

Word about Youth Service's innovative programs began to spread at the end of the first summer camp in 1968. Youth Service's expansion to the Blytheville Air Force Base came about because of an article in the Navy Times. Wing Commander Col. Eugene Minietta at Blytheville had read the article and immediately called Don to discuss starting a weeklong youth camping program at the Air Force base for 1969. However, building a program in another state presented a logistical problem. Don told Col. Minietta that Youth Service would like to expand the program, but could not afford a bus to transport the kids from Memphis to Blytheville, AR. The Wing Commander responded by arranging for an Air Force bus to shuttle the kids for the Monday through Friday camping cycle. With the transportation problem solved, the Youth Service camping program at the Blytheville Air Force Base was underway. Col. Minietta watched the program very carefully during the summer of 1969 to determine if it would be as successful as the one at NAS Memphis.

At the Navy base, tennis shoes, shirts, and shorts were required for base personnel, as well as for Youth Service campers in the gym. However, the Blytheville Air Force Base did not supply those items, and Youth Service did not have funds to buy them. Since the Air Force did not provide them, they would not be able to use the gym. In an unusual gesture of cooperation between the armed forces, the Navy personnel at NAS offered to supply the youngsters attending the Air Force program with shoes and clothing. The Navy officers working with the program said, "Send your bus to the Naval Air Station, and we will give you some supplies, but don't open them until you get to the Air Force Base." Don recalled, "When we arrived at the Air Force base, we opened the boxes to find brand new tennis shoes, shirts, and shorts, all labeled 'U.S. Navy'." Soon afterward, Lt. Gen. David Jones, the commanding general of the Second Air Force, visited the base and saw the kids playing basketball wearing U.S. Navy clothes in the Air Force gym. He quickly asked, "Why do these kids have Navy shoes, shirts, and shorts here on this Air Force base?" Don replied, "Sir, because the base could not provide them for us." Within the next week, all of the campers had new "U.S. Air Force" athletic wear. As it turned out, a little military competition proved to be advantageous for Youth Service.

The Blytheville Air Force Base program was the springboard for providing the Youth Service Camping Program to other bases around the country, yet that role may not have been known at that point in time. Don traveled to Barksdale Air Force Base (headquarters of the Second Air Force) in Shreveport, La., trying to create the same kind of program started in Millington and Blytheville. There, Father Don met again with Gen. Jones, who became a huge supporter of Youth Service and was instrumental in helping the agency expand the camping program to other Air Force bases around the country.

The general reasoned, "After returning from Vietnam, I have so much concern for the youth of this country. I think supporting Youth Service is an excellent example of how the Department of Defense could help these kids." At that point, Gen. Jones initiated an ambitious plan to replicate Youth Service and integrate Youth Service programs in all 15 bases within the Second Air Force and to bases throughout the 15th Air Force command. Gen. Jones once said, "I had confidence that this dynamic, concerned man (Father Mowery) was dedicated to helping young people and if there was any way we could help him, we would."

THE BIRTH OF YOUTH SERVICE, USA

After successful programs at NAS Memphis in 1968 and at Blytheville Air Force Base in 1969, Youth Service, Memphis received approval from military and government officials to expand its programs nationally. However, the organization had to drop its formal affiliation with the Episcopal Church before it could operate on multiple military bases. Created in January 1970, the newly formed Youth Service, USA was non-denominational in structure and now had the proper authorization to work with any military base in the country.

The idea for Youth Service, USA was actually born during a meeting in Lester Crain's living room. As a board member and an ardent supporter, Crain was always a guiding force during Father Don's early years in Memphis. Lester used his background as a Navy aviator and with military protocol to conceive the idea of this groundbreaking program. "Lester was indispensable as a legal advisor and board member and would travel with us on business trips, insisting that he always pay his own expenses. He was also instrumental in setting up programs in new cities," Don recalled.

The organization created corporate charters at two levels with a local Youth Service in Memphis, Inc. and the national Youth Service, USA, Inc. The latter advised and coordinated the tie-in of participating Army, Air Force, Navy, and Marine bases around the country. Separate boards governed each organization. Don remembered:

> I could not have had better boards than I had with both organizations. Each board was composed of hard working people willing to sacrifice their time and make things happen. For that, I am eternally grateful. Again, we were doing the work of helping young people find their direction in life and make them into quality people.

The early national expansion of Youth Service to military bases across the nation was successful largely because of the newly formed Domestic Action Council (DAC) Program. Secretary of Defense Melvin Laird established the Council at the Pentagon in 1969 as the military counterpart of the Urban Affairs Council at the White House. Its purpose was to develop programs in which the military could aid the civilian populace. The Secretary of Defense personally appointed all members of the DAC, which included Joint Chiefs of Staff assistants and Assistant Secretaries of Defense, civilians and other governmental and military people. Youth Service held the unique position as the only non-military, non-federal member of the DAC. The group worked to coordinate government resources in order to promote military-civilian issues. Once established, the Council set out guidelines as to what Youth Service could do operationally in the civilian youth programs.

The DAC was given the task of developing and initiating programs that could alleviate local, regional, and national social and economic problems and to help the nation raise its social and economic standards. As a result, the DAC blessed the establishment of these youth programs in military facilities coast-to-coast. At the same time, several criteria were established, which had to be followed in addition to uniform training of the counselors.

Representatives of the local community and the base officials established each youth program. Youth Service only provided guidance and advice in the start-up phase. Using their local resources, the civilian communities would have to initiate and run the programs with the military, only furnishing facilities and other-in-kind support. This plan emphasized the fact that these programs were a civilian operation. The military officials were very sensitive to any criticism of being "Big Brother" in the Orwellian sense.

Youth Service, USA began a national push in a big way with Don meeting once a month at the Pentagon with the officials of the DAC. Don remembered how he employed his "spiritual networking" abilities to garner support for the program:

> The official sanctioning by the federal government gave Youth Service the direct guidelines we needed by which we could operate and grow our programs. While in Washington, D.C., we called on other parts of the federal government for their assistance, such as the Departments of Health Education and Welfare and Health and Human Services. These departments liked the program because

they were getting extra benefits from tax dollars, and no additional money allocated. It did not cost the government much at all and ran on a non-interference basis. It was a very good partnership.

The military connection was central to everything Youth Service, USA worked to accomplish from 1969 onward. By the late 1970s, through all the weeklong summer encampments, more than 230,000 teenage boys and girls participated annually in the recreational and vocational facilities of the Department of Defense. This was a long way from Father Mowery's first three-day summer camps, where he wanted the boys to experience and enjoy the great outdoors.

ADM Christiansen, the Chief of Naval Training at NAS Memphis, helped spread the word about Youth Service to the other Navy bases by asking Father Don to attend a senior staff meeting at Pensacola to explain the program. Christiansen briefed his old Naval Academy friend, ADM "Smoke" Strean, who commanded the Pensacola Naval Air Station about establishing a program. In a similar vein, ADM Christiansen also contacted the Naval District commander based in Charleston, S.C., creating a program at the Charleston Naval Base. In the military, base commanders change commands about every two years. The new commanders were a positive addition for the Youth Service initiative because they would often look for new and innovative programs to sponsor on their watch. This particularly helped with new start-up programs in Texas, California, and many other states.

Youth Service, Memphis held its annual meeting in April 1969. Over 600 people attended the event held at the Rivermont Hotel in Memphis. The main topic was a review of the 1968 summer youth program, which had reached hundreds of Memphis area boys in a unique and beneficial way. Father Mowery described the role of Youth Service to the audience:

> We took groups of boys to the Navy base and let them live the life of the servicemen for a few days. Some of these boys were school drop-outs who had no future plans. They heard positive messages about staying in school and about obtaining a formal education in order to avoid a police record, which could block their path to a good job.

Father Mowery also told of another important benefit of the program – the effect on the civilian and military volunteers who worked with the boys at camp, as well as the parents of the kids. He related how these volunteers affected the lives of the boys:

> We used the leadership abilities of our workers to reach out and help steer the young people in the right direction. By doing so, they certainly received more than they gave. Mothers of the volunteers often telephoned afterward to thank us for giving their sons the chance to rub elbows with boys who did not have enough to eat, boys whose families did not have an automobile, or enough clothes to go to school. The volunteers quickly realized the importance their work had on the lives of these young men.

One Youth Service counselor shared his feelings about the participants during the meeting:

> Just being on a military base will have an impact on many of these kids. Eating three good meals a day and using these facilities proves to them that the military is not bad. Some of the kids definitely had an attitude change toward the military, and a few may wind up joining the military, but that is certainly not the purpose of it.

At the same annual meeting, CAPT J. E. Godfrey, commanding officer of NAS Memphis, related his thoughts on the program, "Being on the base and having contact with the servicemen definitely does influence the boys, but definitely no effort was made to build a propaganda platform for military recruiters. We know that we do get recruits from Youth Service, but I don't know how many." One camper, who attended the camp and became a Junior Counselor for Youth Service, said he joined the military after being, "impressed with the training and discipline that the Marine Corps offered."

Father Don also met and briefed ADM. Elmo Zumwalt about the Youth Service, USA program shortly after Zumwalt became the Chief of Naval Operations in 1970. Don remembered how the admiral used his influence to help spread the program in the Navy:

> Shortly after the initial briefing, I received a call from ADM Zumwalt's office requesting that I attend a meeting

in San Diego, CA. to brief all admirals assigned to Navy bases west of the Mississippi River. Another meeting was held that year in Norfolk, Va. for all of the admirals east of the Mississippi River. I eventually spoke to every admiral in the entire Navy. I had never seen so many stars at these meetings! ADM Zumwalt eventually endorsed the initiative nationwide and instructed all of the admirals in the Navy to support the Youth Service Program as long as it did not interfere with their primary mission.

Many other key individuals emerged as ardent supporters of the Youth Service program, such as Senator John Warner from Virginia, who became the Secretary of the Navy, and Gen. William C. Westmoreland, the Army Chief of Staff. These two men played vital roles in the national expansion of the Youth Service, USA. A few years later, while Don was attending a meeting at the Pentagon, that relationship was further cemented when Secretary Warner invited Don to travel with him to Groton, Connecticut to take part in a christening ceremony for the USS Groton in August 1973. Warner later became chair of the U.S. Bicentennial Commission, which would factor into the Liberty Celebration in Memphis that Youth Service, USA played a large part. Warner was very impressed with the program and, especially Don's "magic words," "Yes Sir," "No Sir," "Thank You," and "Please."

Father Don served as a Chaplain in the Army Reserve and served on active duty at Fort Bragg, N.C. in 1970. Coincidently, Gen. Westmoreland became ill, and was sent to Womack Army Medical Center at Fort Bragg for treatment. Westmoreland was an Episcopalian, and since Father Don was the only Episcopal chaplain on the base, he became the on call hospital chaplain. That occasion provided Father Don with a great opportunity to speak to the Army Chief of Staff about the Youth Service, USA program.

After learning about the Youth Service program, Gen. Westmoreland immediately wanted to begin the same type of camping program on Army bases. He told Don to "write your own ticket." The general arranged for Don to visit Ft. Monroe, an Army base in Virginia, to begin working with Army personnel. Other bases followed, but the effort to get Army participation proved to be more difficult than the Navy or Air Force, even though Father Don was a member of the Army Reserve. The general also placed him on active duty for a time, so he could tour Army posts in uniform to pitch the camp concept for teenagers. However, Don's initial efforts were largely ignored. The effects of the Vietnam War had weakened the relationship between the military and civilian sectors, leaving the public suspicious of anyone in uniform. Initially, few Army bases were interested in participating from that first tour. Soon; however, six Army bases agreed to sponsor youth training programs because of Don's persistent recruiting efforts. The Army was now fully on board with the Air Force and the Navy.

The Department of Defense (DOD) kept a close watch on operations as Youth Service, USA became more involved with the military. Don met with the DAC officials in Washington, D.C. regularly to brief officials and to ensure them that the programs in various budding locations were legally constituted and meeting their goals. It is interesting that the Department of Defense did not require the base commanders to adopt Youth Service, USA programs. The existence of each program was at the discretion of the local base commander. However, they were encouraged to participate because the program offered many benefits to the youth of this country, as well as the military in which many of the youth ultimately served.

The DAC provided Don with an ongoing list of military bases for Youth Service, USA to visit. Air Force Col. Minietta, who was familiar with the program from his work at the Blytheville Air Force Base, was assigned as project officer to work full-time with the agency. Minietta arranged for these visits, providing Don and his staff an opportunity to tell the base commanders about the program. Don remembered a typical scenario:

> The Air Force assigned us a T-39 aircraft to travel to other bases. We might fly to Grand Forks, N.D. and meet with people on Monday and Tulsa, OK on Tuesday. If the base commanding officer agreed to participate in the program, we would ask him to call a meeting of key people who dealt with young people in the community. These people might include the Juvenile Court judge, representatives of the Boy Scouts and Girl Scouts, and the board of education, among other influential people. We would provide the information to the key people, while at our initial meeting, or come back for a follow-up meeting. The base commander would then endorse the program and offer it to key members in the community. Once introduced to the program and realizing the advantages, people in the neighboring cities were anxious to try the Youth Service model. They were particularly excited about the opportunity of using the neighboring military facility with all of its amenities.

Since Youth Service had its roots in the Episcopal faith, Don would always visit the local Episcopal Church to ask the minister if he would like to help sponsor a youth program, as had been done in Memphis. The church sponsored several programs in this fashion.

After such introductions and logistical work, Youth Service, USA programs emerged one after the other at military bases around the nation. Don soon realized the need for more organizational controls, so geographical regions were created and quite often retired military officers were employed to supervise the programs in certain parts of the country. The Air Force took the lead at an early state, as Gen. Jones commanded over 15 bases. Don's travel schedule increased tremendously. The pace was exhausting at times, but effective. However, having the "chartered" T-39 at their disposal drastically reduced the drive time to important meetings. Youth Service programs grew coast-to-coast on military bases, thanks to Don's logistics work and ever-constant "spiritual networking."

The Memphis-based agency prepared a "how-to" manual, which helped guide the community leaders through the legal and procedural setup processes for their own respective youth programs. Several requirements were unavoidable. First, because of the risk, every camper had to be insured. Fortunately, the group insurance was not expensive during these years and was factored at the rate of about five to ten cents per day per child.

Meanwhile, Youth Service, Memphis expanded its reach into the public and private schools. The agency discovered several years prior that private school families had similar youth problems, but they had more means in which to hire an attorney or psychologist help to deal with their issues. Don recalled preaching one Sunday morning at an Episcopal church where the people were quite affluent. The following Monday morning, he received a call from a parent who said, "I never thought that I would need you, but I would like to meet with you to discuss a serious issue concerning my son." This was not uncommon as Youth Service began working with many wealthy parents to address their own juvenile issues.

The summer program of 1969 was equally successful. The number of Memphis area young people increased to more than 750 for the summer program. Social services for girls were added to the 1969 summer program and Lt. Johanna F. Heimeri, from NAS Family Services, was assigned to lead these activities.

Youth Service recorded one serious incident during the summer of 1969. Twelve-year-old Daniel Lee Davis, a handicapped boy, drowned in the NAS Memphis indoor swimming pool. The boy lived in the all-white Hurt Village housing project. The family was disadvantaged and Daniel's father was dying with cancer. The mother wanted all three of her sons to go to camp; however, one of them had a severe hearing problem and attended special education classes. Youth Service had a policy against serving special education kids at that time because of the risk involved, but she insisted that all three of them attend the camp together. The agency agreed to let the brothers participate and had the mother sign the necessary papers. Don recalled the rules every camper was required to follow and the circumstances surrounding the boy's death:

> The boys were scheduled to go swimming at the indoor pool because the staff felt they had better control over the kids than in the outdoor pools. There was always great concern that no one get hurt. On the first night after eating, the Davis boy marched from the barracks to the swimming pool along with the other boys. When the group arrived at the pool, the written instructions were read aloud and procedures were reviewed. The first rule was no one gets in the water unless permission was granted. The second rule was that no one could enter the deep end of the pool until successfully passing a swimming test, after which, they received a special wristband that identified them as being able to swim in that area.

According to witnesses, young Daniel simply ran and jumped into the deep end, sank to the bottom and never came up. Immediately, the lifeguards pulled the boy out of water and began to resuscitate him; however, it was too late; the boy had drowned. Officials suspected that he may have not heard the instructions or had other health problems, which were undetected at the time. The Memphis newspapers ran a story on the incident, and there was much confusion about exactly what had happened. The mother said she had deliberately told the Youth Service workers not to let her boy swim. However, upon inspection, the paperwork revealed that she had signed an authorization to let him swim along with his two brothers. Don and a Navy Chaplain went immediately to see the mother after receiving the news that her son had drowned. Obviously, the visit was one of Don's most difficult jobs. There were other mishaps and injuries, but all minor in comparison to the fatality. This was the only death that occurred in the program. The family of the drowned boy filed a legal claim against Father Don and Youth Service within a few days of the incident for several million dollars. It was a very unpleasant time for all.

The Youth Service, USA program quickly gained attention and after only two summers, the worthy and growing project gained national recognition. In February 1971, the Freedoms Foundation at Valley Forge, Penn., quite significantly awarded the George Washington Honor Medal to the Naval Air Station and Youth Service, USA for their outstanding work. Father Don and Youth Service won this award for four consecutive years, a distinctive national honor.

TALK IT OUT WITH FATHER DON

Father Don's work with young people went far beyond the camping and job training programs. Most people in the Memphis community came to know Don through his radio show, *Talk It Out With Father Don*. Knowing of Father Don's work with local youth, the manager of WHBQ radio, Jim Bedwell, approached him one day in 1969 and said, "We are the number one radio station for young people in Memphis, and all we are doing is playing music for them and not giving them much exposure that is beneficial. We are thinking about the possibility of having a talk show directed toward these young people."

Initially, Don's response was, "Not on your life!" Don would not consider doing a radio program due to his obligations to the Youth Service agency. However, the station manager persisted and convinced Don of the need and the advantages of spreading the word about Youth Service. He suggested that Don conduct a Joe Pyne-type talk show. Pyne pioneered the confrontational-style talk show in which the host advocated a viewpoint and argued with guests and audience members. However, Father Don believed Pyne's approach was not in line with his ministry and wanted a more positive and friendly call-in style format. Don told him, "I want to have a guest that I can interview – for instance, the chief of police, the Juvenile Court judge, sports figures, community leaders, entertainers, disc jockeys, and other persons of interest."

Bedwell agreed and the radio program began as a live call-in program for young people on WHBQ-AM and FM on Sunday evening January 28, 1970 at 10 p.m. It has remained on WHBQ for 44 impressive years. Interestingly, WHBQ was the first station to air an Elvis Presley record, played by disc jockey Dewey Phillips.

The *Talk It Out With Father Don* radio show became immensely popular. The guest registry, in some instances, looked like a veritable hall of stars, due to the many celebrities who stopped to do the show when passing through in Memphis. "Of course, you never know what a young person is going to say when they call in. We had a 7-second delay, and you had to hear what was said to you. Sometimes, you're working the dials and you didn't always hear every word completely," Don remembered.

The program drew a large listening audience, and Don quickly realized the potential to expand his network faster and across a much broader area. He also invited young people to call him at his office for a private conversation if there was something they wanted to discuss after the program went off the air. This boosted the notoriety and exposure for Youth Service around the region.

The types of questions and topics that aired on the show seem timeless. Don explained the types of calls he received:

> We had kids who were contemplating suicide, kids who were in love and in all sorts of dilemmas. They would all call in and talk about their situations. It was somewhat hair-raising. I had to be able to provide an answer for that young person; live on the radio, and I wanted to make sure my answers were instructive answers that young people needed to hear. The radio show also provided a vehicle for obtaining resources for people in need.
>
> Typical questions we received from young people calling in to Talk It Out included: When should I start wearing makeup? Why won't my parents let me have a motorcycle? What's wrong with drinking or smoking? Is college for me? Should I go steady? Why should I have a curfew?

George Klein, a popular Memphis radio and television personality was a regular listener and avid supporter of Don's Talk It Out radio program in the early years. At one juncture, the radio show combined with a very successful charity event, namely the March of Dimes Walk-a-Thon. Klein participated with Don in the event, which posted record-breaking attendance. The show also broadcast live from the Labor Day Telethon.

Klein was a big supporter and helped promote the agency's image throughout the community. Klein was a one of the most popular deejays in Memphis history and hosted the ground-breaking Talent Party, TV show that aired from 1964 to 1973 on WHBQ. Additionally, Elvis Presley served as George's best man at his wedding. George was one of Elvis' closest friends and a trusted confidant.

Many notable persons listened to Don's radio program and supported the work of Youth Service. Rick Dees, another popular Memphis radio personality, was one of those listeners who helped promote the work of Youth Service. Dees worked for WMPS AM 680 during the disco craze of the late 1970s, when he wrote and recorded *Disco Duck*, the award-wining hit that sold more than six million copies. Rick's success in Memphis, combined with his TV appearances and hit music, led him to relocate to Los Angeles and national acclaim While in Memphis, his participation in Youth Service programs helped to create much needed exposure for the youth agency.

Paul Tudor Jones was another notable listener and a fan of Don's radio show while in high school at Memphis University School. He graduated from the University of Virginia, earning an undergraduate degree in economics in 1976. Jones began working on the trading floors as a clerk and soon became a broker for E.F. Hutton. Jones' cousin William (Billy) Dunavant, Jr., head of Dunavant Enterprises, one of the world's largest cotton merchants, advised Jones along the way. Jones founded Tudor Investment Corporation, which is today a leading global asset management firm headquartered in Greenwich, Connecticut. Jones was also an advocate for the design and implementation of the first ethics training course that became the standard for exchange membership on all futures exchanges in the United States. In 2013, Forbes Magazine listed him as one of the wealthiest men in America. He used his financial success to create the Robin Hood Foundation, which funds more than 240 programs to help the poor in New York City and surrounding areas.

With the radio program gaining popularity, a question soon arose about the hour *Talk It Out* aired. Officials with the Mental Health Association realized that the program was very beneficial, but suggested that 10 p.m. was too late for children to be listening to the program. Many people complained of the difficulty in getting school-aged children to bed. The program moved to a 9 p.m. time slot in order to accommodate younger school-aged children who were frequent listeners.

Over the years, his more notable guests have included celebrities who were national and international stars. In October 1970, Father Don had lunch with Ed Sullivan and his wife, where he had the opportunity to explain the Youth Service program and tape an interview with Sullivan for *Talk It Out*. At the same time, there had been an interview arranged with Arthur Godfrey, who was in Memphis at the time, and Bob Hope called from California on the same day. As a result, on Sunday night, September 27, 1970, Father Don had Sullivan, Hope and Godfrey as guests on the same *Talk It Out* program.

The *Talk It Out* audience spanned over the years from teenagers to young adults and to older parents with children seeking advice and help with personal problems. His first guest, quite appropriately, was Judge Turner of the Memphis Juvenile Court. Judge Turner became a regular guest in the early years of the radio show, which established Youth Service's identity and credibility throughout the Mid-South community. To this day, adult listeners make a point of telling Don how much the show meant to them in their formative years. Father Don now tapes his program and is responsible for arranging the guests each week.

Don remembered when he first started *Talk It Out* he wanted to integrate the Mid-South Fair events into the show format. He talked with Wilson Sparks, the director of the Mid-South Fair, about doing a broadcast from the fair. As a result, Don interviewed performers and fair-goers, which added a new dimension to the broadcast.

Referrals to the agency from *Talk It Out* poured in regularly. One example was a young girl from a needy family, who dropped out of school to work full-time. She was a regular caller and made a special trip to the agency to connect with Father Don. She said she felt that she had no future in her way of living and needed help. The girl eventually joined the Women's Army Corps at Father Don's suggestion and realized her dream of becoming self-sufficient. Later, she honored Father Don by speaking at his retirement reception in 1995.

By the early 1970s, *Talk It Out* was capturing the interest of young people in the Memphis community with an endless number of social awareness topics. One radio show coincided with alcohol awareness week and a member of the Metro DUI Task Force spoke about problems associated with drinking. Other guests on the program included the director of mental health for Memphis City Schools and the director of the Naval Alcohol Rehabilitation Center in San Diego. Guests spoke during the show about teenage problems with alcohol, as well as strategies for those with alcohol dependency problems.

Dick French, station manager for WHBQ radio in the 1980s, said, "I can't imagine anyone who could do a better job than Don. He is an old hand at this now and is free to make his own arrangements for the show. Allowing Don to do these programs with young people is one way of helping us serve the Memphis community." Truly, this long-running radio program has filled a genuine need and still acts as a sounding board for people of all ages. *Talk It Out* has accomplished this by proposing the theory that all young persons need to restore their confidence and need to know that someone cares and is willing to listen."

Don knew many of the young people by their voice or name and met many of them in person. It became a very valuable part of the ministry of

Youth Service. The popular WHBQ radio show remains on the air and has become one of the longest running talk-radio programs in the nation.

Mary Francis Greer worked with Father Don for many years pre-planning and running the show from behind the scenes. She was the key person in coordinating all aspects of the radio programs for Father Don. She arranged interviews with the guests, worked with sponsors, and kept the records of past programs.

One important corporate sponsor who always supported the *Talk It Out* radio show, was McDonald's. Don recalled how effective McDonald's became to the program:

> We always tried to invite guests to discuss things to educate the audience. During the last five minutes of the program, I would give several prepared questions concerning what we had discussed to the listening audience. The caller who had the correct answer would receive a week's supply of McDonald's hamburgers. As a result of the immense popularity of the segment, the kids would listen to every word and fight over the chance to answer the questions. When McDonald's opened a new store locally, we would go and broadcast from their new location. It was a win-win situation for all of us.

One Christmas, Don took the *Talk It Out* radio program to the Shelby County Penal Farm and had a party with the prisoners. The inmates were brought into the gym to hear several entertainers, and McDonald's provided them with hamburgers, French fries, drinks and desserts. During the party, a fight broke out among the prisoners. Since the guards did not carry weapons when they were inside the building, the situation became very tense. One woman was singing Christmas songs and playing her guitar when the scuffle began. She and the other entertainers believed they would become hostages or worse. However, the disturbance ended and the event continued without incident. After the party, Don went from cell-to-cell interviewing the prisoners and recalled, "I asked each of them what they wanted for Christmas. It was no surprise that the reply was most often, 'Freedom!' But, the conversation was therapeutic for many."

Joe Porter, who later became an Episcopal priest, remembered how he came to know Don through the *Talk It Out* radio program:

> At that time, I was young and somewhat alienated from God. I began listening to Don's show and all of a sudden,

I found someone who was making sense to young people. My wife and I had attended church at Grace St. Luke's, but frankly, I was not very interested. Nevertheless, by virtue of listening to his program, I started going to church regularly. What Father Don said was just what I needed to hear at that time. I was fairly young and just out of the Army. I was pretty beat up with life in many respects. He just showed me that life and God are the same. Father Don had a way of integrating God into every experience. As we might say in Mississippi, 'he put the hay down where the goats could get it.' He used the kind of language that was understandable and approachable; language that was conversant and resonant with the life I wanted to live. The God that I had previously known was a God of vengeance, a God who is ready to pounce on people. However, Father Don introduced me to a God who was relevant to life. That was really Don's influence and stimulus for me going through a conversion experience. He helped me to see that God was in every day and in every moment.

Don encountered the best and the worst with his radio program and in his ministry. Once Don broadcast his show from an event at the Mid-South Coliseum. Before the program, Dean Ed Reaves of St. Mary's Cathedral and his wife accompanied Don and Julie to McDonald's on Parkway near the Coliseum to have dinner. Two men inside the restaurant noticed Julie's diamond ring and proceeded to rob them as they exited the restaurant. The men threatened the group with a gun and knife and demanded their rings, keys, and billfolds. To prevent the theft of her ring, and to everyone's surprise, Julie threw her ring and keys over her head where they landed in the bushes behind her. The bandits fled with only a few of their personal belongings, and Julie later recovered her ring from the bushes. Later, they discovered that these men killed someone in another robbery a week later.

Talk It Out became a primary vehicle to expand Don's network to promote Youth Service. One Sunday evening, Father Don mentioned on *Talk It Out* the need to have an old boat repaired, to enhance the recreational ministries portion of Youth Service. A church member from St. Andrew's Church in Nashville donated the boat to the youth program and used a few times at Arkabutla Lake in Mississippi. It was now inoperable. After sharing their dilemma on the radio, Don received a call the next day from the Arrow Glass Boat Co. One of its representatives had heard about the need for a boat, so the company decided to give Youth Service a new boat, motor, and trailer, to continue their water sports activities.

From his experience at Arkabutla Lake, Don knew that a large number of young people wanted to participate in outdoor sports. Therefore, Don needed a base from which to operate an outdoor sports ministry. A friend suggested that he visit Horseshoe Lake in Arkansas because it was near Memphis, and it might serve as a good recreational center for his program. Don visited the lake and thought the area was perfect. He began a search for a house and soon found a man who was being transferred to Atlanta. The man offered his modestly furnished cabin for only $1,500. The house was located on leased property and needed extensive repairs. Don quickly convinced the Youth Service board to purchase the house for the agency.

In addition to the repairs needed for the house, it lacked a dock and pier. Fortunately, Don's friend and board chair Lester Crain's family owned a house with a boat dock nearby on the lake. Don visited them occasionally and would use their dock for activities. The word went out that Youth Service needed a dock and the Navy Seabees quickly answered the call by building them a wooden docking pier and boathouse. A local supporter living at the lake, donated the lumber and materials; another example of "spiritual networking" that had helped Father Don and his beneficiaries all of these years.

Don brought kids to the lake to swim, ski, and ride in the boat during the day. At night, some of the young people slept in the cabin, while others pitched tents in the yard outside. Most of these teens had never been to a lake and were afraid of large bodies of water. They, like many of the early campers, had a fear of snakes and other creepy things, and many of them could not swim. Don and his staff taught kids of all backgrounds how to swim, water ski, and most importantly water safety. "We made sure we had plenty of life jackets for everybody. Many of the young people had not been in the camping program at NAS Memphis, but wanted to experience Horseshoe Lake," he recalled.

Word of the success of Youth Service continued to spread. Early in 1969, Frances Myrick received a call from a representative of the Schlitz Brewing Company, who was referred to Youth Service by Mrs. Henry Jones of the Junior League and Ron Johnson of the Memphis Shelby County Juvenile Court. The company was interested in providing camping experiences for underprivileged children during the summer of 1969 as a part of a national campaign called "Send a Child to Camp." At first reluctant to associate with a beer distributor, Father Don embraced the company's initiative to help the youth of Memphis and realized the potential of such a partnership. As a result, Youth Service helped Schlitz extend the youth program, not only in Memphis, but to other cities as well.

Schlitz's offer to fund youth programs came at a time when money was sorely needed. Later that fall, the chairman of the board, Robert Uihlein and his wife Lori, were in Memphis for the ground-breaking ceremony for a new production plant being built in Memphis and invited Father Don to attend the ceremony. During a lunch meeting afterwards, they discussed the important role Youth Service would play in the program. During 1969, the program sent more than 2,000 young people to summer camp in 14 cities, NAS Memphis and Pensacola Naval bases being the primary locations for these camps. Schlitz established a funding goal to send more than 5,000 children to camps in 1970, which allowed Youth Service to expand to 29 cities.

Initially, The Schlitz Company donated operating funds for Youth Service, USA and paid for travel expenses. They soon provided money to secure an additional staff person to serve as program coordinator to assist Father Mowery. This became an important position because Father Don needed a program coordinator to help him with the demanding travel schedule and the many responsibilities of Youth Service.

Prompted by the involvement of Schlitz, August Busch, III of Anheuser Busch Companies, Inc., wanted an equal opportunity to participate in the Youth Service, USA program. Realizing the opportunity, Father Don flew to St. Louis, where he visited with Mr. Busch. Don remembered after the meeting in St. Louis, "Mr. Busch became very interested and sent an advance team of key executives to Memphis to help us plan a strategy for improving program operations. During their visit, the Anheuser-Busch team presented Youth Service with a check for $50,000 to help cover operating costs and to fund new programs."

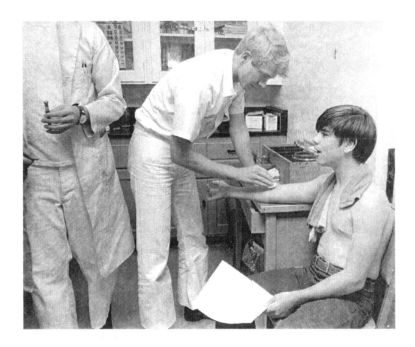

CAMPERS RECEIVE PHYSICAL EXAMS ON THEIR FIRST DAY
AT CAMP

YOUTH SERVICE CAMPERS AT THE NAS GALLEY,
SEPTEMBER, 1969

BOATING ON NAS LAKE WITH YOUTH SERVICE AND BIG
BROTHER VOLUNTEER SEPEMBER, 1969

ONE OF THE FIRST YOUTH SERVICE CAMPING GROUPS
AT MEMPHIS NAS

STRENGTH AND AGILITY DRILLS WERE CONDUCTED AT
EVERY CAMP

YOUTH SERVICE ACCEPTED DISABLED CAMPERS WITHIN
THE FIRST FEW YEARS OF THE PROGRAM

JAY EBERLE ADDRESSING ATTENDEES AT THE ANNUAL
YOUTH SERVICE COUNSELOR TRAINING PROGRAM,
MEMPHIS NAS

YOUTH SERVCE HONOR CAMPERS TRAVELING TO
PENSACOLA, FL, 1970

YOUTH SERVICE PARTICIPANT DAVID LA BARREARE,
SGT. MATEOS AND DON AT AIR FORCE ACADEMY

LESTER CRAIN, COL. EUGENE MINIETTA, JOHN
COLLIER AND DON AT SENATOR HOWARD BAKER'S
OFFICE IN WASHINGTON D.C., 1970

BIG BROTHER MEETING WITH YOUTH AT THE USO,
OCT., 72

FATHER DON IN HIS YOUTH SERVICE OFFICE, 1970

DON RECEIVING A CHECK FROM AN ANHEUSER BUSH
REPRESENTATIVE AT JUSTINE'S RESTAURANT IN MEMPHIS

FATHER DON BROADCASTING HIS TALK IT OUT RADIO
PROGRAM AT THE MALL OF MEMPHIS

CHAPTER TEN

A New Era Of Robust Growth: The 1970s

Youth Service, Memphis and Youth Service, USA experienced mutually ambitious years of growth during the 1970s. Shelby United Neighbors (SUN) continued to serve as a core support vehicle, providing a large portion of funding for the youth agency. St. Augustine Guild continued its volunteering efforts and proved to be of sustaining value to the entities, as did countless individuals and business owners.

After effective meetings in the home of Lester and Brenda Crain, and careful follow-up planning, Youth Service, USA was formally chartered in March 1970. As requested, Youth Service, USA purposely had no official affiliation with any religious organization in order to avoid the idea that the federal government was supporting a faith-based agency. Father Don was elected chairman, and Crain was elected secretary of the first board of directors of Youth Service, USA. The two men and a newly appointed board of directors immediately began coordinating with military leaders from as far away as Colorado, Texas, Michigan, and Florida. Based on early milestones, Don was duly optimistic of success and predicted that in the summer of 1971 there would be 50 to 60 Youth Service programs on military bases nationwide. Lester Crain was a constant guiding force for Youth Service, USA. He assisted with legal advice and conceived many key program ideas in the early days of Youth Service.

When Don traveled to a new city to promote the Youth Service model, he would ensure that the prospective sponsor conform to the agency's standards. Each camping program required a community sponsor (governmental or civic group), a financial sponsor (business or industry), and a military sponsor (the nearby base). In several cases, the women of St. Augustine Guild helped coordinate planning sessions with women's circles in prospective cities in order to help the Youth Service program build the necessary networking relationships. Often, these corresponding groups were civic organizations, such as the Exchange Club, the Rotary Club, Big Brothers-Big Sisters, or the Salvation Army. In cases where there was not an affiliate organization, one was started as a support group.

In the summer of 1970, the new Youth Service, USA programs at various military bases across the country were steadily making effective strides according to plan. This was aided on several military fronts. ADM Thomas Moorer, Chief of Naval Operations, and RADM Christiansen were both impressed with the progress achieved in the Memphis program. After speaking at a NAS Memphis meeting, ADM Moorer asked Don to return with him to the Pentagon for more detailed briefings about Youth Service, USA. ADM Moorer wanted the entire Navy to be involved, provided there was standardized training for all counselors. Secondly, he required that each program have the enthusiastic approval of the commanding officer at each base and third, that the military would not incur additional program expenses.

Youth Service, USA found a competent program coordinator in 1970 and hired retired Navy CDR Russell Sims. The decision to hire retired military personnel worked well because the agency did not have to pay for certain benefits. These men also had many years of experience in management, administration, finance, supervision, and program coordination. Sims was invaluable to the agency because of his important contacts on the military bases, which helped launch key programs around the country.

Aside from developments at the Pentagon, other programs were taking root with the assistance of key people whom Father Don had cultivated. The Episcopal Bishop of Colorado, who had visited Memphis for a Lenten speaking series, spearheaded a program at the Air Force Academy in cooperation with St. Luke's parish in Denver. Barksdale Air Force Base in Louisiana worked with St. Paul's Church in Shreveport. Similarly, Pensacola Naval Air Station and St. Christopher's Church collaborated to foster several program start-ups.

The Second Air Force published its own training manual, setting forth Youth Service program guidelines for their own branch. Top-level Pentagon officials sent out directives urging vigorous pursuit of the objectives of this and related work by people in uniform to help solve domestic social problems of youth near bases around the country.

Though Pentagon officials were quick to commend Youth Service, USA for establishing programs nationwide in such a quick and efficient manner, funding for Youth Service, USA was not always easy to attain. The agency finally secured funding through the combined efforts of Tennessee senators Howard Baker and William (Bill) Brock, and Rep.

Dan Kuykendall. Their support was sparked by another strategic visit to Washington by Father Mowery and Youth Service, USA board members Lester Crain and John Collier.

The Vocational Exposure Program was expanding and young people were on military installations around the country, such as those recently established in California, Maine, and New Hampshire. The prerequisite to this program's installment was that Youth Service would guarantee quality and conformity nationwide. To accomplish this, hundreds of counselor-trainees were brought to NAS Memphis from around the country each spring for an annual weeklong counselor training program.

In July 1970, ADM Christensen relinquished the helm of the Memphis Naval Air Station Technical Training Command to RADM Valdemar Lambert in a traditional change-of-command ceremony. During the farewell dinner to honor ADM Christensen, Lance Cpl. Mike Jones, a former Youth Service camper, shared his success story. The young Marine, who participated in one of the first the youth programs at the Naval Air Station, became a sterling example of a Youth Service participant. He told the audience how he gained critical, life-changing experiences as a teen-ager in the Vocational Exposure Program, eventually joining the military to live out his dream. It was almost a made-to-order illustration of what the agency could achieve in an idealized scenario.

Meanwhile, the program for inner-city youths continued to gain nationwide acceptance. By early 1971, the summer camping programs involved over 20 military installations with boys aged 15 to 18 from cities located near the military bases. Most installations featured five-day stays for each group of young people, in order for them to receive the maximum experience from the program. The campers engaged in various activities from early morning to late at night. These activities encompassed not only sports, but also the chance to live in groups, eat a balanced diet and have a complete physical exam, the first for most of the campers. Additionally, military personnel who were a few years older and whose attitudes and way of life carried teaching value mentored campers. Chief among the principles Youth Service tried to inculcate were physical fitness, citizen-ship, staying in school, developing social skills, and thinking about a direction in life – for all participants, wealthy and underprivileged. Father Don said of the participants, "Not all of these young people are deprived. Some come from affluent families and participated to gain a new under-standing of what it is like to be deprived. They learned that there are other boys their age who don't have one car in the family, perhaps not even one pair of shoes that fit properly."

In the early 1970s, Youth Service, Memphis continued to expand to include more female and minority participants. Working with the Health and Welfare Planning Council, Father Don also saw the need to provide more opportunities, activities, and spiritual guidance for African-American children in the Memphis community. Many of these programs were successful through the help and assistance of the established women's service organization, the Junior League of Memphis.

As early as 1968, representatives from the Junior League of Memphis heard about the program and wanted to know how they could help. The issue prompted Father Don to suggest a program that focused on the predominately African-American Orange Mound neighborhood. The agency obtained a new female group worker, Elizabeth Wade, with funding provided by the Junior League and an anonymous donor. Wade was the first female African-American caseworker for Youth Service and began serving the families of the primarily African-American Orange Mound area in the winter of 1970. Wade formed "clubs," comprised of young girls who met after school at local high school gyms under her leadership.

The Junior League began as one of Memphis' charitable organizations in 1922, within a year of the Church Mission of Help. Many of its members attended St. John's Episcopal Church and learned about Youth Service through its membership base. Their member volunteers were highly organized and committed and willingly giving of their time and energy. These dedicated women served as tutors, chaperones, library assistants, club activity coordinators, arts and crafts instructors, and some helped with office duties at the Youth Service headquarters.

Youth Service in cooperation with the Junior League soon began to create and offer classes in manners, dressing, grooming, personal decorum, cooking and sewing. Additionally, the girls learned how to discuss personal problems and how to make better personal decisions. The Junior League program was based at nearby St. John's Episcopal Church and became successful as different organizations pitched in to help raise money for additional staff. Youth Service worked closely with members of the Junior League for many years.

Wade and the Junior League volunteers became more involved as work with the inner city girls in Memphis progressed. They added personal tutoring, training in money matters and preparation for job interviews to the program format. Wade obtained program space from Beulah Baptist Church to establish a small library to house books and magazines for the female participants. Additional services provided to these teens were very inventive and included focus group discussions, educational games, field trips to local sites, arts and crafts activities, and spiritual guidance. If it were not for local agencies like the Junior League, positive strides could not have been in the lives of these individuals. Don recalled the important role the women's organization played in the success of the inner-city Youth Service program, "The Junior League also provided help in the local schools to better understand the needs of their students and their family situations. Their volunteers and our staff met with teachers in these schools to help select the students. They took great pride in being part of that process."

There are many personal stories that capture the purpose for the Youth Service program. A particular work-study student who was formerly a Youth Service club member considered himself "nothing," but for the interest shown by Youth Service. He later found his purpose in life as a college student. In another story, a 10-year-old boy, arrested five times for shoplifting was being held in Juvenile Court. Fortunately, the boy received valuable counseling and assistance from Youth Service workers. The Welfare Department also referred children to Youth Service.

Local publicity always helped to promote Youth Service's image and programs. The Episcopal circles were well aware of the agency's good work, but broader arenas of society came to learn about the work of the agency.

George Klein's home station of WHBQ was a popular spot with the kids at Humes High School. Klein noted how he helped reach some of the young people in the Youth Service program:

> Father Don would ask me to attend an event and share stories with the kids. I told them they would have to straighten up or wind up in a bad situation. I went to school with Elvis Presley at Humes High School and shared my story of how I made it through my own rough times. I came from a tough neighborhood in North Memphis and my family was not wealthy. It was not easy, but I overcame the obstacles. I told them not everyone would be as successful as Elvis or the Beatles, so if they wanted to make something of themselves, they had to have an education. After Dr. King's death in 1968, some of the young kids in Memphis became more boisterous and harder to handle. Some broke into stores and took drugs more than in past times. Youth Service had the right person in the right place with Father Don, because he could open doors for these young people. He had

that impeccable reputation, and he was doing something
good for the youth of Memphis.

George Klein shared another interesting story that related to Don's
ability to communicate with people on all levels. The story circulated
wildly throughout the Memphis community in the 1970s. George recalled:

> There was a homeless girl in Memphis who was very
> promiscuous. The press called her 'Charlotte, the Harlot,'
> and it was not certain if she was a hooker, a prostitute
> or just an 'easy' girl. The police arrested her for alleged
> immoral activities with several Memphis police officers.
> Because of Father Don's reputation in the community
> and his high profile with the radio show, Memphis Police
> Director Hubbard asked him to talk with her. She was
> reluctant to talk with the police, but she agreed to talk
> if Father Don was present. After several interviews with
> Charlotte, Don and the police interrogators were able to
> determine that many of the stories Charlotte had spread
> were simply fabricated.

Meanwhile, program refining at Youth Service carried on behind the
scenes and through various other cooperative organizations. For instance,
board member and ardent Youth Service advocate John Collier represented the agency at the Shelby County Planning Commission. Collier
served on a specially formed committee to raise money for Youth Service
for programs to support young people aged 18 to 25; an age group that
many believed had been neglected. The group targeted were not only
drug users, but had a variety of social problems. This initiative received
additional funding from the Episcopal Planning Commission, as well as
the Presbyterian, Methodist, and other churches for the following year.

Father Don kept busy making keynote speeches about Youth Service
across the country and continued to build national momentum for the
Youth Service, USA program, brought about by the new partnership
between the military and private non-profit organizations. During the
early months of 1970, Father Don's travel schedule was nonstop. He
spoke to numerous individuals and groups, including local representatives for Shelby United Neighbors, the Kiwanis and Lions Clubs in Little
Rock, the Second Air Force Conference at Barksdale Air Force Base,
and the Mortgage Bankers Association in Chicago. Don also traveled to
the National Alliance of Business in Atlanta, the Girls Clubs of America

in New York City, and visited the Assistant Secretary of Defense at the Pentagon.

While on a speaking engagement in Atlanta, Don shared the speaker's podium with Coretta Scott King, the wife of slain civil rights leader Dr. Martin Luther King, Jr. She expressed her appreciation to Don for expanding Youth Service to assist youth nationwide. Though a tragic event, Mrs. King stated, "I am glad that good things have come from my husband's death."

Support for the national program grew with sometimes unconventional, yet welcome, means. August Busch and his vast St. Louis-based enterprise was a good example. Mr. Busch wanted a program started in a local military hospital in St. Louis and wanted his staff members to come to Memphis and develop multi-year plans for the program. In turn, the arrangement provided training for his team in the practice of generating successful goals and objectives. Incidentally, Bill Timmons, a Baylor School classmate of Father Don's, and President Nixon's legislative advisor, introduced the president to Don's work with Youth Service.

When Youth Service, USA became operational, the board in Memphis took the position that they would provide the template and mechanisms for the national programs, but let the local people in their associated organizations operate the programs long-term. Therefore, the Youth Service board did not own the national programs, and many them operated under different names. The non-Memphis programs appointed their own counselors, selected by a local civic group. For example, the board of education coordinated sending the campers to camp at the Pease Air Force Base program in New Hampshire.

Though each program varied nationwide, a formal graduation ceremony was recommended for each participant completing the program. Clothing played a symbolic role for campers in all of the programs. In Memphis, competitive squads wore yellow, blue, green or maroon shirts given to them when they arrived. After they received their personalized graduation certificate, they donned the unity-generating white T-shirts bearing the logo of Youth Service. Parents, benefactors, and interested business people and politicians received graduation invitations. Those who did not have a means of travel were transported in a city bus chartered by Youth Service. Each visitor was paired with a camper for a tour of the program because Don wanted supporters to see the facilities firsthand. After the graduation, people began to talk about the good things they had observed that day. Don recalled the positive feedback from the young people and the community:

It was gratifying to hear all the good comments that were said about the young people. We put these young people in an adult world and they responded in an adult way. They were proud of their accomplishments. This is an investment in the youth of our community. The young campers realized they could make something better of themselves by hard work.

YOUTH SERVICE, USA
COUNSELOR TRAINING PROGRAM

The first annual Youth Service Counselor Training program was held in 1970 in order to replicate the Youth Service model in other cities and bases around the nation. Designed and supervised by the Youth Service staff, over 100 counselors from more than 20 youth programs involved with military installations nationwide took part in the Counselor Training Program at NAS Memphis. This initiative was designed to serve thousands of youngsters at weekly camps across the country.

During the weeks prior to the scheduled date of the campers' arrival, training sessions conducted for counselors included participants from President Nixon's Youth Opportunity Program. Momentum clearly was building both locally and nationally. Three one-week sessions convened in Memphis at the beginning of each summer. Given this flexibility, the counselors could select the week that suited their schedule. Often, a military staff member from his or her base would accompany the civilian trainees to learn more about the program. Many of the counselors were schoolteachers who worked for the youth program during the summer.

The training included seminars and workshops, where the attendees shared new ideas. Many counselors tapped into the valuable experience from participants of past programs. The depth of progress made in racial reconciliation was profound. During one session, Father Don stated one of the primary purposes of the integrated program: "In Memphis, we try to let black and white boys who have never associated with each other learn to live together. It is a new adventure for many to learn from one another."

The annual counselor training was comprehensive and included drug abuse and delinquency programs, briefings on youth indoctrination, legal issues, leadership, and medical services. Representatives from the Memphis Naval Air Station, the Shelby County Sheriff's Department and Youth Service staff provided discussions during their training in Memphis.

One special guest speaker was Maj. Gen. James F. Hollingsworth, commanding general of Fort Jackson, S.C. Gen. Hollingsworth played an early key role in extending the Youth Service program to Army installations around the nation. In a gesture of support, the general placed the Army leadership staff at the Navy's disposal during one of the initial training conferences. This was quite surprising, given the good-natured rivalry among the participating military services. Because of his enthusiasm for the program, Hollingsworth eventually became a member of the Youth Service, USA board.

Gen. Hollingsworth expressed his confidence in the youth by saying:

> In basic training, we strive to teach young men to find and recognize themselves. We must teach our young men to take advantage of their strengths and convince them by example to overcome their weaknesses. We try to teach soldiers to live, work, study together and to take on and accomplish difficult tasks together. We must build in this desire to accept difficult tasks in brotherly love and with respect for each other. Finally, we try to teach a man to do things well. If these young people do not know the good things of life, then we must teach them. Americans have a duty to their adventurous youth who are displaying initiatives, yet looking for someone to assist them and guide them. We must get more people around the country involved in the future of America.

A partial list of military bases represented during the one-week training sessions in Memphis included:

The Air Force Academy, Colorado Springs, CO
Dyess Air Force Base, Abilene, TX
Little Rock Air Force Base, Little Rock, AR
Fort Jackson, Columbia, S.C.
Jacksonville Naval Air Station, Jacksonville, FL
Pensacola Naval Air Station, Pensacola, FL
Barksdale Air Force Base, Shreveport, LA
Blytheville Air Force Base, Blytheville, AR
Charleston Naval Station, Charleston, S.C.
Carswell Air Force Base, Forth Worth, Texas
Fort Bragg, Fayetteville, N.C.
Wurtsmith Air Force Base, Oscoda, MI

Charles G. Allison, Chairman of the Presidential Classroom for Young Americans, also spoke at the Counselor Training program at the Naval Air Station. The counselors for this training would conduct government tours and teach participants government procedures. Mr. Allison met with Father Mowery and Charles Novak, civilian director for Youth Service programs at the Memphis Naval Air Station, to share President Nixon's support for the Youth Service initiative. Air Force Col. Eugene Minietta, who represented the Second Air Force, accompanied Allison and discussed the outlook for Youth Service, USA program.

Meanwhile, the partnership between Schlitz Brewing Company and Youth Service continued during 1970. The jointly formed goal for the Memphis program was to send 500 to 750 deserving youngsters from the Memphis area to camps each summer and initiate a program with business people in Memphis to help select the youngsters. The company also funded 50 additional youngsters through an incentive program within their retail stores. Youth Service also worked closely with the Memphis Juvenile Court and the Memphis Police Service Centers in selecting youngsters for the camps.

A longtime group worker with Youth Service, Joe Bean, selected many of the young people for the Memphis camp. The idea was to make the best possible selection from those who needed the most help; quality instead of quantity was the goal. Bean worked with teenagers in the eastern part of the city and in close cooperation with all of the social service agencies.

Father Don needed additional counselors and group workers who had experience working with young people. One of the best resources for Youth Service was the Memphis City Schools. Often, schoolteachers who were not teaching in the summer served in these important roles for the agency. Clyde Saunders, one of these teachers, served as director of that summer's War on Poverty Committee (WOPC) program for Youth Service.

Due to the additional funding from August Busch, Youth Service was able to hire additional staff to work with the youth in 1970. Twelve work-study students were employed through Memphis State University to assist the summer staff. Eight additional camp counselors coordinated activities at the Memphis Naval Air Station, Blytheville Air Force Base, AR, and the Pinecrest Presbyterian Camp at LaGrange, TN. During that summer, Youth Service began using additional Junior Counselors in the camping programs. These young people were specifically selected because of their ability to work with youngsters and received a stipend for their work.

Youth Service boys and girls also attended the Tennessee ecumenical church camp at Pinecrest, sponsored by the Tennessee Episcopal Young Churchmen. In that ecumenical spirit, Idlewild Presbyterian Church sponsored activities including arts and crafts and allowed the use of their gym and educational and recreational films for the participants. Youth Service also traveled with a group of young people to Hot Springs, AR. Another group traveled to Nashville to tour the state capital. Clyde Saunders, project director, recalled Youth Service working in some capacity with over 1,400 young people during the summer program of 1970.

Several non-Episcopal groups pitched in to assist with the programs and provide additional resources. Second Presbyterian Church provided funding for one college graduate who worked for Youth Service. She served as a summer worker in charge of the recreational activities at Idlewild Presbyterian Church. Other organizations paid for caseworkers, which allowed the programs to expand to meet a seemingly never-ending demand. Another illustration of outside help was the mother's club at Lauderdale Courts public housing, sponsored by the First Methodist Church. The members of this club assisted caseworker Nell Bell in the northern parts of the city.

Though the young people attended the summer camping programs generally one week of the year, they were not forgotten after their visits. The Youth Service program became a year-round concern – particularly with the Memphis operation, but also with Youth Service, USA. When the teenagers returned home, youth workers remained in contact and continued to work with them, aided by family social workers and local school systems and job placement personnel.

Father Mowery added:

> In addition to the camps, we provided group workers to serve people in the neighborhoods, with juvenile court and in the homes. We established important relationships and used many other avenues to reach inner city and suburban youngsters 15 to 17 years old. These young people were the most likely to turn to crime as a way of life if somebody did not reach them and show them they had better choices.

Campers in the Memphis program who displayed leadership, positive attitudes, excelled in recreational and educational activities and had shown an ability to work with young people in need, were chosen as "Honor Campers." Campers were also encouraged to write letters of their experiences to base commanders. Those judged the best writers were also candidates for the Honor Camper distinction. The Honor Camper position was the highest standard a young person could achieve as a Youth

Service graduate. Two Honor Campers were selected from each camp; one by the campers and the other by the staff. Over 20 of these specially selected young men traveled by bus to Nashville to visit the state capital in 1970.

The next year Honor Campers flew to the Naval Air Station in Pensacola, FL. As guests of that major Navy base, they spent a day on the aircraft carrier USS Lexington, treated to a day of deep-sea fishing, and saw the Blue Angels aerobatics unit perform. Additionally, these Honor Campers received a chance to become a Junior Counselor for the camping program the next season. Retired USN project officer Charles Novak, who headed the recreation services for NAS Memphis, also gave honor Campers trophies. Novak later served as the administrative director for Youth Service, USA.

Don needed to transition from bus to air transportation for the Honor Campers to visit these distant locations, but it was impossible for civilians to fly on military aircraft. However, the commanding general of the National Guard agreed to transport the campers to and from Memphis and Pensacola after Don shared with him a copy of the Domestic Action Council guidelines.

Youth Service held recreational activities at community clubs on Saturdays, school holidays, during the summer, and during the school season. Counselors always stressed individual counseling for each young person in the program in order to provide positive reinforcement and guidance. These activities were part of the recipe of ingredients to help develop a strong and responsive program.

Youth Service programs were extremely cost effective and utilized every resource in order to make the most of all funding streams. Federal grant funding became an integral part of the growth of the Youth Service, USA programs. By September 1970, more funds from the Office of Economic Opportunity (OEO) through the WOPC program were committed to the summer programs. Youth Service became quite involved with the WOP initiative and with Sonny Walker, head of its Atlanta region.

Though federal funding provided a jump-start to many of the programs offered by Youth Service, challenges to the organization were always present. The money supply coming from the War on Poverty Committee ended in October 1970. As a result, Father Mowery became concerned about replacing these funds in order to support the ongoing programs.

By December 1970, the War on Poverty Committee was dissolved and was replaced by efforts of the Community Action Agency within the Memphis and Shelby County governments. Proposals for new funding were submitted to the members of the Shelby County Court and the

Memphis City Commission to garner support for Youth Service and the continuation of funds for expanded summer programs. "Because of our 'spiritual networking,' thankfully, we were funded," Don recalled.

Amid the hard work, occasionally there was time for a few much-needed leisure trips. Father Don took a group of Civil Air Patrol cadets to the Air Force Academy to tour the facility at Colorado Springs, complete with sightseeing in Colorado. The Air National Guard provided transportation and a group of Memphis donors pitched in to pay for the trip.

As the year 1970 closed, Youth Service officials could thank a litany of groups in Memphis for their support. These groups included the Memphis Episcopal churches, the Shelby County Episcopal Planning Commission, Immanuel Lutheran Church, Second Presbyterian Church, Christ United Methodist Church, Shady Grove Presbyterian Church, Beta Sigma Pi, Schlitz Brewing Company, WLOK, WHBQ, WMPS, WDIA, and WMC radio stations. Additional contributors were Kappa Kappa Gamma, Youth Service Whitehaven, The Junior League, St. Augustine Guild, Goodfellows of Memphis, Inc. and of course, the War on Poverty Committee.

As 1971 dawned, John Collier became the new president of the board of directors for Youth Service, USA. One of the most important occasions of the year was the Annual Meeting of Youth Service. Held in conjunction with the 30th anniversary of the USO, the two organizations joined in February for this most important meeting. The meeting was unprecedented in that it was the largest assembly of supporters in the history of the two organizations. More than 600 people attended the event at the Holiday Inn Rivermont. The principal speaker for the gathering was Assistant Secretary of Defense Roger T. Kelly.

Kelly, who served as Assistant Secretary of Defense for Manpower and Reserve, drew military personnel and social service officials from across the country to hear the progress made by programs spawned by Youth Service, Memphis and the new Youth Service, USA. Secretary Kelly commended the programs when he told the crowd, "These organizations have provided a vehicle for alleviating problems of the community by utilizing military resources. The seed that was planted in Memphis has been replicated across the country and has been quickly adopted by the various branches of the Armed Forces."

Secretary Kelly revealed that in 1969 there were just three Youth Service programs in place. In the summer of 1970, 20 youth programs operated around the country with the cooperation of the military. He also pointed out that nearly 350,000 young people had already benefited in some way by these programs. In later years, that number rose significantly. Father Don recollected, "Secretary Kelley knew we had begun operating outside conventional bounds with the camping program and using the Memphis Navy base. However, the Secretary liked what he saw and vowed to help give the program the proper authority to conduct the programs legally."

Additionally, officials with the Department of Defense realized a year earlier that there was more to the concept than just Youth Service. Other programs were inspired from the publicity that Youth Service was garnering in national publications. Communities around the country were seeing the exposure and the innovative angles the agency used to build a workable template step-by-step nationwide.

Roger Kelly became the chairman of the Domestic Action Council and helped the organization as it matured to become a clearinghouse for new ideas. He spearheaded plans to use military resources to improve the quality of life in American cities, while still maintaining a strong defensive posture. As a result, military people were beginning to adopt social reform in tandem with its acceptance across wider society. The goals of the DAC were accomplished without impinging on military resources because charities and public service organizations provided most of the funding to support the youth programs on military bases.

Secretary Kelly offered these inspiring remarks at the meeting:

> I have a deep and abiding faith in the young people of this country. What I hear from them reinforces the beliefs I have in this job. They consider the threat to the nation's security as two-dimensional; the potential foreign aggressor nation and the potential, and often imminent, decay and breakdown within the social fabric of American cities. They are frustrated that they will not be able to do anything about it, and that is a frustration difficult for them to accept.

In Memphis, the Youth Service, USA pilot program found sufficient footing to springboard to area military installations because, Kelly said, "Father Mowery would not let the idea die, and brave people like ADM Ernest Christensen dared to receive it." At the meeting, Secretary Kelly awarded ADM Christensen a plaque and a medal on behalf of the Memphis community for his pioneering work by allowing Youth Service to use the facilities at the NAS Memphis. He cited the admiral's dedication, "that has played a meaningful role in uplifting the youth of Memphis." Secretary Kelly also cited the Youth Service program as a pacesetter between the military and civilian groups, all stemming from Father Mowery's pilot camping and vocational education projects.

Members of the first Youth Service, USA Board of Directors in 1970 included:

> Bishop John Vander Horst
> Bishop Edwin Thayer of Colorado
> The Reverend Robert P. Atkinson of Memphis' Calvary Church
> Spence L. Wilson of Holiday Inns, Inc.
> Attorney J. Lester Crain, Jr.
> John S. Collier, of Collier Insurance
> Al Whitman, financial executive

EXHAUSTED CAMPERS AFTER A LONG DAY OF ACTIVITIES
AT YOUTH SERVICE CAMP, 1969

YOUTH SERVICE COUNSELOR INSTRUCTING CAMPERS TO
CHANGE INTO THEIR TEAM SHIRTS

MRS. J.B. COOK WITH FATHER MOWERY AT A THANK
YOU PARTY FOR YOUTH SERVICE DONERS, 1969

YOUTH SERVICE SUPPORTER MRS. J.B. COOK HOSTING
A PARTY FOR CIVIL AIR PATROL CADETS

CAMPERS IN THE NAS GYM, AUGUST, 1970

CHARLES ALLISON, PRES. CLASSROOM FOR YOUNG
AMERICANS, FATHER MOWERY AND COL. EUGENE
MINIETTA JUNE, 1970

GEN. HOLLINGSWORTH ADDRESSING YOUTH
COUNSELORS AT NAS MEMPHIS, JUNE, 1970
(PHOTO BY THE COMMERCIAL APPEAL)

FATHER DON AND U.S. REP. DAN KUYKENDALL, 1970

A MEETING WITH (L TO R) GEN. COLE, GEN. JOHNSON, GEN. JONES, FATHER MOWERY, GEN. WALLACE, AND GEN. BROWN

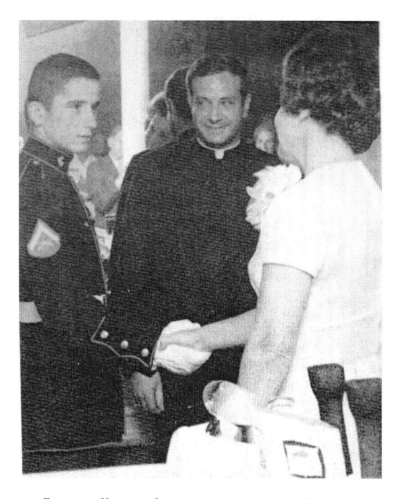

FORMER YOUTH SERVICE PARTICIPANT, MARINE
CPL. MICHAEL JONES, FATHER MOWERY AND MARGE
CHRISTENSEN, WIFE OF ADMIRAL E.E. CHRISTENSEN,
JULY, 1970

YOUTH SERVICE DEDICATED STAFF MEMBERS, FRANCIS
MYRICK AND MARY FRANCIS GREER, 1970

SHELBY COUNTY MAYOR BILL MORRIS AND GEN. DAVID
JONES, CHAIRMAN, JOINT CHIEFS OF STAFF, AT THE
PEABODY HOTEL IN MEMPHIS, APRIL, 1979

CORETTA SCOTT KING WITH FATHER DON SPEAKING
AT THE NATIONAL ALLIANCE OF BUSINESS IN
ATLANTA, GA

FATHER DON, FRED SMITH, CHAIRMAN AND CEO,
FEDEX, AND CHUCK TISDALE, WHITE HOUSE
REPRESENTATIVE, AT THE PEABODY HOTEL

CHAPTER ELEVEN

Expansion On Two Fronts: 1971 – 1974

The awards Father Don and Youth Service received became an immediate and publicly visible indicator of the success of the Youth Service
program. Garnering the principal award from the Freedoms Foundation
was undeniably a milestone indicator of achievement. Father Don and
several military officers from NAS Memphis journeyed to Valley Forge,
Penn. in 1971 to receive the coveted honor. Among the delegation were
stalwart board members Lester Crain and John Collier, as well as Col.
Eugene Minietta, Project Officer for the Second Air Force and CAPT Jack
Godfrey, commanding officer at NAS Memphis. Youth Service shared the
Freedoms Foundation honor with NAS Memphis in the governmental
activities division.

Previous recipients of the prestigious award from the Freedoms
Foundation included Hugh O'Brian, George Foreman, H. Ross Perot,
Anita Bryant, Paul Harvey, and Eric Hoffer. Youth Service was the only
program recipient for this distinction. In fact, the citation for the Youth
Service program was the sole "principal award" given during the ceremony
that year. The Tennessee General Assembly also recognized the lofty work
of Youth Service in House Resolution No. 90 on April 13, 1972.

The Memphis Commercial Appeal published an article in 1971 that
profiled Youth Service in general, but also alluded to the role of the
Department of Defense's DAC, that allowed nationwide exposure. That
story was very different from years earlier when Youth Service set up its
program on the Navy base in almost total anonymity.

With the support of the DAC, Youth Service, USA quickly began convening with leaders in the highest circles and echelons of the nation. One
such circle was The Fellowship, headquartered in Washington, D.C. This
non-governmental faith organization counsels heads of state and was at

that time lead by Doug Coe, who started the Washington Prayer Breakfast. The organization was situated in a scenic house in Baltimore called The Cedars and was composed of many influential people from all walks of the government and military. The board of Youth Service, USA often met at the Cedars to discuss ideas and make plans for youth programs. Father Don's "spiritual network" of individuals and organizations was being strengthened not only locally, but also nationally.

The word was clearly spreading that the camping experiences, and all of the related programs involved much more than recreational skills. They also carried from the beginning a focus on education and personal development for young people. All participants received physical exams, learned dental and personal hygiene and became acquainted with foods they had never encountered. Each participant met with young military personnel who were learning new jobs themselves, which helped the campers see that learning was the key to future personal development. The service personnel also benefited by being able to share their military and newly acquired vocational experiences while in uniform. Meanwhile, on the spiritual and ethical side of the equation, Navy chaplains of various faiths were always there to provide moral leadership and counseling for young people in the program.

The depth of such a program, recognized by the Freedoms Foundation, had also at its core an increased emphasis to motivate the young people toward a better way of life as they pursued cultural and educational opportunities They improved racial relations and provided the campers an increased sense of mutual understanding. The majority of the sessions carried an equal ratio of African-American and white participants and proved to be a rewarding experience for all. Father Don always wished for the campers to become better acquainted – to break the ice and overcome any differences. Over 700 boys were scheduled for the camping program in Memphis alone during the summer of 1971. The selection process was important for the success of the program. For example, campers who arrived as friends were broken up, to allow them to interact with different people for diversity and personal growth. From this concept lay the roots of what later became the Bridge Builders program in the late 1980s.

By this juncture, Youth Service, USA had grown into a full-fledged outgrowth of Youth Service, Memphis, Inc. It cannot be overstated that without the Memphis program, Youth Service, USA could not have existed, for it was the baseline template for success. Father Don and the board were unanimous in their approval to move the nationwide program full speed ahead. CDR. G.T. Denmark, project officer for the Memphis Naval Air Station, enthusiastically endorsed the program stating, "The week-long encampment at a military base gives a teenager a whole new outlook on life."

Attorney and board member Lester Crain, a central figure along the path to growth and significance, was the logical choice to head the new liaison committee for Youth Service, Memphis and Youth Service, USA. Despite the liaison, the two similarly named organizations retained a very distinctive identity. Youth Service, Memphis continued to retain its affiliation with the Episcopal Church, while Youth Service, USA operated as a non-religious based denominational agency working with military bases.

Youth Service continued expansion plans for its growing list of programs. In 1971, the Memphis Police Department and the Juvenile Court submitted a proposal to obtain federal funds from the Department of Justice's Law Enforcement Assistance Administration (LEAA) for programs at NAS Memphis and Blytheville Air Force Base. Federal funding was not easy to acquire, but officials remained optimistic because grants for similar youth projects had been awarded in Michigan, New Hampshire, Florida, and California. Ultimately, 75 percent of the funds for the programs in the early 1970s were supplied through the LEAA grant, Shelby United Neighbors, and private funders providing "start-up" money.

The Community Action Agency (CAA) replaced the prior War on Poverty committee as a major funding source to Youth Service. The CAA was able to enlarge the project for 10 weeks during the summer of 1971 with much-needed funds. Foster Adams with Youth Service and Roscoe Overton of the CAA were central participants in the program and pushed the CAA for future grant funding.

Despite an occasional windfall, funding remained a constant challenge for the agency. Father Don learned that the Big Brother activities at the USO would have to be reduced as funds began to decrease on that front. Nevertheless, plans for a USO/Youth Service Patriotism Parade, where service personnel and young people would march together, continued as planned for the spring of 1971.

Youth Service, USA served as the primary model for other youth programs around the country, but new programs varied in activities and available local resources. Over 35 cities with military bases were now working with the organization in various phases. Representatives from several of the cities often visited Memphis and patterned their programs after the successful model created at NAS Memphis. Though similar, each Youth Service, USA program had its own requirements, attributes, and board of directors. Because of this, several of the programs were year-round instead of only during the summer months.

Every national youth program launched by Youth Service encountered its own share of challenges, primarily for funding and in winning the support of the local communities. Col. Marvin Anding, a retired base commander at Barksdale Air Force Base in Louisiana, told of how the local citizens had to be persuaded to sponsor a youth program. "You definitely have a selling job in order to overcome their reluctance to get involved." Nevertheless, the Barksdale Air Force Base program that summer had over 200 boys participating in the Vocational Exposure Program for 13 to 18-year-olds. The colonel related the difficulty in recruiting enough civilians involved in raising money. Thus, the Memphis template was quite difficult to replicate in cookie cutter fashion.

Father Don routinely visited the poorest sections in a particular state, while planting the seeds to launch new youth programs around the country. He regularly met with the youth, representatives from local government, and school and military officials in the areas in which he traveled. Because of his efforts, additional Youth Service, USA programs were planned and organized at military installations near San Francisco, San Diego, Seattle, Chicago, Boston, Philadelphia, Dallas, and other cities throughout the United States where military bases were located. In one highlighted moment, Father Don visited Fort Stewart in Georgia and gave an informative briefing to Georgia Governor Lester Maddox about the program. Together they flew over the base in a helicopter to view the facilities. Afterwards, the Governor was fully committed to the Youth Service initiative.

Meanwhile, Youth Service, Memphis was having its best summer camping program yet, due to more participation and assistance from Navy and Marine Corps personnel. Returning military men, wounded in Vietnam, volunteered and served as youth counselors in the 1971 summer program at the NAS Memphis. These men could perform light duty and were a welcomed addition to the training staff.

During that summer, Don began working with the local Crippled Children's Hospital, which allowed them the opportunity for some of the disabled children to attend the camp. Six children were selected to attend per week, while volunteers from St. Augustine Guild provided chaperones and transportation from the hospital to the camp. Several Marines at the base who had been helping with the camping program took a particular interest in this project in hopes that this activity would become a nationwide program. Twenty-five disabled boys participated in the day-long visits and tours of the Naval Air Station. The West Tennessee Chapter of the Easter Seal Organization for the handicapped, led by Buddy Wright, regional director for the West Tennessee area, sponsored many young people for Youth Service programs. Wright, who himself was confined to a wheelchair, stated that the purpose of the visit was to "train the boys to perform with others and in turn, be accepted by their fellow peers."

As Youth Service, Memphis and Youth Service, USA programs continued to expand, the respective boards determined that Father Don needed an assistant. A job description for the position was developed and a search began to fill this position. Additionally, the board determined that the agencies needed new offices in order to operate most effectively. At the same time, the members realized the need to keep the corporate offices of these two organizations together, so they could continue to collaborate and share valuable operational and growth ideas.

Certain funding boosts seemed providential as August Busch in St. Louis, who had a pre-existing relationship with the organization, presented another check to Youth Service, USA to shore up critical areas of need. At the same time, the Youth Service, USA board was awarded a grant for $55,000, which was earmarked for program expenses and trips to visit various communities throughout the country. This funding helped to establish Youth Service programs on other military bases.

The president of the Youth Service, USA board in 1971 was ADM Christensen, and retired Col. Minietta served as vice president. Board members Al Whitman, Spence Wilson, John Collier, and Lester Crain continued to help to raise the necessary funds to support Youth Service, USA programs and planned for their continued success. Because of their efforts, new sites sprang up like mushrooms.

The Memphis agency received over 400 referrals from the Memphis/Shelby County Juvenile Court and Board of Education in 1971, nearly 100 referrals from the Department of Public Welfare, and approximately 2,500 referrals from churches, organizations, and interested individuals. Over 700 youths participated in Youth Service operated camps at NAS Memphis, Blytheville Air Force Base, and Camp Pinecrest. Additionally, Father Don's weekly radio program, *Talk It Out*, heard Sunday nights on radio WHBQ, continued to draw referrals to the organization. The radio program was even commended by Wallace Johnson, chairman of the board of Holiday Inns of America, for its role in "helping keep young folks on track through better communication with adults." Johnson also arranged for Father Don to meet with Reverend Billy Graham about the Youth Service program, further expanding his "spiritual network."

In addition to the camping, group work and individual counseling during the year, Youth Service provided nearly 600 local families with comprehensive casework in order to strengthen their home life situations. Additionally, two newly formed mothers' clubs met on a regular basis in support of Youth Service programs and initiatives. With more visibility and exposure, funding increased and programs grew in number.

After witnessing the many successes, other support groups gathered around Youth Service, including radio station WHBQ, Kappa Gamma Alumnae Sorority, Kiwanis Club, and various church denominations. All were involved in supporting the programs and touching the lives of local young people. Auburndale School (now St. Benedict School) adopted Youth Service as a project and individual homerooms prepared Christmas baskets for approximately 40 families, which included clothing, food, toys, and gifts. The Arnold Air Society of Memphis State University provided 50 families with much-needed food baskets that Christmas. These people and organizations helped support a nationwide effort for inspiring responsible attitudes and actions and developing leadership in young people.

The outreach spread beyond local Episcopal churches. Whitehaven Methodist, Whitehaven Presbyterian, Idlewild Presbyterian, and Beulah Baptist were among churches that donated equipment, supplies, and facilities to the agency. The Big Brother activity continued with the cooperation and support of the local USO, which permitted 1,600 "little brothers" who needed male companionship to be paired with 780 service personnel from NAS Memphis. Various church groups and women from the St. Augustine Guild were responsible for providing wholesome lunches, while the Navy provided transportation.

A renewed partnership between Big Brothers and the USO was underway in 1972. Military "brothers" paired up with two "little brothers" for a day of fun and camaraderie. Military men and several college students served as "Big Brothers" and were asked to be friends and examples to the youngsters, but not counselors. Typical activities included roller skating, a trip to the zoo, lunch, a football game, and other activities. Visits to various local attractions, as well as the outings, were critical to the growth and development of young people in the program. The youngsters also provided community service by cleaning litter around Overton Park and on school grounds. Some of these youngsters had never experienced life outside of their limited worlds. Some had never left downtown Memphis, eaten a salad or been in an elevator. Others had never seen the animals in the zoo. Youth Service selected the 12 to 16-year-old youths in the program because they needed a mentor in their lives. Many were significantly enriched by these ongoing experiences.

Father Don used his well-established network to strengthen programs in need, especially when he learned that the Community Action Agency monies were no longer available for 1972. He immediately contacted the

Rockefeller Foundation, General Electric, National Jaycees, and several federal agencies about potential funding for Youth Service, USA. CAPT George Gregory, the commanding officer for NAS Memphis, helped lay groundwork for the 1972 summer program. They set aside additional resources for the Youth Service project, which provided a much-needed expansion over the previous year.

Father Mowery traveled to Arizona to meet with Governor Jack Williams and several other youth organizations in the state. Additionally, he unveiled the possibility of having Youth Service programs established on 40 college campuses nationally through the Mott Foundation. Don explained, "There is no reason that the program housed on military bases could not work on college campuses."

A newly created program called "Rap Session" aired in February 1972 over WHBQ-TV. Several young people on the program discussed the upcoming "Expo 72," which was an outreach endeavor of the national Campus Crusade for Christ. Networking with these programs provided a steady stream of interest and referrals for Youth Service week to week.

The March of Dimes Walk-A-Thon, one of the largest and most high-profile non-profit events in Memphis, was held in March 1972 and Youth Service and WHBQ served as two of the sponsors. Father Mowery and Lewis Priddy, district leader of the March of Dimes, were among the principal organizers, and Don promoted the event on his radio show. The organizers expected perhaps 4,000 people to attend the Memphis Walk-A-Thon, but through the efforts of Don and other volunteers, more than 14,000 people actually took part in the 20-mile walk. Several members of the Youth Service board and staff also participated. Don drove a dune buggy-styled Jeep to kick off the event. Taped on the sides were signs that stated "Walk It Out Today – Talk It Out Tonight on WHBQ." Father Don used the dune buggy to pick up and transport people to first aid stations. Interestingly, the person to cross the finish line was a young person from Youth Service. The young man ran 17 miles and walked the last three miles. When the tally was taken of contributions, the March of Dimes' fight against birth defects was enriched by more than $100,000 that year.

A novel idea initiated by the local board was to raise money to purchase a Winnebago-type van and convert it into a rolling classroom that would go from site to site, taking the program to yet more young people in Memphis. A federal grant from the Office of Economic Opportunity (OEO) eventually provided the needed funds for this venture. The OEO Atlanta office liked the idea and increased the original grant, which enabled the agency to purchase the vehicle. Memphis Rep. Dan

Kuykendall of Tennessee was instrumental in helping secure these funds to make the idea of a mobile classroom a reality.

The Youth Service, USA program had grown from three military-based programs in 1969 to 20 in 1970, to 38 in 1971. Father Mowery then estimated 100 programs would be in operation by the end of 1972. Other platforms became offshoots of the Youth Service program. For example, longtime supporter Calvary Church in Memphis asked Youth Service to operate the Wisconsin School Day Camp. Calvary financed the program and supplied volunteers for children involved in reading sessions, arts and crafts, bible lessons, sports, and swimming in the summer of 1972.

A celebration in 1973 commemorated Father Mowery's 10-year anniversary as executive director of Youth Service, Memphis and director for five years of Youth Service, USA. Roman Catholics, Presbyterians, Baptists, Jews, Methodists, Episcopalians, and people from all walks of the faith attended the event. Privates and generals, sailors and admirals, politicians, social workers, lawyers, business executives, clergy, young people, even a few octogenarians all came to honor one man for his work with youth – The Rev. Donald E. Mowery.

For many present, Father Don had helped turn their lives around. Others had received from him sorely needed personal advice and reinforcement. ADM Christiansen told the audience that gathered, "Most of these accomplishments can be attributed to the driving energy of one man who kept plugging away against considerable odds. It is fitting that we honor Father Don, for he has inspired all of us to become better people. They said it couldn't be done, but he showed them it could." Other guest speakers included Congressman Dan Kuykendall, who noted, "Of the countless youth programs I have seen across the nation, none had the scope and brilliance of Youth Service, USA."

Lt. Gen. Russell E. Dougherty, USAF and Commander of the Strategic Air Command (SAC), expressed his appreciation on behalf of the 75,000 grateful people throughout the SAC for the "unique and magnificent work Father Mowery has done for the communities in which our bases are located." Additionally, many of the young men and women who were at one time campers in the program or those he had helped along the road of life attended, offering their heartfelt thanks for his work.

Don recounted to those in attendance how the program was first established. "In April 1968, while looking down from my Youth Service office window, I saw Memphis burning. Older teenage boys were looting and rioting. Something had to be done to get them off of the streets and make them productive citizens."

At the special event, Don also received the Governor's Certificate of Merit from Tennessee Governor Winfield Dunn. Memphis Mayor Wyeth Chandler also awarded Don with the city's Distinguished Service Award. The Office of Economic Opportunity, the USO, the Presidential Classroom, and fellow clergy additionally honored Father Don. Tennessee Senator Howard Baker praised his work and wished Father Don "another 10 years at the helm."

A perfect capstone to the anniversary event was the graduation ceremony for those who completed the summer program at NAS Memphis. Youth Service, USA Project Coordinator CDR. George Denmark presented certificates to campers who had completed a full week of activities. ADM Al Sackett, the newly appointed Chief of Naval Technical Training, commended the participants and the program for its goals of education, motivation, recreation, and conversion of the nation's youth power into a viable workforce.

For the campers, graduation from the Youth Service camping program was a time for looking back and recalling the good times they enjoyed with their newfound friends. Campers compiled their own invitation lists and would use the base telephones to invite family members or school mentors to join them for this special event. The guests would have lunch with the campers in the dining hall, while the campers acted as hosts. After lunch, they would all convene in the chapel for the formal ceremony. As the graduation ceremony ended, the campers received certificates, along with pictures of their camping group and small American flags. They proudly began their trip home after the ceremony, for many a somewhat reluctant journey.

Traveling and planning absorbed much of Father Don's time. In March 1972, the board extended an invitation to The Reverend James Jelinek from St. Bartholomew's Church in Nashville to assist Don with certain aspects of Youth Service. Shortly after his arrival to Memphis, he and Father Don introduced a new thrust toward offering a Comprehensive Youth Service Model, which would require additional staff and called for greater emphasis on working with complete families rather than only group counseling of young people. Young persons included in the group activities would come from the families where the caseworkers received support as a family unit.

A Youth Service caseworker would interview the family for a case history and psychological testing was provided if needed. The caseworker and group worker would work together with the family unit. Staff conferences for the diagnosis of problems and possible treatment plans were part of the process. Treatment plans would include family counseling, vocational guidance programs, and placement of individuals in counseling with peers for personal growth. The mobile classroom was used in Memphis to assist young people and their families. This program was an outcome of meetings with the directors of social services at Memphis State University, Dr. Paul Schwartz, and Andrew Fox. However, they ensured that this initiative did not detract from the basic mission of the agency.

With the Vietnam War winding down, public attention turned toward the domestic sphere to help citizens improve the quality of life in America. Father Mowery traveled often to meet with officials of the Domestic Action Council and other federal agencies to create additional exposure for the Youth Service programs. The Council continued to support Youth Service to build formal youth activities for civilian as well as active duty and reserve components of the military services.

Father Don cited an example of this civilian collaboration, as when several Green Berets helped 40 migrant families in California find work and a place to stay. The Department of Defense liked this type of program, and Father Mowery was pleased with the direction that the DAC was taking in formulating policies and programs instead of leaving it up to the political organizations to run the programs. In this way, local people could help solve local problems.

The chairman of the DAC thought the idea of using retired executives to help clients and agencies would be effective. In other words, a retired CPA could help a Youth Service program with budget problems, and a retired field commander could help with planning and overseeing the youth camps. Another perspective of the Chairman was that for each $4,000 Youth Service raised, the Council would match that money to fund expenses and personnel needed for the agency. This enabled Father Mowery to add another full-time person to his staff that year.

Father Mowery went to Sacramento, CA in 1972 and toured Mather AFB with Defense Secretary Melvin Laird, who expressed commitment to the program and who was very helpful in setting up Youth Service projects across the country. Youth programs also sprang up at the Washington Navy Yard, Bolling Air Force Base and Andrews Air Force Base in Washington, D.C.

A Department of Health Education and Welfare (HEW) grant helped fund the Youth Service Counselor Training Conference at NAS Memphis, the meeting's fourth straight year, in a joint effort with the Department of Defense's DAC program. Held during the first three weeks in June 1972, the training conference featured William "Sonny" Walker, Southeast Regional director of the Office of Economic Opportunity (OEO), who told the participants in his opening address:

I believe Youth Service, USA illustrates the crucial importance of the private sector. It has always been the key to community participation, as it is composed of the community gatekeepers. Your willingness to expand the definition of community to include the disadvantaged in any form is more important than all the laws that can be passed.

Other guest speakers for conference that year included RADM Allen A. Bergner, chief of Naval Technical Training; retired USAF Col. Eugene Minietta, director of Youth Programs, Inc., of Orlando, FL; Air Force Brig. Gen. Earl Brown, Department of Defense; Andy Fox of Memphis State University's School of Social Work, and Dr. Paul Price, director of MSU's Department of Recreation.

Additional contributors included Robert Gemignani, Commissioner of the Youth Development and Delinquency Prevention Administration of the Department of Health Education and Welfare. Gemignani visited Memphis to help secure funds for a Youth Service symposium, which climaxed the Annual Counselors Meeting in February 1973. It hosted a large gathering of people to discuss Youth Service programs across the country including several dignitaries from Washington, such as Secretary of Defense, Elliot Richardson, who was invited to be the keynote speaker.

Dr. Charles Newton of Memphis State University and author of the Comprehensive Youth Service Model participated in the symposium and explained the results of the two-year juvenile delinquency study sponsored jointly by Mississippi, Arkansas and the Tennessee Council of Governments, and the Memphis Youth Guidance Commission. Some 146 agencies who worked with youth in these states were involved. The DAC encouraged these agencies to find the most efficient ways to meet the needs of all young people. The Council determined policies, target areas and priorities through its various committees. Dr. Newton viewed Youth Service as one of the main agencies involved in the initiative. This system would provide a channel of communication between youth, the social work community, and the government. The Comprehensive Services System also prevented an overlap of services to youth in the Memphis area.

In February 1973, the Navy League and the Memphis Chamber of Commerce sponsored a major promotional event to acknowledge the Youth Service program. Youth Service, USA supporter ADM Thomas Moorer, Chairman of the Joint Chiefs of Staff, was quoted at the luncheon, "Memphis is a place you can visit and speak your mind and they'll understand." RADM William Thompson, the Navy's Chief of Information, used the occasion to announce plans to make a movie depicting the Navy's new and growing Youth Service, USA program.

A team of Navy photographers arrived at NAS Memphis from the Pensacola Naval Air Station and spent three weeks publicizing the Youth Service activities. The Navy titled their film *Promising Young Americans*, which proved to be an important resource in developing other Youth Service programs for the Navy. The 30-minute documentary film chronicled of the story of Youth Service, USA. It was completed in August 1973 with a five-man film crew, that recorded the boys' activities during their week-long encampment at NAS Memphis. A year later, the Air Force produced its own film, using the Air Force base in Sacramento CA as their success story. The Air Force film simply titled their film *A Week of Summer*.

Interestingly, the documentary films about the Youth Service programs made no mention of the economic status of their participants. As Don explained, "We did not like to use words such as 'underprivileged' and 'disadvantaged' in describing our young people." Despite their best efforts to curb the reference to these negative terms, a story ran in one base newspaper about the program with large headlines that read "Slum Kids Get Week at Base." Many of the young people who attended the camp saw the story and asked if they were slum kids and disadvantaged. "Of course, they were disadvantaged, but you don't have to tell them to their face," Father Don said. Nevertheless, Youth Service used the films to emphasize the fact that the agency was there to help the young people any way they could. These documentaries helped sell the program across the nation and by 1973, Youth Service, USA had over 90 programs under development.

Another important meeting followed the Navy League's event. The annual meeting for Youth Service at the Rivermont Hotel in March 1973 was a joint effort between Youth Service and the USO. The event marked a tribute of thanks to the military for their valuable assistance to Youth Service. Secretary of the Navy John Warner was slated to be the guest speaker, but had to cancel his trip the day before the event. His replacement, Deputy Undersecretary of the Navy Joseph A. Grimes, Jr., said at the meeting, "You are giving hundreds of youngsters a vision of themselves they could have in no other way." He gave high praise to Youth Service, citing how the interaction between the two groups helped create a cohesive, working bond between the military and civilian communities. Undersecretary Grimes spoke extensively on the social benefits of the two programs and thanked the attending organizations for their efforts. Following the Undersecretary's speech, retired USN ADM Christensen, who had become president of the Youth Service, USA board of directors, formally recognized Mr. Grimes for his contributions to the two programs as they toured the NAS Memphis program.

Meanwhile, Youth Service had again received notice of having won a Freedoms Foundation Medal for Good Citizenship in 1973. This marked the third year that Youth Service was a recipient of the esteemed Freedoms Foundation Award. During the foundation luncheon, Youth Service also received the George Washington Honor Medal Award for the camping program and for the radio program, *Talk It Out*. In line with other national-level awards, Father Mowery also received the Sertoma Club's Service to Mankind Award for "unselfish service deemed best for Memphis and the community."

Father Mowery the same year most notably received a congratulatory letter from President Richard Nixon, who commended Don for his role in providing much-needed leadership and guidance to hundreds of young men since the inception of Youth Service, USA. The president wrote:

> Dear Reverend Mowery,
>
> It was a pleasure to learn recently about your distinguished service to the community as executive director of Youth Service, USA, Inc. I understand that you were recently honored by the citizens of Memphis for your role in providing much needed leadership and guidance to hundreds of young men since the inception of the organization.
>
> The Volunteer spirit has been one of the great strengths of the American Heritage, and your outstanding achievements demonstrate how much our nation has benefited from that tradition.
>
> On behalf of all your fellow citizens, I welcome this opportunity to commend you for your dedicated efforts and to extend my best wishes for continued success in the years ahead.
>
> Sincerely,
> Richard Nixon

The president's letter boosted the credibility of Youth Service beyond measure. Having President Nixon in his circle of important resources displayed the depth and breadth of Don's "spiritual networking" ability even within federal government circles.

Always using his networking skills, Father Mowery obtained surplus equipment, which the federal government had available through the DAC channels. When he attended the interagency DAC meeting in Washington, D.C., Father Mowery was able to obtain vehicles for the use of his field workers from the Army Defense Depot, also overseen by the Council.

Though the process of planting new programs nationwide was a difficult one, base cities where the Episcopal Church had a presence were often easier for Youth Service, USA to establish a program. Such program planting required demographic research and the utilization of important contacts in the local communities. One example was in the nation's capital.

Youth Service had its eye on starting a key program in Washington, but first had to convince Bishop John Walker, who presided over Washington's National Cathedral. This bishop was well-known and respected nationally, therefore his influence was important. Don remembered, "We were well connected with Rep. Harold Ford of Tennessee, who told me that if we had Bishop Walker on our team we should be successful in the Washington district."

Walker was invited by Calvary Church in Memphis to preach during the Lenten series. While in Memphis, Father Don took Bishop Walker on a tour of NAS Memphis to view the program firsthand. Bishop Walker was so impressed that he agreed to support a start-up youth program in Washington and even joined the Youth Service board. Later, Don met with Washington, D.C. Mayor Marion Barry and Rep. Harold Ford, who together were instrumental in helping start programs at Anacostia and Andrews Air Force bases.

There were other favorable experiences, from Episcopal Bishops in San Diego, Knoxville, Nashville, Denver, San Antonio, Miami, and other locales, when funding for expansion was being sought. Establishing programs took time, effort, and a little finesse, all the same. Using his position as an advantage, the bishop in Tennessee would call counterparts in other cities and ask for their audience, mentioning that he was a Youth Service board member.

In 1973, Father Mowery contacted "Bud" Wilkinson, a coach with the Fellowship of Christian Athletes (FCA) ministry. He believed the Youth Service program, through FCA, could be brought into the high schools nationally. Wilkinson liked the program and agreed to serve on the board of Youth Service, USA. Don also traveled to California to meet with famed Coach John Wooden at UCLA in order to brief him on the Youth Service program. Coach Wooden eventually joined the board as well.

The fifth annual Youth Service, USA Counselor Training Conference at NAS Memphis again drew counselors from across the nation. The objective for this conference was "the conversion of youth power into manpower through education, motivation, and recreation." Officials compared the program to a "1,000-mile journey that must begin with one step." As a part of the summer youth program in 1973, two groups of young girls spent several days and nights at NAS Memphis. The coed experience was a first for the program at the NAS.

Twenty-eight members of the Department of Defense's DAC convened in Memphis at the Naval Air Station in July 1973 to gather useful information and practices, which might be important to other military installations across the country. Members of the delegation received a thorough tour of the programs at NAS Memphis. Most members of the Council came from Washington. Among those attending included:

Carl W. Clewlow, Acting Assistant Secretary of Defense for Manpower and Reserve Affairs

James E. Johnson, Assistant Secretary of the Navy for Manpower and Reserve Affairs

Lt. Gen. Wallace Robinson, Jr., director of the Defense Supply Agency

Frank A. Bartimo, Assistant General Counsel for Manpower and Reserve Affairs

William Beecher, Deputy Assistant Secretary of Defense for Public Affairs

Dr. Theodore C. Marrs, Deputy Secretary of Defense for Reserve Affairs

James P. Goode, Deputy Assistant Secretary for Manpower and Reserve Affairs

John Burrows, Office of the Assistant Secretary of the Navy

The attendees were guests of the Memphis Navy League and the Military Affairs Council of the Memphis Chamber of Commerce for an evening reception at the Defense Depot Officers Club. ADM Al Sackett, chief of Naval Technical Training conducted a series of command briefings on local military DAC programs. Assisting ADM Sackett in the tours were CAPT G. K. Gregory, NAS Memphis Commanding Officer, and CAPT David C. Beer, Commanding Officer of the NAS Naval Hospital. Ms. Ella Turner, executive director of the Memphis USO and Col. Harry Moore, Commanding Officer of the Memphis Defense Depot, also presented during the conference.

Father Mowery was invited to appear on NBC's *The Today Show* from New York in July 1973; just about the time the organization was gaining early national exposure. Naturally, Don seized this unique opportunity and remembered, "The response that I received from this program was really overwhelming. I received hundreds of letters, many of them in response to my use of the 'magic words,' 'Yes, Sir, No, Sir, Thank You, and Please.' I received more letters about those words than any other things I said that day." Don explained the summer camp program and fielded questions from host commentator Frank McGee. Interestingly, Barbara Walters and Burt Reynolds were backstage in the same makeup room. Burt was impressed with the Youth Service idea and told Don about his ranch near Jupiter, FL. He also invited Don to bring some young people to visit the ranch. Because of his appearance on *The Today Show*, Don received letters from viewers all over the country commending the program and expressing their appreciation for promoting such a great idea.

Don's travel schedule was exhausting during the 1970s. He recalled several special events while visiting Washington that summer:

> I was at the Pentagon meeting with former Senator, then Secretary of the Navy, John Warner who complimented me on instilling the 'magic words' in the young people and that we needed more of that. Another trip took me to Andrews Air Force Base where I met briefly with Secretary of Defense Elliot Richardson and ADM Hyman G. Rickover, known as the father of the modern nuclear submarine industry, for four days of events.

In a separate ceremony, Don attended the launching of the USS Lipscomb. A few months later, he attended the launching ceremony of the nuclear submarine USS Memphis in Norfolk, VA. Don also traveled to Washington in December 1973 to address a national convention on youth recreation and then spoke at the National Junior League Conference in Houston, TX, attending with Memphis Police Director, Jay Hubbard.

Activities continued with notable figures. Secretary of the Navy John Warner served as guest speaker at a Youth Service luncheon on November 12, 1973. In a similar vein, Father Mowery welcomed the Secretary of the Air Force John L. McLucas to Memphis to view the Youth Service, USA program.

On the home front, creative efforts continued to bridge gaps between teens on the streets of Memphis and law enforcement officials. In October 1973, Captain Wendell Robinson of the Memphis Police Department outlined a Halloween project called "Meet and Treat." This was the result of collaboration between WHBQ, officials from the Department of External Affairs of the MPD, Father Mowery, and Capt. Robinson. With the cooperation of the candy companies in the community, approximately 60 squad cars were given a supply of goodies. When a young person waved and spoke to a police officer, they were awarded with a treat. This gesture helped create a better image of police officers among the young. Father Don promoted the project on his radio program and as a result, about 100,000 pieces of candy were given away that Halloween. As an acknowledgement of his community work, Father Don became chaplain for the Memphis Police Association and was a regular speaker for training programs at the Police Academy.

After several trips to visit officials at the Pentagon, Don met with members of the Department of Justice and found them to be quite interested in the Youth Service program. While briefing Roger Kelly, Asst. Secretary of Defense, Don had planned a visit to brief President Nixon and the head of the LEAA on Youth Service programs. Bill Timmons, one of Don's high school friends, was instrumental in helping set up this important meeting with the president. Timmons became the Special Assistant for Legislative Affairs to President Nixon and later a consultant to large industries such as Budweiser and General Motors. When Don told him about Youth Service in Memphis, Bill said, "President Nixon would love to hear about this. I want you to come up and brief him about the program."

Once again, networking was critical to the success of the Youth Service programs. Don remembered, "Every time I went to Washington, I would go to Bill's office. He was very supportive of our program." In 1974, Timmons arranged for Don to meet with President Nixon. The Watergate debacle had caused several postponements, but a day and time were finally set. Unfortunately, Nixon resigned from the presidency the day before the scheduled meeting. Don missed the opportunity to meet with the president, a meeting that was sure to bolster support for the youth programs.

Another program involved longtime Youth Service staff counselor Larry Holmes. He helped oversee the new and growing farm project, which had been started the previous summer with a handful of teenagers. Holmes planned a larger scale program using approximately 12 acres of local land, donated by his mother for this purpose. The young people were paid from the harvesting of crops and sale of the produce. Holmes remarked, "There is value in teaching young people to farm and at the same time, letting them work in a gainful manner."

Because of these innovative programs, the agency continued to receive national awards. The Freedoms Foundation Award luncheon in May 1974 featured a banquet in which Youth Service and the Naval Air Station received recognition certificates for their summer camp projects. Additionally, Youth Service, USA received a George Washington honor medal award for "Citizenship-Youth Emphasis" for the innovative program to inspire self-improvement, provide moral guidance, motivate youths toward a meaningful lifestyle and promote positive attitudes.

Youth Service supporter Gen. David Jones was appointed Chief of Staff of the Air Force in 1974. This distinguished member of the board of Youth Service, USA had commanded the Second Air Force and ultimately received a presidential appointment to become Chairman of the Joint Chiefs of Staff in 1978. Don remembered, "Through our 'spiritual networking,' we could not have had a better board member than Gen. Jones and could not have been as successful without his influence."

The sixth annual Youth Service Counselor Training Conference convened in 1974 at NAS Memphis and drew representatives from the Pentagon, as well as those from various programs across the country. The conference enabled participants from hundreds of communities in 30 states to experience educational training, recreation, and moral guidance in a dynamic new atmosphere. All the military branches displayed a positive inter-service competition and now supported the Youth Service, USA program. A related Youth Service, USA report showed almost 100 youth programs operating in the U.S. during 1974, adding thousands of participants to the various national programs. The programs generated services valued at $3.2 million through private funding to these youngsters.

Thus, through its triumphs and points of urgency, the Youth Service programs flourished overall in the first half of the 1970s, thanks to energetic and creative guidance from its leadership, board members, supporters, and the military contingent.

YOUTH SERVICE CAMPERS RECEIVING DENTAL
CHECKUPS, MEMPHIS NAS, 1971

YOUTH SERVICE VOLUNTEER SGT. ALVIN SHUTTERS RECEIVES
AN OFFICIAL SHIRT FROM HIS GRATEFUL CAMPERS, JULY, 71

ST. AUGUSTINE GUILD MEMBERS, (L. TO R.) NANCY
TIELENS, THERESA HARDISON, PAT COVINGTON,
POLLY LEMMON, JUNE, 1972

BUDDY WRIGHT, HEAD OF THE EASTER SEAL PROGRAM
SHOWN WITH CAMPERS

THE SWIMMING POOL AT THE NAS WAS THE FIRST
SWIMMING EXPERIENCE FOR MOST OF THE CAMPERS

PADDLE BOATING ON THE NAS LAKE WAS A POPULAR
ACTIVITY FOR THE YOUNG CAMPERS

VOCATIONAL EXPOSURE ALLOWED THE CAMPERS TO
LEARN ABOUT A VARIETY OF JOBS ON THE BASE

VISITORS OFTEN CAME TO SEE THE RESULTS OF THE
YOUTH SERVICE CAMPING PROGRAM

YOUTH SERVICE GRADUATION CEREMONY AT
THE NAS CHAPEL

YOUTH SERVICE, USA BOARD MEMBERS ATTEND A
MEETING AT THE CEDARS IN WASHINGTON D.C

YOUTH SERVICE GIRLS PROGRAM AUGUST, 1974

FIRST GIRLS HONOR CAMPERS

RADM S.L. GRAVELY JR., THE NAVY'S FIRST AFRICAN-
AMERICAN ADM AND DEP. UNDERSECRETARY OF THE
NAVY JOSEPH A. GRIMES, JR., IN MEMPHIS

YOUTH SERVICE, USA BOARD MEMBERS BOARDING A
PLANE DONATED BY MARTIN-MARIETTA FOR MEETING IN
WASHINGTON

ONE OF THE FIRST CAMPING GROUPS AT NAS MEMPHIS

NEW YOUTH SERVICE HEADQUARTERS AT 2600
POPLAR, MEMPHIS, TN

MARCH OF DIMES WALK-A-THON, 1972 (L TO R)
FRANCIS MYRICK, FATHER DON, GEORGE KLEIN AND
DAVID LA BARREARE

HORSEBACK RIDING WAS ONE OF THE MANY ACTIVITIES
FOR YOUTH SERVICE CAMPERS

GENE TURNER WITH FATHER DON ON ACTIVE DUTY AT
FT. BRAGG, NC

FEMALE YOUTH SERVICE PARTICIPANTS, MERIDIAN
AFB, 1973

FATHER MOWERY APPEARING ON NBC'S TODAY SHOW
WITH FRANK MCGEE, JULY, 1973

FATHER DON WITH SUPPORTERS,
STAFF, ADVISORS AND VOLUNTEERS

CMDR. TWEEDY PRESENTING YOUTH SERVICE AWARDS,
NAS MEMPHIS

FATHER DON'S 20TH ANNIVERSARY AS THE HEAD OF
YOUTH SERVICE

CAMPERS CLEANING THEIR BARRACKS BEFORE THE DAY'S
ACTIVITIES. ACCOUNTABILITY WAS ALWAYS STRESSED

CAMP COUNSELORS, MEMPHIS NAS, 1973

ANOTHER PROUD GROUP OF YOUNG PEOPLE READY TO
ENJOY THE ACTIVITIES AND LEARN LIFE LESSONS

A MARINE VOLUNTEER EXPLAINS EQUIPMENT OPERATION
TO THE CAMPERS

LINING UP FOR CHOW AT THE MESS HALL

CHAPTER TWELVE

The Power Of Spiritual Networking:
1975 – 1980

In 1975, many organizations rightfully recognized Father Mowery for his 20 years of ministry, which began in 1956. This recognition came from the successful maturity of people from local community agencies and national supporters. That growth encompassed an increasing sphere of cooperation and influence. Many local organizations donated time and money toward the ever-broadening efforts, including new partners such as Nationwide Insurance Company, Auburndale School, and Boy Scout troops from all over the city, Memphis State University's ROTC program, the Goodfellows organization, and several non-Episcopal church groups. The Memphis Ministerial Association, of which Dean Ed Reeves was president, noted that memorial giving to Youth Service was seemingly at an all-time high.

Assistance also came from welcome unofficial sources of well-known, helpful individuals. A case in point was the popular WKNO Memphis children's local TV personality, Charles Scruggs, who was known affectionately to Memphians as "Mr. Chuck," became very interested in Youth Service and helped promote the agency.

Another ardent supporter was Milton (Milt) Kauffman, who owned Gooding's Million Dollar Midway. Kauffman, who was also a Jewish Rabbi, brought his carnival midway each year to the Mid-South Fair. His benevolence allowed hundreds of Youth Service kids to visit the fair who otherwise would not have been able to attend. In addition to free admission, they received food and rode unlimited midway rides. Youth Service counselors had the freedom to invite young people within their network. Since the counselors transported them in their cars, some of them attended the fair every day, so all of their assigned youngsters could participate.

Don recalled, "To my knowledge, we were the only group in Memphis that received these privileges from Milt Kauffman. He was a great resource to our program. We would have our workers plan and organize the fair activities before the youth arrived, so their experience would be well-balanced." The young people were encouraged to view the educational exhibits because there was an opportunity to expose them to many interesting cultural things in addition to the rides at the fair. Don served for many years on the board of the Mid-South Fair. From that experience, he met many influential people, such as Johnny Cash and his wife June Carter Cash, Arthur Godfrey and Ed Sullivan. When entertainers were here to perform at the fair, Don would use the opportunity to invite them to be on his *Talk It Out* radio show.

Longtime Calvary Church rector and Youth Service board member Dr. Don Henning expressed his support of the agency and the work it was accomplishing, citing the growing dimensions it had reached across the country. Dr. Henning believed in the need for personal integrity and training of young minds toward personal discipline and to a life of personal service. He noted, "We should thank God for organizations such as Youth Service and the dedicated people who give of themselves to help young people."

Additional interest for the work of Father Don and Youth Service heralded from other local religious quarters, including several personages outside the Episcopal Church. Two organizations – Campus Crusade for Christ and Young Life, the national youth outreach to high schools, also became strong supporters.

Another friend and important advisor in Don's "spiritual network" was Father Anthony-Gerald "Lee" Stevens, a member of the Order of the Holy Cross, who often advised Don on matters regarding the Youth Service ministry. Don had known Father Stevens since his early days in Chattanooga and Nashville. Stevens had served at the monastery at Sewanee before becoming resident monk at Iona House in the Diocese of West Tennessee. Later Stevens founded the Mbalotahun Leprosy Relief Program in Liberia. He devoted the rest of his life to aid the remote leprosy clinic and colony, where he claimed to have "lost his heart forever" to its people.

After having lunch with Don and Julie at their home in 2006, Stevens departed to Liberia for the last time at the age of 94 to establish a new indigenous religious order for men, the Community of Love in Jesus (CLJ). This was a very fitting name for this order as this dearly loved man influenced many such communities wherever he went, especially as spiritual advisor for the Diocese of West Tennessee. Father Stevens died at the age of 95 in 2007 in his little cell at the St. Francis monastery in Bolahun, Liberia.

Father Stevens was an important connection to Memphian John Paul Jones, father of Paul Tudor Jones, previously mentioned in Chapter Nine. Paul Tudor Jones had acquired land in Africa and became familiar with Father Stevens' charitable work there through his father's meeting with the popular monk. Together with Father Stevens, Paul Tudor Jones and Jones' high school friend and board member Reid Sanders, Youth Service gained many influential supporters.

Credit for the success of Youth Service, Memphis can be traced to trusted advisors such as Father Stevens as well as people within its own ranks. The important subgroups of Youth Service included strong committees in finance, programs, personnel, membership, and public relations, in addition to liaisons with Youth Service, USA and specialty committees, which all helped to make Youth Service one of the most innovative youth programs in the country.

YOUTH SERVICE GARDEN PROJECT

Not all efforts to change the minds of youth dealt with crime and delinquency. Ideas for a variety of educational opportunities cropped up at every turn. Contributors such as retired USMC Col. Bill Holmberg proposed several ideas that added depth to the Youth Service program offerings. He knew the military, Washington power circles, the Memphis community and was one of Don's most trusted advisors. Holmberg served as a member of the Domestic Action Council and was an executive with the Environmental Protection Agency (EPA). Father Don referred to Bill as, "one of the kindest people I've ever known. He was very interested in helping people and became one of the most valuable and influential members of the Youth Service team." Bill was responsible for the outdoor garden project initiative, as well as several groundbreaking initiatives over the years.

Through Holmberg's orchestrating efforts, Father Don invited Alan Zeithammer, a newly hired employee with the EPA who had experience in gardening, to speak to the Youth Service Board during the planning stages. Zeithammer, a college-trained agricultural expert, was raised on a farm in Minnesota. He explained that the EPA was interested in having a model farm in Memphis to teach young people from the inner city about organic agriculture. The Shelby County Penal Farm, which had been using its prisoners for farming since the end of World War II, was a logical site. Father Don contacted Tommy Hill, Superintendent of the Penal Farm, who agreed to the concept. Hill said, "We have the land you need for the program, and we have the labor to plow and cultivate the soil for planting." Father Don discussed the idea with the County Mayor's office and the Penal Farm staff, who ultimately made the Garden Project a reality.

The project served a dual role: as an educational experience and as a job training program. It began with two primary groups. The first group came from young people recruited by Youth Service, and the second group consisted of selected prisoners who were serving sentences at the Penal Farm. City Councilman Bob James, attorney Lucius Burch, cotton executive William B. (Billy) Dunavant, Jr., and Shelby County Mayor Roy Nixon all supported this successful farm project, which ultimately provided jobs, food and an opportunity to teach urban youths about farming.

The Garden Program officially began the first week of May 1975 with the assignment of garden plots to the Youth Service participants. Two young men who both had studied agriculture filled the available counselor positions. However, teaching the participants how to become gardeners was the only remaining issue. Most inner-city kids were not interested in gardening and did not care about hoeing and weeding a garden in the hot sun. While it was a stiff challenge, Youth Service staff went to work convincing the young people, while Hill worked with the prisoners on the value of the program.

Father Don reflected on how the prisoner group operated:

> Officials for the Penal Farm selected the prisoners based on their record of good behavior and if they had families nearby. The Ministerial Association had just built a new chapel at the Penal Farm, so we invited the prisoners in the program to the chapel on Sunday morning. We also provided transportation for their families to attend church with them; this was certainly something new. Following church, we had a picnic lunch, where the prisoners could spend the afternoon with their families and work in the garden. We provided shaded places for them to spend time together, so it was good for the family and for the prisoner.

The model project eventually drew visitors from around the country, including farmers and gardeners from states as far away as Maine and Iowa.

Father Don's "spiritual network" again proved invaluable during this time. Lester Gingold of Sears donated tools and gardening equipment, while the Memphis Depot workers erected a fence to secure the property. Officials with the Memphis Defense Depot also furnished a van and two surplus pickup trucks free of charge for the Garden Project. The Memphis Board of Education provided mobile classroom units where the gardeners and their family members could learn about new ways to prepare and preserve food via the Agricultural Extension Service. Local grocery stores agreed to buy any excess food produced from the Garden Project with the money going to benefit the prisoners' families. The Marine Reserve had been especially helpful in supplying large tanks of water for the project, and the Shelby County Fire Department agreed to keep the "water buffaloes" filled.

Because of these efforts, Father Mowery was invited to speak to a meeting of the National Recreation and Park Association in Las Vegas. The seminar highlighted the Penal Farm demonstration project and gained national exposure for this successful program. Because of its innovative success, the Youth Service Garden Training Project received an honorable mention in the 1986 American Community Gardening Association, National Community Gardening Contest.

Paralleling this heightened interest across the breadth of the community, the agency's staff and boards continued to expand with the addition of Gerald Stigall, who was hired as a permanent Youth Service staff member. He was a graduate of Vanderbilt University and a member of the National Honor Society, president of the Key Club, and an Eagle Scout. Insurance industry executive John Collier, served as treasurer on Youth Service, Memphis and Youth Service, USA boards. He became a liaison between the local and national agencies and regularly reported on the progress and developments of both organizations.

Notoriety was augmented heavily on a national basis when Youth Service, USA garnered another Freedoms Foundation Award in 1975 for youth leadership activities on military installations. The recognition cited how Youth Service, USA motivated young people toward a sense of direction and provided moral and vocational guidance.

Father Don garnered the Americanism Award from the American Legion that year. More notably, he also received a congratulatory letter from President Gerald Ford for his work nationally with Youth Service, USA. The president acknowledged Don by saying, "Your work has indeed been in the finest American tradition of voluntary action. It provides an example for your fellow citizens, and it reminds each of us of the proud heritage we share."

Another acknowledgement came from USAF General Russell E. Dougherty, commander of the USAF Strategic Air Command. Gen Dougherty stated, "Youth Service has played a key role in our total effort to assist local communities surrounding our bases with meaningful, needed domestic programs. What Father Don has started is good for all of us. We greatly respect our fine association with him, doing God's work, God's way."

Youth Service, USA continued its outreach to attract national supporters. Charles Novak, program director for the national agency, often traveled to Washington with an eye toward coordinating conferences for summer programs around the country. Father Mowery visited the National Bicentennial Commission in 1975 and was invited to brief President Ford on the progress of Youth Service programs. While there, he met with former Secretary of the Navy John Warner, who had become Chairman of the National Bicentennial Commission. The Commission would play an important role with Youth Service, USA in the bicentennial celebration in Memphis later that year.

Regionally, the Episcopal Layman's Conference for Tennessee gathered at the DuBose Conference Center near the University of the South at Sewanee each fall. Even though clergy normally could not attend, Father Don spoke at the 1975 conference. Don wanted to use the occasion to emphasize the work in Memphis with Youth Service, so others could replicate the program.

To prepare for the Layman's Conference, Don asked automobile executive Milton Schaffer if the agency could borrow his GMC motor home for the trip to Sewanee. Schaeffer agreed to loan the van and assigned a driver to the trip. Shelby County Sheriff Bill Morris, City Councilman Bob James, the president of the Memphis Board of Education, and 10 other key people from various occupations rode in the motor home to the event. At the conference, each one spoke of their positive experiences with Youth Service programs. Testimonials of the participants had a tremendous and lasting impact on everyone attending.

Based on Father Don's speech at the Tennessee Layman's Conference, Bob Van Doren, a layman from St. George's Episcopal Church in Nashville and an officer of First American Bank there, approached Father Don afterward and requested that a youth program be started in Nashville. As providence would have it, Van Doren transferred to Memphis to live and work. He brought with him a love for helping youth and became a member of the Youth Service Board of Directors. Bob was moved spiritually by what he had heard at the conference and soon resigned his bank position, attended seminary, and eventually became an associate minister at St. John's Episcopal Church in Memphis.

United Way officials viewed the agency as very efficient; able to operate a large program on a military base at a relatively low cost and became impressed by its impact on youth, but Youth Service, Memphis required more money to operate its many activities. Their request of $200,000 from United Way for 1976 was only a portion of its total needs. Therefore, Youth Service, Memphis found itself in another funding shortage. Father Don prayed that assistance and fortunately, the Memphis City Council and Shelby County Quarterly Court approved funds in September for the camping program.

THE LIBERTY BICENTENNIAL CELEBRATION

In addition to the ongoing youth programs, Youth Service was chosen to help coordinate the "Liberty Celebration" to be held at the Mid-South Coliseum and in conjunction with the Liberty Bowl game in December 1975. The Bicentennial Commission in Washington, D.C. sanctioned this event and Youth Service, USA was the major sponsor. The Commission, headed by Senator John Warner, was familiar with the agency's excellent work and reputation, so the Liberty Celebration in Memphis was to be the official kickoff for the National Bicentennial.

The idea to build the Liberty Celebration around the Liberty Bowl football game was another idea conceived in the living room of board member Lester Crain. Father Don and Lester believed that this country was founded on Christian principles and as a result convinced Liberty Bowl Director Bud Dudley to consider Youth Service as a part of the festivities. Dudley had brought the Liberty Bowl game to Memphis from Philadelphia and had been the director of the annual sporting event for many years. The game was traditionally held in late December on what always seemed to be one of the coldest days of the year. Dudley had wisely chosen to weave the message of patriotism into the Bicentennial celebration and asked Youth Service to take the lead in organizing the event.

The Liberty Bowl game that year pitted Texas A&M against UCLA, but a highlight preceding the game was a 90-minute Liberty Celebration at the Mid-South Coliseum featuring country music luminary Charlie Pride as Master of Ceremonies and Maj. Gen. Thomas Stafford, commander of the Apollo-Soyuz space mission, as a special guest speaker. The Everett R. Cook chapter of the Air Force Association and the board of Youth Service sponsored a Liberty Celebration luncheon honoring Gen. Stafford who spoke at the officer's club at the Defense Depot in Memphis. Miss America, Tawny Elaine Godin, also made a guest appearance for the event.

Youth Service sponsored a citywide poster contest to promote the Bicentennial event and students submitted spaced-themed entries from the city and county schools. A special panel of volunteers judged elementary and high school entries. The winners received a luncheon at the Moonraker Restaurant in neighboring Germantown and had their posters displayed on the walls during the party. McDonald's gave winners cash prizes, and Gen. Stafford was on hand to pass out the awards to the talented students.

Bishop Fred Gates served as program chair and Ken Carter of the First Assembly of God Church conducted an interchurch choir of hundreds of Memphis voices accompanied by the UCLA college band. Gwen Awsumb served as chair of the local committee and helped secure approval of this high profile event through the National Bicentennial Commission. The Air Force Association also played an important role.

Notable speakers provided inspiring words for the celebration, and several marching bands and church choirs performed at the halftime show, with over 2,000 Boy Scouts and Girl Scouts in uniform. Color guards and flag processionals marked the festivities. Limousines, donated for the occasion, transported visiting dignitaries.

An unexpected logistics issue plagued the program planners prior to the event. A national group of patriotic college students under the name Re'Generation was slated to perform at the celebration. However, an airline strike at the time crippled the travel plans of keynote guests and performers. Former Youth Service camper David LaBarreare, who was working in fuel services at the Memphis International Airport, pitched in with a creative idea that a new air service, Federal Express (now FedEx), might help transport the guests. Don immediately called Federal Express and asked for the chairman of the board, Frederick W. (Fred) Smith. However, Art Bass, president of the company at that time, returned the call and began efforts to help. Eventually, the problem was solved, but that phone call led to an ongoing relationship between Fred Smith, Art Bass, and Don Mowery. Interestingly, Fred Smith wanted to meet the person who had the temerity to call and make such a request. Years later, Bass praised Don for his work, "There are few things in this community that can rival the efforts you expend helping those whose lives play an important part in our collective futures."

The accolades continued for the work of Youth Service. The Navy League presented Father Mowery with a special commendation at its annual meeting in 1976. Additionally, Youth Service received another Freedoms Foundation Leadership Award in that year at Valley Forge, PA.

On a personal note, The Reverend Roy Stauffer, pastor of Lindenwood Christian Church, introduced Don to his future wife, Julie Bailey, in 1976. Julie grew up in Memphis and was attending Lindenwood Christian Church at the time. Don recalled the occasion of their first meeting:

> I was so busy traveling that I did not marry until I was 51. Roy Stauffer and I were good friends. We were both single, so he invited me to attend a singles night event one Friday night at Lindenwood. I was one of the speakers and told the audience about the Youth Service program. I spotted a pretty woman sitting on the front row and told Roy that I would like to meet her. Julie and I hit it off and dated for a long time before we married. She became instrumental in keeping me organized and was a wonderful ambassador for what we were doing with the agency. Julie became my right hand and on many occasions assisted St. Augustine Guild with their many fundraising and social events.

On a local staff level, Youth Service acknowledged long-term staff person Nell Bell as one of those particular persons who demonstrated her love and compassion for young people during her 18 years of sustained service to the agency. It illustrated that, no matter what lofty levels it attained far and wide, Youth Service ultimately boiled down to the work of these valuable people.

Such was the case when Father Don introduced, "John," a young man who had attended camp twice, as both an Honor and Junior Camper. After a year of floundering without direction, he joined the Navy and commented that the "magic words" that he had learned in camp had served him well over time. Another boy, who had been economically disadvantaged, served as camp counselor. He later received a recommendation from Senator Howard Baker for admittance to West Point Military Academy.

Only three years old as a company, representatives of FedEx learned of the activities of Youth Service and met with Don to discuss how the growing business could assist the program. That interest grew over time as FedEx became integrally involved with the youth organization at the highest levels. As the relationship grew with Fred Smith and Art Bass, Don was invited to perform the christening of the first Boeing 727 cargo plane as it entered service of the cargo carrier. An enthusiastic crowd of FedEx employees and guests met the plane when it landed on the tarmac after circling ceremoniously over the airport. The Booker T. Washington High School band played to the large crowd gathered for the festivities.

The following prayer for the special occasion was brief, but reflected Father Don's goodwill and support for the organization:

> Now we dedicate everything we do at this time to your glory, and ask that you continue your blessings on this company, its friends and business associates, and all those who are gathered at this time for the occasion of the christening of this great airplane. For this, we ask in Jesus' name. Amen.

Later that year, FedEx began funding to Youth Service, which greatly helped the operational coffers. Several FedEx executives became members of the Youth Service board through the years. Father Don also performed the dedication for the FedEx Greenway Training Center for pilots.

Youth Service board member and former FedEx executive Brian Pecon called the christening ceremony of the DC-10 airplane, "a significant turning point in Father Don's longstanding relationship with the company and founder Fred Smith." Smith became a staunch supporter of the Youth Service programs and served on the board during the capital campaign in 1989. As a result, the two have remained good friends throughout the years.

In conjunction with Father Don's work to solve the growing problems relating to the youth of this country, Charles "Chuck" Colson of Prison Fellowship and Watergate notoriety visited Memphis during 1976 and spoke to the Memphis Area Council on Crime and Delinquency. Don recalled, "Each time we had a VIP visit our program in Memphis, long time supporter, Milton Schaeffer, who owned Bluff City Buick, loaned us one of his vehicles. I called on Milton many times and one day, he donated a new car to Youth Service to transport visiting guests. He had a big heart and helped us in many ways."

The January 1978 issue of Reader's Digest mentioned a program that exposed teenagers to prison life by allowing them to speak directly to prisoners and seeing for themselves exactly what happens in prison from the inmates themselves. The program later became known as the Scared Straight series nationally. Youth Service counselors presented this program to the Memphis Council on Crime and Delinquency, which was studying the idea of having such a program in Shelby County. This format, later known as the Youth Service About Face Program, followed these general lines and will be treated in chapter 14 in full form.

By February 1978, the Vocational Exploration (Camping) Program grew a new affiliation with the AFL-CIO Human Resources Development Institution in which some 60 to 90 young people from 16 to 21 years of age were placed in various businesses in the city. This was part of a larger national program aimed at providing training in jobs for young people during the summers. The manager of the Caterpillar Tractor Company was a key contributor who worked with Youth Service and employed some of its graduates.

The AFL-CIO Labor Council also helped develop a summer youth employment program funded by the Employment and Training Administration of the U.S. Department of Labor. Youth Service provided summer jobs for 80 high school juniors and seniors. There were 110 spaces for Memphis youths – 20 through the Juvenile Court Diversion Program and 10 through Big Brother and Big Sister programs. The object of this effort was to expose young people to a variety of vocations in the private sector and to educate them to the realities of the world of work. The youths received an allowance equal to the minimum wage. Four Youth Service supervisors ran the program and staged group meetings, provided job and career counseling, and provided administrative support for the young participants.

It should be noted that most of the participants in the Camping and Vocational Exposure Programs did not have the economic backing to attend college; therefore, some considered the military to be a viable alternative. While Youth Service in no way intentionally recruited for the armed forces, some participants did join the military service when they came of age and a few entered the military academies. "The military wasn't for everyone, but we helped guide them in the process if they displayed the desire, ability, and aptitude," Don explained.

Father Don and the Youth Service staff constantly sought to create new programs and enhance existing ones with the help of local organizations. For instance, Larry Turner, a newly hired counselor with wilderness experience at George Washington National Forest in Virginia, worked to create an outdoor leadership program similar to the Outward Bound program.

Other programs in the late 1970s included educational field trips sponsored by the Pink Palace Museum. Director Robert Walker head of the Memphis Fire Department allowed the agency to use several fire stations for group meetings. The youths also enjoyed ice-skating at Overton Square and Libertyland Amusement Park. A cooking school for some of the young people was made possible through the help of Dick Fisher's school, *What's Cookin,* which was attended by both boys and girls. The agency also provided water skiing lessons and other water sports during the summer for groups of young folks just across the Mississippi River at Horseshoe Lake in Arkansas. Contributors donated all of these activities to the program.

Success stories abound for those who attended the ongoing vocational camping opportunities. A former Youth Service Junior Counselor, who by age 25 started a very successful business, told of his being involved in the program in 1979. "Bill" said the program and the Honor Camper's trip to Pensacola, FL had given him direction he could not have received otherwise. That former camp counselor recalled, "I will never forget the moral fiber that was given to me during my association with the agency." He also expressed hopes of becoming more directly involved with the organization in the future.

Positive notoriety was spreading to the extent that Father Don and his staff were asked to intervene in troublesome areas around the country with their creative templates of care, transformation, and positive community change. In one ambitious instance, Youth Service, USA worked to help tackle poverty and the explosive situation that was taking place in Liberty City near Miami. Because there was need in almost every community, national youth programs were growing all the while. Father Don recalled his visit to Liberty City to meet the Episcopal Bishop:

> The bishop was fascinated with what we had to offer and with what the church was doing in the way of social programs toward preventing delinquency. Our trip ended more successfully than a recent visit by President Jimmy Carter, who was forced to leave due to the highly charged racial tension in the area. I became very good friends with Charles (Chuck) Tisdale, an African-American, who served as Mayor of Bridgeport, CT. and who was a liaison to President Carter during this time.

According to Don, Tisdale helped calm the people and make acquaintances with city leaders in the Miami area. Youth Service also pitched in and called upon its networking contacts at FedEx, which had a large hub in Miami. FedEx was supportive of the effort and not long afterward, Youth Service, USA, was eventually able to establish a large and successful job-training program in Liberty City through a military association with the Coast Guard.

Father Mowery continued his "spiritual networking" with vital trips to Washington during the Carter administration. On one visit, Don discussed Youth Service programs with Bill Milliken, who was then president and founder of Cities in Schools (now Communities in Schools, Inc.). From his pioneering movement to foster high school graduates, Milliken helped initiate what were called "Street Academies." He served on the board of directors for Leadership Foundations of America and provided vital support and advice to Don. Support from key influencers such as Milliken was vital to promote the growth of Youth Service.

One of the biggest promotional events for Youth Service occurred on April 27, 1979 when USAF Gen. David Jones, recently chosen as Chairman of the Joint Chiefs of Staff by President Jimmy Carter, came to Memphis and presented the Air Force documentary film, *A Week of Summer,* which highlighted the significant achievements of the organization. Proclamations from Shelby County Mayor Bill Morris and Memphis Mayor Wyeth Chandler declared the day as "Youth Service Day" in Memphis. The event helped raise awareness for the agency to an entirely new level.

Sponsored by the Memphis Chamber of Commerce, the event was held at the historic Peabody Hotel, which was closed at the time, but because of the special day, Don received permission to reopen the beautiful historic hotel for this celebration. There was no operating kitchen, so Danvers and Shoney's donated the food. The event drew over 800 attendees including important dignitaries from around the country. Officials with the City of Memphis presented keys to the city and Shelby County to Gen. Jones, who was the featured speaker. Also speaking at the event was Charles Tisdale from the White House Staff and Federal Coordinator for the "Cities in School" program, and Tony Jackson, director of National Programs for the Community Services Administration. Participants heard Gen. Jones comment, "I have never received a warmer welcome than this one in Memphis. This event is a tribute to Youth Service, Father Mowery, the Episcopal Church, and the Memphis community."

FATHER DON WITH HIS STAFF, SUPPORTERS
AND VOLUNTEERS VISITING THE CAMP

NAS CAMPERS FLANKED BY THEIR COUNSELORS

FATHER DON, MARY LOU GALICIAN, GEN. THOMAS
STAFFORD AND BEVERLY SOUSOULAS AT THE LIBERTY
CELEBRATION, DEC, 1975

AIR FORCE SHOWING OF YOUTH SERVICE FILM,
A WEEK OF SUMMER, AT THE PEABODY
HOTEL APRIL, 1979

CHAPLAIN DON AND LT. MASSIEU ON
ACTIVE DUTY, 1970s

FRED SMITH, FATHER DON AND FRED'S MOTHER SALLY
HOOK, AT THE CHRISTENING OF THE FIRST FEDEX
BOEING 727, 1976

FATHER DON AND FRED SMITH AT THE PEABODY HOTEL
FOR THE SHOWING OF THE YOUTH SERVICE FILM, 1979

INDIVIDUAL ACHIEVEMENT AWARDS BEING HANDED OUT
DURING A GRADUATION CEREMONY BY THE COMMANDING
OFFICER FOR MEMPHIS NAS

FATHER MOWERY PRESIDES OVER THE GRADUATION
CEREMONY AT MEMPHIS NAS CHAPEL

ALBERTA GAINES, LONG TIME SUPPORTER AND YOUTH
SERVICE BOARD MEMBER

CHAPTER THIRTEEN

From Job Training To Bridge Builders:
The 1980s

The decade of the 1980s served as a key, formative period for the varied Youth Service career programs. Youth Service received substantial local and governmental support, and the program over the decade matured nationally. It is noteworthy how a given program evolved into new refinements, but many of these initiatives were firsts and others were untried. Officials of Youth Service created many new and innovative programs that often assumed lives of their own in other areas of the country.

In 1980, Youth Service was in the process of renovating their new Memphis headquarters building on South Goodlett Avenue. John Collier chaired the new building committee, and contractor Henry Haizlip, Jr. oversaw the renovation. The Reverend Wallace Pennepacker of St. John's Church graciously allowed Youth Service to share their quarters during the yearlong process. The agency settled into several rooms on the third floor of St. John's Church. The donated attic space had no air conditioning, which rendered the quarters almost untenable in the warmer months. During that unseasonably hot summer, the temperature in Memphis reached an all-time high of 108 degrees, which was part of a remarkable and memorable 15-day stretch of temperatures above 100. Many times, the staff would have to go home during the workday to change clothes due to the oppressive heat.

Funding for the programs of 1980 slowed substantially due to a series of unexpected budget cuts. Since the city and county had been providing money for this program, any decrease in funding affected the residential camps for Youth Service. However, the year would be a benchmark for other positive public relations efforts.

In other important staff developments, Lt. Col. John Edwards, who had retired from the Air Force, came to Memphis to become deputy director of Youth Service, USA in October 1980. While in the Air Force, Col. Edwards developed a Youth Service program at Wright-Patterson Air Force Base in Dayton, OH. Don related, "John was very involved in our program and did a great job. He was a valuable asset because he knew the programs, as well as military protocols." Edwards was instrumental in helping Youth Service, USA grow into a multi-million dollar program from the financial experience he had gained in the Air Force. He brought many new and creative ideas to the table and took some of the traveling off Don's plate in the process.

As the national program grew beyond what anyone could have fathomed at the beginning, specialization and allocation of staff efforts at Youth Service had to be more closely coordinated than perhaps ever before. More structure proved necessary as the dual programs matured in both their scope and array of initiatives.

Former military officers were key contributors to the work of Youth Service. Their management skills and experience in program design and implementation proved invaluable to the growth and success of Youth Service, USA. A partial list of these important additions to the Youth Service Staff includes:

James C. Kasperbauer, retired USAF Lt. Col., program director, Memphis

Ben Woodworth, retired CAPT USN, program director, Memphis

Hal Dortch, retired Col. USAF, program director, Nashville

Sid Hatfield, retired USAF, program director, Knoxville

Hugh Don Gregg, retired Lt. Col. USAF, program director, Chattanooga

Robert E. Pruitt, retired, retired Col. USAF, program director, San Antonio

Nathan Kniker, retired Major USA, program director, St. Louis

Hal Yaskovich, retired Col. USAF, program director, Washington, D.C.

John Krosnes, retired Lt. Col., director of development

Marvin "Barney" Barnett, retired CAPT USN, program director

Jim Bassham, retired Lt. Col. USAF, program director

George Douglas, retired Major Gen. USAFR, program director

The Vocational Exploration Program provided a more structured educational approach for young people ages 14 to 18. Young people learned about various jobs and the path they needed to take to be successful in a particular career. This program motivated and encouraged young people to stay in school and to make realistic choices in preparation for their future careers. This effort provided linkages to other programs offered year-round and allowed for follow-up assistance for the participants by full-time instructors and support personnel. The Private Industry Council funded the initiative, but required continuous support from the private sector. Undergirding these efforts, NAS Memphis and Youth Service enjoyed long-standing partnerships and continued to serve hundreds of young people every year in the 1980s. Interventions into the lives of these young people created hope and a chance for a new direction in their lives. Stories abound of the young men and women who survived these tenuous teenage years.

Don recalled an interesting story of two such participants in the Memphis program. During the summer months of 1980, two 15-year-old boys, "Robert" and "Terry," went on a burglary spree in the city. For Terry, it started with stealing from Walgreen's when he was 13. When the two met, they began to "egg" each other on until they committed their first offense together. After their arrest, the police estimated that the duo had broken into more than 50 businesses. In many ways, they were typical boys. Both lived with their mothers in single-parent households. They expressed little interest in sports and indicated they were frequently bored at home.

During the burglaries, the boys took electronics, office supplies, and anything they found of value in the offices. They divided the loot and hid the stolen items in their respective houses. At first, they were overly cautious, but became bolder as they discovered how easy the crimes were to commit. Robert was most concerned about running into a security guard and getting "his brains blown away." Their ability to escape detection only reinforced their self-esteem and efforts. Terry enjoyed the challenge of getting into the buildings, and Robert was usually the lookout. A plain-clothes police officer, driving by a business at 3 a.m., saw them as they entered a building and put an end to the criminal career of the daring duo.

Reform school and prison was a probable path for the two boys, but after a review of the case, Juvenile Court decided to let them work off their sentence through the Community Service Program. Youth Service supervised the boys, as they were required to perform 450 hours of community service each. Both young men were glad to have the opportunity to work off their offenses and were thankful that they were not placed in juvenile detention centers.

Robert related how Don had affected his life:

> Father Don is the difference in me trying to get my 'head straight.' He has a way with kids. You feel relaxed around him because he is not a domineering type. He knows how to promote a better outlook on life. You know he has the power to throw you back into jail, but you feel he is your friend. He does not represent authority the way probation officers do.

Father Don shared other stories of youngsters who had been involved in crime. One story involved a young man who had unknowingly broken into an occupied home. The homeowner quickly discovered the boy and because of recent burglaries, kept a gun handy. While attempting to escape, the homeowner pointed the gun at the young man and shouted for him to stop. Fortunately, he did because the homeowner said later that he was prepared to pull the trigger if he had not stopped. The youngster eventually worked through his problems and later received a college degree in psychology.

Marine Pfc. Don Franklin told the Youth Service board of his experience as an Honor Camper and a Junior Counselor before he went into the military. He could not afford college and planned, from what he had learned in the Vocational Exploration Program, to make the military a career. He thanked the board for making it possible for him to participate and credited his time at the Youth Service camp for his life-changing decision to join the Marines, another success story for the program.

A new, revised Job Skills Training and Employment Program (JSTEP) for youths 18 to 24 years of age began in the early 1980s. This program grew out of the base tours where Don noticed the empty chairs in the classrooms, especially in the courses on mechanics. Filling those empty chairs with Youth Service participants was a creative alternative. With the help of Father Don's friend, ADM Christensen, they both realized that the military could train the Youth Service people along with their own students without adding costs to the government. Don used his networking skills with area business and recalled, "We chose unemployed individuals who had the 'smarts' to accomplish goals in the classroom and who could learn the military way. The beauty of the plan was that it wouldn't cost the military any more money to add a few of our people to a class that was half-full."

As the Jobs Training Program expanded, it soon was discovered that some of the young people could not read and comprehend the printed training manuals. In response, Youth Service assigned several of its staff members to live at the Memphis Navy base with the young trainees. The staff taught the participants English, math, and reading comprehension in the evenings after they completed the day classes. Without the remedial assistance, these participants could not have completed the courses, and because of this intense tutoring, some of the youngsters achieved the same educational level as their military counterparts.

The Youth Service job-training program was greatly enhanced when Tennessee Senator Bill Brock became the U.S. Secretary of Labor. After receiving a call from Secretary Brock, Don was invited to Washington to brief the Secretary about the new job training program at NAS Memphis. After learning more about the project, Brock and federal military authorities helped support placing the training program on bases across the country.

Don recalled, "The military supported us in the national expansion of this program, but only if we used the same model and could guarantee the same results at the other bases across the country. Their support made the programs work." Over time and in stages, Youth Service, USA orchestrated a staged-in sequence of similar programs with young people in other locations around the nation.

In January 1981, Youth Service, USA applied for a grant from the Department of Labor through the Comprehensive Employment Training Act (CETA). CETA was a federal law enacted by Congress to train workers and provide them with jobs in the public and private sectors. The program extended more control for job training to individual state governments and offered work to those with low incomes and to the long-term unemployed.

Father Don became good friends with Dr. Warner Dickerson, who was appointed by the Tennessee governor to head federal social programs in the area. Dickerson also worked closely with the schools in Tennessee, helped support the CETA grant funding and later served as the head of the Memphis NAACP. He played an important role in navigating the process of obtaining federal funding for state programs. Father Don explained, "Dr. Dickerson had confidence that if the state invested money in Youth Service and its programs, they would get their money's worth."

Another important supporter was well-connected Memphis attorney and City Councilman, Louis Donelson. The Governor later appointed him State Comptroller and through his efforts, helped open the funding gates on several occasions. Because of these and many other efforts, Youth Service, USA became a recipient of a contract to operate several on-the-job training programs at NAS Memphis. Local companies such as FedEx, Holiday Inns, and Cablevision helped with the planning for the job training program. The Youth Service Job Training and Employment Program in Memphis served as the model for other on the job training programs across the country. Additionally, the counselors, staff, and volunteers acted as role models for the young people they helped. The valuable work of these dedicated people would be difficult to replicate today.

As illustrated in this narrative, Youth Service had a special knack for using existing facilities rather than building or purchasing new ones. This key element was essential as program costs continued to escalate. Included in a list of free or in-kind services was the Sheriff's bus for transportation, meals arranged with military bases, the use of underutilized land tracts at the Penal Farm land for gardening, obtaining jobs for youngsters at existing factories and commercial enterprises, and even passes and tickets to events that were not full to capacity.

The Youth Service Job Skills Training and Employment Program was accorded a more structured form by the summer of 1981. There were as many as 60 trainees participating in this path of opportunity at any given time locally. Those who applied for the job training program through the CETA grant had to express a desire for the training and job commitment in order to enroll. The six months of skills training at 35 hours per week included counseling for an hour per day that included advice on how to seek a job, develop self-respect and respect for others, how to properly dress for work, and cultivate a positive attitude.

More than 120 positions from private employers were promised to the local program. The positions were in job fields such as air conditioning, plumbing, maintenance, welding, janitorial service, electrical, clerk typist positions, auto mechanics, and warehousing. CETA program officials interviewed the young applicants and then tested them for adaptability. The young people would then make applications involving a week-long process at the CETA office. After their clearance for the training program, they went through further training and counseling at NAS Memphis. To anticipate growth of this important initiative, three additional job sites were added to the Job Skills Training and Employment Program. They included the Memphis Defense Depot, the Corps of Engineers, and the National Guard facilities in Memphis.

According to established rules, JSTEP trainees could leave the program at any time. Graduation did not guarantee a particular job to the trainee. However, if the graduate did not like the job selected for them, there were always backup jobs with other businesses for which they could apply. The program more or less acted as a clearinghouse for the employers and trainees. All participants received $3.35 per hour during their training. They would then apply for a specific job at one of the businesses, which had committed to the program. This process became a national standard for other cities through the Youth Service, USA network. For example, the Episcopal Bishop in Miami was very supportive of the program. He voiced his comments in a newspaper article that described how the first trainees in the Miami project earned jobs as mechanics with the Ryder Truck Company.

The Job Skills Training and Employment Program began to train more women in non-traditional jobs, but some women did not find industrial and warehouse work appealing. Father Don recalled explaining the concept to the first women in the program. "We told them that if they put on steel-toed shoes and a work uniform, they could make a lot more money driving a forklift than working as a secretary." Once the women became more familiar with "blue-collar" skills, many realized how they could be successful and not have to worry about dressing up for an office job. During the months of on-the-job training by the military, the women would receive a small additional stipend because most of them had expenses relating to childcare.

Another important part of the Job Skills Training and Employment Program was not just the training for the job itself, but included instruction in appearance and attitude when they went for a job interview, as well as lessons on how to manage a household budget. Because many participants lacked money or even a job, they had little reason to know details about how to handle financial matters, Social Security or taxes.

The success of the Job Skills Training and Employment Program spread quickly to other locations such as Wright-Patterson Air Force Base in Dayton, Ohio under the leadership of Lt. Col. John Edwards. The Youth Service program on Wright-Patterson Air Force Base added an emphasis on youth employment, where youngsters received pay for working 8 to 20 hours a week. This was directly tied to their schoolwork to give them job experiences and more motivation to stay in school. Walter R. Williams, Jr., as chief of the Equal Employment Opportunity Commission at Wright-Patterson, helped direct and reformat the project in conjunction with the Youth Service camps.

Youth Service, USA began to experience growing pains regarding aspects of the program in 1981. Several board members believed that there was a lack of unified organization within some of the national programs. Specifically, organizing and operating multiple federal and local programs in different states proved difficult at best. Father Don understood these concerns because, early in his tenure, he knew the challenges of dealing with the federal bureaucracy. The inconsistencies rested in the fact that all three branches of the military had different programs. The terminology varied, the local community groups were different, and the local funds available for each project came from different sources. Additionally, some projects at the national level were in danger of losing their funding at the local level.

The summer youth employment and training program not only provided jobs, but also added competency-based instruction for 200 youths ages 16 to 21. Annually, more than 150 young people participated in this format at NAS Memphis, and more than 50 youths received training at the Memphis Defense Depot at a given time.

The Memphis City Council and the Shelby County Board of Commissioners reduced funding for the NAS Memphis program in 1981. Additionally, the change in command in Memphis and at other military facilities made it necessary for Father Don to "resell" the program to new leadership. This was challenging because it was the privilege of the base commanders if they did not want to offer base facilities because of mission priorities or added maintenance and utility costs. These factors caused the local youth program, as well as the national programs to wax and wane at many of the bases. Therefore, the tightening of military budgets in recent years and the physical lack of personnel, called for new approaches to keep the camps open for youngsters.

Youth Service applied to the Neely Foundation for more money to fund a new type of "intensive" outdoor camping program. Based upon the success of the program at the Naval Air Station, Youth Service and Army

Green Berets decided to introduce a survival-based program at Arkabutla Lake in northern Mississippi. This program taught wilderness survival skills for junior and senior high school teens. They received specific training and counseling in personal, physical, and moral development.

Don used his connections with the Army Reserve to initiate the program and recalled how the survival camp program began:

> I contacted the Special Forces at Ft. Bragg, NC and asked about instituting a program. A contingent of Green Berets came to Memphis and staffed the survival camp program at Arkabutla Lake in northern Mississippi. We had ten weeks of survival camping during the summer of 1973. The U.S. Army Corps of Engineers was responsible for initiating the program and the Army Special Forces, Green Berets, provided survival equipment and training expertise. The teens lived in tents and survived by living off the land.

These programs not only helped motivate youths to become physically and mentally fit, but challenged them to develop leadership and responsibility as well. The Youth Service staff always built the foundation for a purposeful, constructive, and worthwhile life. They incorporated recreational activities to encourage young people to develop leadership skills, sportsmanship, teamwork, and physical fitness. Another important aspect of every Youth Service program was group counseling, which was conducted daily in the areas of interpersonal relations, values, ethics, and career planning.

Several success stories stand out as a testament to the success of the job training program. A Youth Service newsletter chronicled Elizabeth Chambers' success story with the Youth Service Job Skills Training and Employment Program. Prior to her enrollment, Chambers, a single mother, spent most of her time raising her three children and watching television the narrative stated. After watching a Youth Service television commercial, Chambers' life was never the same. She joined the program and immediately began training as a warehouse forklift operator at the Memphis Defense Depot. Though the difficulty of a non-traditional job would have scared many people away, Chambers was eager to work and thrived on the challenge. The secret, she said, was that she was "working for something better." "Something better" meant job opportunities, quality day care for her children, transportation to the training site, and training in a skill that could mean a steady job. Most importantly, it meant proving that she could take on the challenge and come out on top. It translated into a major step forward in her quality of life that could only come from a new level of self-respect. At her graduation ceremony in St. Mary's Cathedral, Chambers addressed the gathering and spoke of how she prospered in the Youth Service program. During an awards ceremony in Memphis, Elizabeth became one of seven young women honored by Governor Ned McWherter for her exceptionally hard work and determination. That year, several hundred graduates received certificates at the cathedral for their accomplishments.

The graduation ceremonies for the Job Skills and Education Training Program in Memphis were held at St. Mary's Cathedral and were much more elaborate than the Vocational Exposure (Camping) Program, with hundreds of guests in attendance. They were very important events, filling nearly every seat in the cathedral. Flowers and pageantry adorned the church, while the Navy Band from the Naval Air Station played and the color guard presented the flags. Songs filled the air and special guest speakers offered encouragement to the graduates as they accepted their diplomas. A large reception normally followed each graduation, which included members of St. Augustine Guild and members of the Board of Youth Service.

One of the graduation speakers during these events, Memphis City Councilman Myron Lowery, provided words of wisdom from one who had once been directly involved with the agency. The holder of two master's degrees and a former work-study student with Youth Service, Lowery described to the audience how the program provided him with his earliest work experience and how there was no better role model for the youth of the city. Lowery was later recognized by the U.S. Jaycees as one of the Ten Outstanding Young Men in America.

Genevieve Thomas, another graduate of the Job Skills Training and Employment Program, believed her graduation certificate was her ticket out of government assistance programs and into the business world. Thomas was one of the Youth Service job trainees who worked for no pay in exchange for practical experience and placement counseling upon completion of the six-month training program. Mrs. Thomas said her children motivated her through all the months of training. "I couldn't see them going to school in raggedy clothes," she said in her address. "I wanted something better for my family."

The Memphis Housing Authority hired Thomas as a secretary. She recalled, "I felt like I was doing everything possible to let people know that I would be an asset to their organization." When she was 17, Genevieve was in the top percentile of her class and involved in extracurricular activities. Despite her situation, she commented, "I knew that I would someday be someone if I did not give up." Her emotional address inspired an audience of several hundred parents, friends, and supporters.

There were other personal accounts such as Dianne Carter, who obtained a job at the IRS Service Center because of the program. She remembered Youth Service providing day care, which gave her the ability to continue training. "It was very rewarding, even though I wasn't getting paid as an employee," Carter said. Another graduate, Jackie Crosby, worked as a personnel-staffing specialist for the Service Center. She recalled that the center hired four of the seven Youth Service trainees who completed data transcribing training that year.

Phillip Burnett, then president of the Board of Youth Service, Memphis, recalled that approximately 85 percent of the graduates in the program ultimately found meaningful jobs. "This program offers a valuable resource for Memphis and assists people who would otherwise not have an opportunity." Burnett also served as head of the Cotton Council and was responsible for introducing Billy Dunavant to the Youth Service program and Board.

Retired Air Force Col. Bill Freeman, who worked with the Memphis Mayor's office, recalled his association with Youth Service when he was commanding officer of the Memphis Defense Depot. He first met Father Mowery in 1978 when he allowed Youth Service counselors to use the swimming pool for the summer at the Defense Depot. Later, he became involved in the Job Skills Training and Employment Program. Col. Freeman handpicked his Depot supervisors for the first program and wanted to give it every advantage. He often said, "When you teach a young person a skill, we all gain." The training for the first group was so successful that other Depot supervisors were asking him to assign trainees to them. Freeman started with a group of 15, which grew to 60 young people at one time in that training program.

In Tennessee, Governor Lamar Alexander liked the program so well that he thought it should be a year-round activity in the city school systems. Soon, similar job training programs sprang up in Chattanooga, Knoxville and Nashville, as well as Little Rock, Baltimore, Sacramento, and Miami.

Don also became acquainted with Thomas Pownall, who was Chairman of the Board for Martin-Marietta Corporation and an influential person in Washington. Don remarked about one trip to Washington to visit Pownall:

We wanted more non-military and private sector members for the Youth Service board. To entice him to come on board with us and out of desperation, we had a young lady pose for a picture at his office door with a large bag of popcorn and a sign that read, 'Things are Popping at Youth Service,' and that did it – he joined our board. We received a pleasant surprise when Martin Marietta Corp. then made the first contribution of $50,000 for the expansion of the Youth Service, USA training programs across the country.

Pownall offered assistance at every opportunity and reiterated his commitment to Youth Service when funding became tight. He wrote in a letter to Don, "Though it has not been easy, you have managed to keep your organization in good shape and expanding its efforts. It is obvious that nothing has ever diminished your enthusiasm for the work you are doing, and I admire you for it." Through his company, Martin-Marietta, Pownall also provided transportation for Youth Service board members to attend several events in Washington.

In 1981, Father Don and Youth Service, USA received the Outstanding Public Service Award given by the Secretary of Defense, Casper Weinberger. The award is the second highest award presented by the Secretary of Defense to a civilian during peacetime. Former recipients of this award include Laura Bush and Hillary Rodham Clinton.

The presentation was made during a luncheon at the Shoreham Hotel in Washington, D.C. to thank those who assisted Youth Service, USA. The American Defense Preparedness Association (ADPA) hosted the sold-out event for the Youth Service Board of Directors. Gen. David C. Jones, Chairman of the Joint Chiefs of Staff, was a guest of honor as ADPA recognized him for his work for young people through Youth Service. Others at the head table included:

> Secretary of Labor, Raymond Donovan, with a delegation from the Department of Labor (DOL)

> Eighth District Congressman, Harold Ford

> Former YSUSA Board President, RADM E. E. Christensen

> Director, Region IV, Community Services Administration (CSA), USN (Ret.); William "Sonny" Walker

President of the National Office for Social Responsibility (OSR), Robert Gemignani

President, Youth Service, USA Board, John S. Collier

President, Washington Chapter (ADPA), Al Hobelman

Special Assistant to President Regan, Morton C. Blackwell

Vice Chief of Staff, Gen. Robert Mathis, USAF

Chief of Naval Personnel, VADM Lando W. Zech, Jr., USN

Vice Chief of Staff, Gen. John W. Vessey, Jr.,USA

The delegation from Memphis included Youth Service, Memphis and Youth Service, USA board and staff members, as well as members of the Memphis State ROTC detachment.

Others who had assisted Youth Service along the way were acknowledged at the event. Former Assistant Secretary of Defense, Roger T. Kelly, was honored by ADPA for his work in establishing the Domestic Action Council. Additionally, Charles Tisdale, former White House staff member, was recognized for helping coordinate a cooperative effort between YSUSA, CSA and DOL.

In his presentation speech, Gen. Jones, representing Secretary Weinberger said, "Not only in the Memphis area, but throughout this country, Youth Service, USA has reached more than 300,000 youths since the program's inception in 1969, and there are many success stories." Mike Vestal from Memphis State ROTC and Lance Corporal Don Franklin, USMC, both former Youth Service participants, told the crowd of their involvement with Youth Service and the influence the organization had on their lives. Also attending the event was Red McCombs, a valuable supporter of the Youth Service, USA programs. McCombs was founder of Red McCombs Group in San Antonio, co-founder of Clear Channel Communications, owner of several new car dealerships and former owner of the San Antonio Spurs, Denver Nuggets, and Minnesota Vikings.

In 1982, Youth Service, USA experienced a dramatic increase in programs. More than 100 military installations had opened their doors to more than 400,000 youth and young adults since the pilot program began. Hundreds of trainees were involved in the Youth Employment and Training Program. Ninety percent successfully completed the program, and 45 percent were immediately placed in jobs. The national momentum continued for the job-training component. In April 1983, Father Don presented an overview of the job-training program before the Joint Chiefs of Staff at a prayer breakfast in Washington. During the breakfast, Don revealed his plans to begin similar platforms in more states that had a military presence.

The year 1983 was of great personal consequence, as it marked Don and Julie Bailey's wedding. After dating for several years, they were married by Bishop Alex Dickson, who had just previously been consecrated Bishop of the Diocese of West Tennessee April 9. In fact, Bishop Dickson instituted the marriage as his first official duty the next day at 7 a.m. on April 10 at St. Mary's Cathedral. They had planned the early morning ceremony to avoid disrupting the regular 7:30 a.m. morning worship service. The wedding attendees included a large number of friends, well-wishers, and supporters. Don was touched when he looked into the congregation and saw Lester Crain's wife, Brenda with her daughter Kim who served as a counselor for Youth Service summer program. Dean Ed Reeves of St. Mary's Cathedral and Doug Bailey of Calvary Church assisted during the marriage ceremony. The newlyweds then left to catch a plane for a cruise departing from Miami the same day.

Julie worked in public relations with the UT Medical Group and became a valued assistant in Don's work with youth. She was his personal advisor and trusted confidant on many of the issues Don faced during the second half of his career in Memphis. She also was a member of the St. Augustine Guild and worked tirelessly to find ways to make money for the programs. Julie coordinated dinners and served as host for influential donors at many events. One such event was the first annual dinner and auction held at the Memphis Hunt and Polo Club, created through her initiative.

Supporters such as Bishop Dickson played an important role in promoting the work of Youth Service and often traveled with Don to annual meetings such as those held at historic Old St. Paul's Church in Baltimore and the Cedars in Washington. Dickson became a very active board member despite the demands of his position as bishop. Dickson always had an interest in youth. Before becoming bishop, he was head master for All Saints Episcopal School in Vicksburg, MS.

Meanwhile, the work of Youth Service pressed onward that year. In Memphis, the vocational trainees were introduced to the world of education from Shelby State Community College, where they attended training sessions each week for which many received credits. Since funding for the Memphis summer program was always tight, the summer camp at the Naval Air Station cut costs by reducing the number of days for the program. In a gesture of support, the Memphis Police Department, Shelby County Sheriff's Department, and the Tennessee Highway Patrol pitched in and provided officers, all of whom worked as camp counselors. The officers wore counselor clothing throughout the week, and then totally surprised the campers by showing up in full police uniform at the graduations, revealing their true work identities.

Other types of support added to the creative nature with which Youth Service operated. Local corporations usually provided cash, but also gave in-kind donations. These gifts were often delivered in a variety of ways. For instance, one year, Stein Mart Department Store gave a tenth of its sales for a given day, the largest shopping day of the year, as a gift to Youth Service.

It was common for the Youth Service board to hire retired military personnel. One prominent figure joining the agency was retired USAF Col. Frank Dawson. Dawson first met Father Mowery in 1974 when he was serving as Professor of Aerospace Studies at Memphis State University. He was still an active duty Air Force officer during this time, heading the Air Force ROTC program at Memphis State until 1976. A former Air Force fighter pilot, Dawson was seeking an opportunity to serve a worthwhile cause after his retirement. Frank had teaching and training experience and an MBA from Auburn University, so Don hired him to serve as director of operations for Youth Service, USA and Youth Service, Memphis. He served in that role from 1983 to 1997 and headed several major initiatives during his tenure. Frank was responsible for hiring and training staff, designing programs, writing grants, job market research, and he was the organization's military liaison. It was Dawson's job to work with the military to match their training capacity with the job needs in the nearby cities. President Reagan's new emphasis on job training from 1981 to 1989 made it a much easier for Dawson to build momentum for job training programs around the country.

Dawson recalled his role in heading the Youth Service Job Skills Training and Employment Program (JSTEP):

> I went several months trying to figure out what I would do after I retired. It was hard for me to take off that uniform. In 1982, I attended a meeting with Father Don and John Edwards who were developing a new job-training program in Memphis. The program collaborated with the military and civilian communities to create job training for 18 to 24- year-old young people.

My first job was to direct JSTEP in Memphis, but we soon established other programs in Nashville and several other cities. Typically, we went into a civilian community and determined where potential jobs were located. We then contacted the local military base and talked to the commanders about the job-training program. It was not difficult to sell the program because of Don's record of accomplishment of having three Joint Chiefs of Staff on his board. That usually attracted their attention. All of the area military bases had excess capacity and most of them could use extra labor. Additionally, it did not cost them anything.

Once we received approval from the base commander and identified the types of training to provide, we set to work building the program. The types of training depended on what jobs were available in the community. Every community had different industries and needs. For example, in Nashville, we worked with the Air National Guard to train aircraft painters. The money to fund these programs came primarily from the Private Industry Council, which was a part of the U.S. Labor Department, and private donations.

Initially, we had between 25 and 30 participants in each job-training program. Some of these programs ran for only a couple of years, depending on the funding, while others ran until the Private Industry Council money ran out. In total, we provided job training for about 7,000 people nationwide through JSTEP.

Father Don considered Frank Dawson a true gentleman and one of the most valuable and respected members of the Youth Service staff because he knew the programs, the military system and the Memphis community well. Dawson worked with Don for 14 years and retired from Youth Service in January 1997. He built and managed 10 JETEP training programs around the country while marketing the program to the Private Industry Council. These programs were located in Memphis, Nashville, Knoxville, Chattanooga, San Antonio, Biloxi, St. Louis, Atlanta, Washington, D.C., and Augusta. Each program had special challenges that required the expert managerial skills and persistence of Col. Dawson to make them successful.

Other important additions to the Youth Service staff during this time included retired USN CAPT "Red Horse" Myers who helped design many of the Youth Service, USA programs. Sandra DeGraffenreid became the first program manager for personnel development for the Youth Service, Memphis Vocational Exploration Program. Counselors with this department provided counseling and follow-up work on referrals from Juvenile Court, parents, schools, and other agencies. They made home and school visits, provided individual and group counseling, conducted community clubs and maintained client cases designated by the agency. In addition, they attended professional conferences and seminars, recruited participants for the Vocational Exposure Program, the job skills training and employment programs and even transported clients to and from activities. Another key addition to the Youth Service staff was Gene Banton, who directed regional operations, supervised programs and handled grant-writing duties for the agency.

Youth Service continued to expand in outreach and influence in 1984. Civilian and military officials from Washington, D.C. became regular visitors to Memphis in an effort to discover what programs would work for the youth of this country.

By the fall of 1984, Father Don reported that over 100 young people were involved in the Vocational Exploration Program funded by the Private Industry Council. Chosen by the Memphis Board of Education, these youths had to meet certain criteria to be admitted to the eight-week program. Attendance each day averaged 99 percent, which was exceptional, considering that most of the young people had to take public transportation in order to reach the school. The Private Industry Council reported that Youth Service had the finest system of its kind in the city and urged the agency to double the enrollment.

Another venture, the Job Skills Alumni Program was awarded a research and development grant in October 1984 by the Human Development Services Office of Children and Youth and by the U.S. Department of Health and Human Services. A dozen former students formed an advisory committee and were committed to assist with job training for future candidates. Graduates of that program numbered 478 that year, despite the burden placed upon them due to the commitment involved. Despite the added pressure, teaching young parents to cope with stress helped break cycles of child abuse, one of the main objectives with parenting skills and family budgeting.

During the 1980s, hundreds of successful young people graduated from the Job Skills Training and Employment Program and the Vocational Exploration Program at NAS Memphis, where they were exposed to various occupations and a new way of life. In April 1984, Father Mowery received a visit from Jim Coyne, special assistant to President Ronald Reagan. Coyne headed the president's program on private sector initiatives and was quite impressed after a visit to the Youth Service training sites in Memphis. Coyne commended Youth Service for creating such an innovative platform and reported to President Reagan on the success of this initiative. As a result, Father Don received a presidential citation for his work from President Ronald Reagan at the White House Garden.

In July 1985, Secretary of Labor, Bill Brock, praised the Youth Service Job and Skills Training and Employment Program in remarks he made to the National Urban League in Washington. That year, over 600 young people were trained and placed in jobs across the country.

Along the course of Youth Service's remarkable history, Don and Julie Mowery remember a stirring number of providential interludes that helped in its development. One such occurrence involved Bill Holmberg, who helped to create the Youth Service Garden Project.

While passing through Memphis on a return trip to Washington, Bill called Don from the airport to say hello. Don and Julie immediately went to the airport for a brief meeting before Bill left on his connecting flight. During their visit, Don needed Bill's advice about an issue involving a segment of people who questioned the appropriateness of having young people live and be trained on military bases. Bill remarked, "There is one person who could help us solve this problem, and that is Senator Ted Kennedy." At that moment, Julie looked up and exclaimed, "Look who is coming down the airport corridor - it's Ted Kennedy!" Bill knew the senator, so he approached Kennedy and asked him if he had a few minutes to talk. They all discussed the issue over pizza at one of the restaurants in the airport and the problem was solved. "This encounter at this precise moment was most amazing; I call it "spiritual networking," remarked Don.

Father Don was a "salesman" early in life. Even as a priest, he found himself in a position of having to "sell" the youth programs to anyone who would be a potential investor. Don was always reaching out to serve the Memphis community. He was always active in Memphis business circles because of the private donations needed to fund the annual budget. As a result, the Sales and Marketing Executives of Memphis, Inc., acknowledged Don as the winner of the Outstanding Community Sales Award in April 1986. Don became the 25th recipient of this prestigious award, which had been presented annually since 1962. Past winners of this award include Fred Smith, founder of FedEx; William B. Dunavant, Jr. of Dunavant Enterprises; Abe Plough of Plough, Inc.; Kemmons Wilson, co-founder of Holiday Inns, Inc.; Norfleet Turner, chairman of the Board of First National Bank; A.F. "Bud" Dudley, executive director of the Liberty Bowl Football Classic and many other important Memphis business executives.

Don was always on-call as an agency director to speak before organizations, clubs and groups where he "put out the call for assistance." As a result, Youth Service readily accepted donations of cash, equipment, vehicles and property that supported the work of the agency. After seeing a Youth Service display in the lobby of the Buckeye headquarters building, Sarah Virginia Henington, a chemist at Buckeye Cellulose Company, donated a house to Youth Service in 1986. The property was then sold and the funds effectively used by Youth Service. Henington decided to donate more of her family property and eventually donated several hundred acres adjacent to Holly Springs National Park in northern Mississippi for the Youth Service cause. Eventually, additional funds were generated when the timber was harvested and sold. All of the proceeds went to Youth Service. Support continued to flow in from other sources as well, bolstered by the fine reputation of the agency in Memphis circles.

Corporations and federal entities continued to assist Youth Service. Ralston Purina provided a grant that placed young people in jobs with the Air National Guard. The U.S. Army Corps of Engineers provided for 30 young people to work 40 hours per week at the Corps.

Education continued to be a major theme for Youth Service, Memphis. A new career planning initiative began in 1986, designed to prepare junior high school students for competition in the workforce. The competency-based curriculum emphasized systematic career planning, basic education skills, and course selection. Program objectives were to introduce about 250 young people to the world of work through a structured career-planning curriculum. The goal was to have at least 90 percent of the students successfully complete the program. Another goal was to have at least 85 percent of students achieve a rating of 75 percent on competency area indicators. Other objectives were to broaden the individual participants' perception of life's determination factors, generalized expectancy of success and a positive sense of self. In addition, they were to learn basic educational skills through computer-assisted teaching. Counselors used career planning to guide youths with successful role models. The schedule was for an 18-week program with young people receiving compensation for their participation.

Other organizations in Memphis grew because of the efforts of Youth Service. Emmanuel Episcopal Church and Center, an Episcopal urban outreach program serving Foote and Claiborne Homes communities served as an outreach program of Youth Service for years and was one of the only safe havens where neighborhood kids could meet and play. Bishop Dickson asked Youth Service to operate the Center until The Reverend Colenzo Hubbard took over as priest and became its executive director in the 1980s. Hubbard began to create his own programs and the Center began to transition away from Youth Service. Hubbard has successfully led the neighborhood Center, assisting families with their spiritual needs since that time.

Youth Service used local as well as national resources to build its youth programs. Military leaders and Pentagon officials familiar with the national programs always offered their full support. In 1986, ADM William J. Crowe, Jr. was elevated to the status of the new Chairman of the Joint Chiefs of Staff and became a new member of the Youth Service, USA Board of Directors. The appointment of such high-ranking military officials to the board was noteworthy, as ADM Crowe was the third Chairman of the Joint Chiefs of Staff to serve on the Youth Service, USA board, following Gen. David Jones and Gen. John Vessey, Jr.

The constant need for funding streams continued to challenge the agency. Several fund-raising events brought in money to support the youth programs already in place. In December 1987, local businessman William (Billy) Dunavant, Jr. and board member Lester Crain co-hosted a large fundraising event for Youth Service at the Racquet Club of Memphis. The same year, another fundraising initiative came in the form of what was known then as the Graceland Gala. Jack Soden, president and CEO of Elvis Presley Enterprises, wanted to continue the tradition that Elvis began in 1963 of supporting Youth Service. Major donors, invited to the program in honor of Elvis, received a special dinner on Valentine's Day, and in return had full access to the Graceland mansion. The money received from this annual event served as a down payment for the new Youth Service headquarters on Goodlett Avenue.

In March 1988, the Youth Service board decided to hold a formal Capital Campaign fundraiser to expand their programs and dubbed the event "Assuring the Future." The goal to raise $2 million was ambitious for this time, and many people believed this goal was unachievable. The Capital Campaign was scheduled in conjunction with a tribute dinner in celebration of Father Don's 25 years with Youth Service. Billy Dunavant, Jr., Campaign Chairman, along with Lester Crain serving as Gifts Chairman, headed this ambitious endeavor held at the Hyatt Regency in

East Memphis. International financier and advisor John Tigrett hosted the kickoff party at his penthouse overlooking the Mississippi River and downtown Memphis. This reception preceded the larger Capital Campaign at the Hyatt. John's wife, Pat Kerr Tigrett and Don's wife Julie arranged for all of the decorations for this festive gala at the Hyatt. Tennessee Governor Ned McWherter, as well as the city and county mayors attended the signature event. Marine Sgt. Mike Jones, a former Youth Service camper, gave a testimonial of his experiences with the program. The occasion was a great success, primarily due to the efforts of these and many other people in the community. The funding goal was reached within a few weeks of the event. Incidentally, the funds received from the Capital Campaign enabled the agency to establish the endowment used to create the Bridge Builders program at Youth Service.

Don also received a special recognition letter from President Ronald Regan in conjunction with his twenty-fifth anniversary celebration and the Youth Service Capital Campaign.

Dear Father Mowery:

I am delighted to extend warm greetings and congratulations as your friends and colleagues at Youth Service in Memphis salute you for 25 years of helping youth in Memphis and across the nation.

This tribute is truly well deserved. From its fledging days as a camping program in Fuller Park for a handful of underprivileged youngsters to its status today as a diverse program with countrywide impact, Youth Service, USA has touched the lives of thousands of people for the better. For a quarter century you have offered these maturing men and women counseling, vocational guidance and, above all the knowledge that someone cares. Thanks to your leadership and apparently limitless energy, your program has now been replicated in communities across America and is recognized as a model of successful public-private sector cooperation. You can be proud of your many years of accomplishment; most of all, I know, you are proud of the accomplishments of the generation of young Americans you have served.

Again, congratulations. Nancy joins me in sending best wishes for a memorable celebration and continued success. God Bless you and everyone you assist.

Ronald Reagan

Other congratulatory letters offered heartfelt thanks for the contribution Father Mowery and Youth Service were making to the youth of America. Many high-level officials praised the work of the agency. ADM Crowe, Chairman of the Joint Chiefs of Staff wrote:

> You can be justifiably proud of all that you have achieved through the Youth Service organizations on behalf of less fortunate Americans. Under your dynamic leadership, the youth service programs have awakened communities of the need to provide avenues whereby the hopes and dreams of all young people can be realized.
>
> The men and women of the armed forces have been with you since the early days, and it has been an exemplary and satisfying partnership. Together, that partnership has been able to implement recreational and vocational programs across the country, which foster pride in self, a belief in God, and a love of country.
>
> Your success in the youth development area speaks for itself by the number of lives you have influenced. Many of them have found employment in their local communities. Others, I am happy to say, have enlisted in the armed forces and are serving their country in all parts of the world. Others have continued their education in the civilian sector of our society.
>
> My deepest appreciation and blessed best wishes to you as you continue your service to the local communities and to our nation. May the next quarter-century bring even greater accomplishments to you and to the youth service programs.

Don's ability to relate to people from all walks of life was evident as he continued to build his "spiritual network." He decided early on that he needed a unique approach for breaking the ice with people in high-level positions and chose to offer his hosts freshly baked homemade cookies as a goodwill gesture. Don recalled how he arrived at this strategy:

> When you network with people, generally, their schedules are very tight and you have just a few minutes of their time. My wife, Julie makes good chocolate chip cookies, so I started taking cookies with me to my out of town meetings. When I would arrive, my host would usually ask if I would like some coffee. I would decline, but I would offer them a cookie from a batch Julie had just made for me in our kitchen in Memphis. All of a sudden, the ice was broken.

Don's cookies became popular with the White House staff and other government officials, but he did receive a bit of teasing for the home-spun tactic. Regardless, the cookies worked magic for Don, as he used the goodwill gesture before all of his important Washington meetings. Don began giving cookies to President George W. Bush, Vice President Dan Quayle, and the White House staff. Interestingly, White House security asked what was in the box Don was carrying, but never checked the contents. After having cookies with President Bush, he proclaimed to Don, "From now on, you are the Cookie Priest."

Father Don gave the invocation when President Bush came to Memphis for the Points of Light ceremony. Don remembered the president saying on his arrival, "Good, the Cookie Priest is here today." Besides being a good icebreaker for Don, offering cookies made him unique. Because of this initiative, Don received a special thank you note from President Bush and his wife Barbara.

> Dear Reverend Mowery:
>
> Barbara and I want to thank you for those wonderful chocolate chip cookies you sent us. Pat Plemons delivered them last Friday during our visit. Thanks for thinking of us. Barbara joins me in sending you our very best wishes for a happy, healthy 1987!

Don continued to travel extensively spreading the word about Youth Service and assisting communities with their own programs. For many years, Don and Julie attended the annual Blue Ridge Institute meeting in

Black Mountain, N.C. The national meeting, held every August, included social welfare agency directors, primarily in the South, along with hundreds of people involved in social program work. These events allowed Don to meet and network with many key people throughout the country. The Salvation Army band performed, and top-notch national speakers shared their stories with those in attendance. Don attended the weeklong Blue Ridge meeting for 18 years as head of Youth Service.

Youth Service, USA programs continued to spread rapidly throughout the country, causing Father Don and his deputy, John Edwards, to travel at a frantic pace. If Don was not planting seeds for a new program, he was helping community leaders sustain their own youth programs. This work took an immense amount of his time. Nonetheless, he always found time to visit friends and especially his mother in East Tennessee.

Don recounted, "My father died in 1977 and soon afterward, my mother married an old high school boyfriend when they were both in their eighties. She lived in a retirement community in Chattanooga, and those later years were some of the happiest days of her life."

In August 1988, Don attended the Blue Ridge Institute and stopped in Chattanooga to visit his mother. The timing was providential. Don and Julie had just had dinner with his mother and celebrated Don's birthday that evening. Later that night, while they were staying in one of the guest rooms at the retirement community, Don heard a fateful knock on the door and was told by a nurse that his mother was having a heart attack. Don recalled the event as if his mother had forecast the moment of her death. "I immediately rushed down the hall to her bedside where she literally died in my arms, on my birthday."

Though a time of personal loss for Don, the programs of Youth Service continued forward. By the late1980s, the Job Skills Training and Employment Program had established a training site at the Veterans Administration Hospital in Memphis. Using their facility, the program could provide training at a fraction of the cost without having to rent or buy a building. The Memphis Job Skills Training and Employment Program annually trained over 300 people in vocational and job retention skills. Various government agencies throughout Shelby County provided training under government supervisors, while Youth Service instructors trained their clients in pre-employment, employment and work maturity skills, remedial math and English. As graduation approached for the participants, Youth Service provided employment assistance and job placement. On average, more than three quarters of the participants earned full-time employment in the private sector. Additionally, the taxpayers did not bear the costs, since corporations, foundations and private donations funded this unique program.

While at the VA Hospital, Youth Service program participants were assigned to work in such challenging areas as building management, dietetics, nursing, personnel administration, psychiatry, rehabilitation medicine, social work and supply services. Due to limited funding for their services, the participants were registered under the Volunteer Services Program where the only compensation they received was parking and one meal a day. In return, they provided 13,745 voluntary service hours toward patient care and received a special letter of appreciation from the VA Hospital in 1985. The Youth Service participants received many commendations from supervisory personnel for their willingness to learn the assigned jobs and their interest in performing to the best of their ability.

In May 1989, Vice President Dan Quayle's office advised Father Don that the vice president would be making a trip to Nashville to view the Youth Service program there. As a result, Don and the vice president toured three training sites set up at Nashville's Air National Guard facilities. Lester Crain, John Edwards and several other board members, accompanied Don to meet the vice president in Nashville. A short time later, Vice President Quayle invited Don to Washington for further discussions regarding Youth Service.

THE BRIDGE BUILDERS PROGRAM

Youth Service, Memphis experienced a radical change in the way the agency dealt with the youth starting early in the spring of 1988. The traditional methods for working with young people of different races were changing. A new generation of youngsters was emerging and thus, new ideas on how to reach them were discussed. Becky Wilson, who was then a lawyer with the District Attorney's office, proposed one such idea. Becky learned about Youth Service from her husband Spence Wilson, who served on the Youth Service, USA board and was also the son of Holiday Inn's founder, Kemmons Wilson.

The concept for the Bridge Builders Program was born after Becky Wilson accepted an invitation from Shelby County Mayor Bill Morris to accompany a group of people on a bus tour of North Memphis. The purpose was to study the poor neighborhood conditions, particularly in the area surrounding North Side High School. Wilson was appalled at the sight of blight, trash and poverty during the trip,. She realized that her children and their friends likely were unaware of the terrible conditions in which many citizens in Memphis had to live. Wilson began to think of how her children, who attended private schools, would be growing up and dealing with people from these poverty-stricken areas. She wanted to do something about this situation on an even larger scale, as well. Guided by Mayor Morris, she learned that Youth Service was one group in Memphis that could help with her vision to bring together these two diverse groups.

Wilson then shared her idea for the new social program with Father Don. They began to discuss ways that youth with different backgrounds could work together through Youth Service to heighten awareness and to instill a harmony among African-American and white youth. Her idea was to build stronger "bridges" of understanding and racial harmony.

Youth Service used "Bridge Builders" as the name for this program after Wilson's remark that she wanted to be a bridge builder in the community. Interestingly, Youth Service had been including white and African-American youths in many of its programs since the mid-1960s, but Wilson's plan went much further. In her approach, there was a sweeping new design. Participants were selected from area high schools, bringing together students from private, predominantly white high schools and joining them with students from public, predominately African-American high schools. The students would then experience various activities, while working together and learning about each other in the process.

In April 1988, Father Don introduced Becky Wilson to the Youth Service, Memphis board. She described her idea to bring together young people from Briarcrest, one of the prominent East Memphis private schools and Northside High School, which is located in one of the poorest areas of North Memphis. She hoped the planned three-week summer program would build better relationships among the young participants. Wilson told the board, "The future leaders of Memphis are living in very segregated environments. It seems we are asking a lot of our future leadership and expecting them to make good judgments and decisions for the whole community." Her idea would bring students together to learn about each other and expose them to valuable leadership skills that would help them improve their personal lives and build a stronger community base. The Youth Service board unanimously agreed to try it, and the Bridge Builders program was born. The board approved funding for the program from monies received from the capital campaign, previously led by Dunavant and Crain. Once accepted by the board, Bridge Builders started operating under the umbrella of Youth Service and the agency became the foundation from which the program grew.

The new initiative was not successful at the very start. There was little interest from the teachers or the students when Father Don and Becky Wilson first approached Northside with the idea. They received a similar reaction from the officials at Briarcrest and practically had to beg for a few kids from each of the schools to try the new program.

Students from Briarcrest High School and Northside eventually joined the pilot program after the concept was fully outlined and after obtaining a few volunteers to assist. Youth Service took them to NAS Memphis where, much like the program some years before, they lived together in a barracks and engaged in a number of recreational, educational, and personal development activities. The youths also had a chance to talk about their individual differences, as they grew more familiar with one another. They discussed food, diet, hairstyles, and dress. Interestingly, the African-American kids from North Side could not understand why the white Briarcrest kids would pay money to attend a private school when they could attend the public schools at no cost.

Forty young people were involved in the first Bridge Builders program. The new project experienced similar resistance the next year when it expanded to include two additional schools. Nonetheless, Bridge Builders quietly began to gain interest, mostly among the more affluent families who wanted their children to experience how the less fortunate lived. The Bridge Builders program slowly gained the respect of these two schools from the success of the first session, and plans were made for additional retreats and collaborating with other schools.

The original idea of attending a special retreat together and learning more about each other through close interaction grew into a more formalized arrangement with added features over time. Becky Wilson served on the Youth Service board and during their transition from Youth Service to BRIDGES. Father Don summarized Wilson's value to the program:

> This program would not have been successful had it not been for Becky Wilson. She was very sincere and determined to make this a success. She was concerned that her children and the children from other families had this valuable experience. She was a good partner, and I really enjoyed working with this dedicated woman.

The Bridge Builders Program described itself then as a "comprehensive youth leadership training program designed to promote communication, understanding, and trust among developing leaders from different backgrounds." The program took root and developed a more formal stance. It brought together future leaders from different socioeconomic and ethnic backgrounds and fostered positive decision-making, while it promoted good morals and values. Additionally, Bridge Builders (BRIDGES) began to collaborate with a number of local schools and opened each high school football season with a series of "Bridges Classic" games and activities generating racial harmony, cooperation, and mutual respect.

The Bridge Builders program was such a success that Youth Service, Memphis eventually transitioned into BRIDGES beginning in 1996. The newly named agency ultimately expanded the youth leadership program to other high schools in Shelby County, as well as several other states across the country.

Bridge Builders sponsored a forum series and invited highly prominent national presenters to speak at the Cook Convention Center during the mid-1990s. Father Don recalled these events as some of the most memorable times during his career as head of Youth Service.

Bridge Builder Speakers

Danny Glover – Actor, film director and political activist.

Barbara Walters – World-renowned broadcast journalist, author, and television personality.

Sam Donaldson – Reporter and news anchor, serving with ABC News from 1967 to the present.

Jack Kemp – American politician and a collegiate and professional football player. He served as Housing Secretary in the administration of President George H. W. Bush, having previously served nine terms as a congressman.

Bryant Gumbel – TV journalist and sportscaster. He is best known for his years as co-host of NBC's *The Today Show*.

Charles Kuralt – American journalist most widely known for his long career with CBS, first for his *On the Road* segments on *The CBS Evening News* with Walter Cronkite and later as the first anchor of *CBS News Sunday Morning*.

Coretta Scott King – American author, activist, and civil rights leader. The widow of Dr. Martin Luther King, Jr. She also held a prominent role in the Women's Movement.

USA Gen. Norman Schwarzkopf – Retired United States Army general who served as Commander of the Coalition Forces in the Gulf War of 1991. Also known as "Stormin Norman."

James Carville – Political consultant and commentator, attorney, and media personality, who is a prominent figure in the Democratic Party.

Mary Matalin – Political consultant and wife of James Carville, well, known for her work with the Republican Party, serving under President Ronald Reagan and campaign director for George H.W. Bush.

Dave Barry – Pulitzer Prize-winning author and columnist who wrote a nationally syndicated humor column for *The Miami Herald.*

Bill Cosby – Actor, author, television producer, educator, musician and activist. A veteran stand-up comedian and performer.

William Raspberry – Pulitzer Prize-winning syndicated American public affairs columnist.

Father Don had the opportunity to talk with many influential people around the country through his network of military, government and clerical leaders. As president of the Youth Service, USA board and as president of the Air Force Association, Gen. George Douglas also knew what buttons to push to make things happen. Don had long discovered that strategically aligning himself with the military had its advantages. The Air Force Association supported the community and the military bases, always providing vital support.

Another key contributor was Bishop John Allin, Presiding Bishop of The Episcopal Church in the United States. Late in 1989, Bishop Allin invited Don to Nashville to discuss the Youth Service program in Memphis and around the country. A couple of weeks later, Father Don received a call from Bishop Allin. Don described the conversation as if it was yesterday:

> My phone rang and Bishop Allin, who was good friends with President George Bush Sr., said he was calling from the president's office in Washington. He and the president were in a discussion about what the Episcopal Church was doing for social issues, so I briefly described to him our work with Youth Service, Memphis and around the country through the Department of Defense. President Bush became very interested and asked if I could come to Washington to give him a personal briefing. Within a month, I met with him to explain the idea. He liked the concept and encouraged the development of programs around the country.

Father Don had another encounter with President Bush in November of that year. Lionel Linder, editor of *The Memphis Commercial Appeal* newspaper, and his staff had heard President Bush talk about people needing to be "Points of Light" in this country. He suggested that Memphians create their own Points of Light campaign to improve the local community. The editor publicized the idea in the *Commercial Appeal* and asked for nominations of people to be Points of Light, based on what they had done for their community. The initiative became very popular and people began sending names of friends, schoolteachers, and leaders of non-profit organizations and civic-minded volunteers about what they were doing. Several of them were selected, and a story followed about how these people made a difference. President Bush heard about the initiative and visited Memphis to present an award for their efforts, which became one of the first Points of Light for the national program.

On the day before Thanksgiving 1989, Mr. Bush arrived in Memphis to present a Point of Light award to Lionel Linder of the *Commercial Appeal* from the Point of Light Foundation headquartered in Washington, D.C. Don also delivered the invocation for the event on the lawn of the *Commercial Appeal*. What began in Memphis spread nationally and today the organization continues their mission, "to inspire, equip, and mobilize people to take action that changes the world."

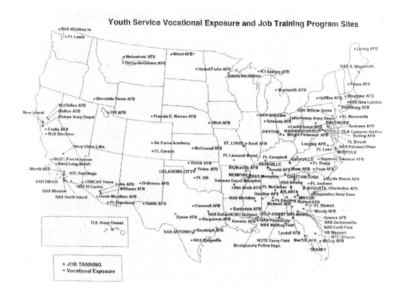

MAP OF YOUTH SERVICE, USA PROPOSED PROGRAM
SITES, 1980s

MEMPHIS CITY COUNCILMAN, MYRON LOWERY,
FORMER YOUTH SERVICE FIELD WORKER WHILE
ATTENDING COLLEGE

VISITORS OBSERVING JOB TRAINING
DEMONSTRATION IN MEMPHIS

MEMPHIS CITY COUNCIL MEMBERS AND GUESTS VISIT
THE YOUTH SERVICE JOB TRAINING PROGRAM

JOB TRAINING GRADUATION CEREMONY AT
ST. MARY'S CATHEDRAL

PARTICIPANTS AND COUNSELORS FROM ONE OF THE
FIRST BRIDGE BUILDERS CLASSES, 1989

SHELBY COUNTY COMMISSIONER JIM ROUT TALKING
WITH CAMPERS AT MEMPHIS NAS

SHELBY COUNTY, TN MAYOR BILL MORRIS WITH
FATHER MOWERY, 1988

TN GOV. NED MCWHERTER, FATHER MOWERY, JAY
EBERLE, FRANK DAWSON AT THE GOVERNOR'S OFFICE
IN NASHVILLE

(L TO R) GOV. DON SUNDQUIST, PRES. BUSH,
UNIDENTIFIED WOMAN, REP. HAROLD FORD,
FATHER DON, REP. JOHN TANNER, 1989
(PHOTO BY THE COMMERCIAL APPEAL)

VICE PRESIDENT DAN QUAYLE VISITING THE JOB
TRAINING PROGRAM IN NASHVILLE, TN, 1989

VICE PRESIDENT DAN QUALE WITH FATHER MOWERY
AT THE WHITE HOUSE

MEETING AT THE WHITE HOUSE WITH PRESIDENT BUSH,
FATHER MOWERY, GEN. GEORGE DOUGLAS, PRES. YOUTH
SERVICE, USA BOARD, AND JOHN EDWARDS, 1989

"If there are people who still don't recognize that the youth of the future is out there, I hope they take heed to the clarion call that's going on. We have to save, essentially, this generation."

—Becky Wilson, founder of Bridge Builders, a Youth Service program.

BECKY WILSON, FOUNDER OF BRIDGE BUILDERS, 1988

BILL MORRIS VISITING CAMPERS AT NAS

BILLY DUNAVANT, FATHER MOWERY AND PHILLIP
BURNETT, PRESIDENT, YOUTH SERVICE BOARD, 1988

BILLY DUNAVANT (SEATED), ADM. HARLOW, FATHER
DON AND MSGT. MIKE JONES AT THE CAPITAL
CAMPAIGN CEREMONY, 1988

DOUG BAILY, RECTOR, CALVARY CHURCH, BISHOP
DICKSON, ED REAVES, DEAN, ST. MARY'S CATHEDRAL.
DON AND JULIE'S WEDDING, 1983

BISHOP ALEX DICKSON, JULIE MOWERY AND FATHER
DON AT JOB TRAINING GRADUATION

DON AND JULIE ON THEIR HONEYMOON

DON AND JULIE RELAXING AT HOME, 1987

FATHER DON AFTER RECEIVING THE DEPARTMENT OF
DEFENSE OUTSTANDING PUBLIC SERVICE AWARD FROM
GEN. JONES, MAY, 1981

FATHER DON AND VIRGINIA HENNINGTON (SEATED)
(L. TO R.) JOHN EDWARDS AND JIM WARNER
(STANDING), 1986

FATHER DON AT THE MICROPHONE FOR THE TALK IT
OUT RADIO PROGRAM, 1980S

FATHER DON INVERVIEWING A GUEST ON TALK IT OUT

FATHER DON WITH JOB TRAINING PROGRAM
PARTICIPANT, 1984

FATHER MOWERY AND JOHN EDWARDS, MAY, 1981

FATHER MOWERY WITH U.S. CONGRESSMAN HAROLD
FORD IN WASHINGTON D.C., MAY, 1984

Father Mowery with U.S. Congressman Steve Cohen

Gen. John W. Vessey, Jr., Chairman,
Joint Chiefs of Staff 1982-1985, Gen. Wallace
and Father Mowery

GEN. VESSEY, FATHER MOWERY AND GEN. JONES AT
THE SHORHAM HOTEL IN WASHINGTON, MAY, 1981

JOB TRAINING GRADUATE BEING CONGRATULATED BY SHELBY
COUNTY COMMISSIONER D'ARMY BAILEY, 1982

JOB TRAINING GRADUATION

CHAPTER FOURTEEN

About Face And Retirement: The 1990s

By the dawn of the 1990s, Don entered in his 27th year with Youth Service, Memphis and 20th year with Youth Service, USA. His many accomplishments stand as a testimony to the success of the programs he helped launch through all of these years. The Camping and Vocational Education program, as well as JSTEP ensured Father Don and Youth Service a place in social service history, but the About Face program, the last in this trilogy of successful initiatives, is equally deserving.

The About Face program evolved out of an earlier iteration of the Youth Service, Memphis' Camping and Vocational Exposure program and was first referred to generically as a youth "boot camp." Teaching young people a greater respect for authority was always a goal of every Youth Service program, but About Face was different. This program relied heavily on education, exercise, personal development and discipline. It was an intensive "tough love" program for teenagers primarily from the Memphis community and was considered a "scared straight"- type of training. Conducted at NAS Memphis, About Face targeted young people who had already been arrested as many times for drug offenses. Most of them had little education and were accustomed to living a life of getting things through criminal activity or by dealing or using drugs.

The program was conceived with the help of Father Don's network of valuable advisors, which included Dr. David Abshire, John Edwards, and Bill Holmberg, who served as catalysts for this innovative program. Like Don, Abshire is an Episcopalian, who had attended the Baylor School and were joint recipients of Baylor School's Distinguished Alumni Award in 1978.

Abshire is a West Point graduate and was a decorated company commander during the Korean War. He served as Assistant Secretary of State for Congressional Relations and as special counselor to President Ronald Regan. Abshire also served as Ambassador to NATO and vice chair of the board of the Center for Strategic and International Studies (CSIS), an organization he co-founded with ADM Arleigh Burke. Another interesting note is that he co-founded the Trinity Roundtable with The Reverend Dr. Daniel Matthews, who was the rector of Trinity Church Wall Street in New York City. Abshire remarked at the time, "There are enough Episcopalians in Washington that we should get them together and discuss things of mutual interest for our well-being." The Trinity Roundtable, which was the result of this meeting, has a combined religious and governmental emphasis. Father Don recollected, "I was invited to join this prestigious group and went to Washington for the Roundtable meetings held at The Capitol. The Roundtable is composed of many "movers and shakers" in Washington and continues today."

Abshire became a tremendous resource to Youth Service because of his knowledge of Washington and the workings of the Department of Defense. Early on, Abshire realized how Youth Service could help support national social programs for young people. He realized that one of the biggest problems facing youth was drug usage, and he keenly understood the Youth Service programs relating to vocational exposure and job training. From this knowledge, Abshire helped develop a program that the agency could conduct in coordination with the DOD to help young people with drug problems.

Father Don and Abshire discussed the idea of this new youth treatment and prevention program during Don's visit to Washington. After several meetings within Father Don's valued "spiritual network," and through the power of the cookies he always took with him to Washington, Don was able to bring the right people on board as supporters. When Don returned to Memphis, he discussed the concept with officials at NAS Memphis and Juvenile Court. The program received a green light and carried a catchy military name – About Face – hoping the intensive training would turn their lives around.

Father Don reflected on the early days of the program:

> The Navy gave us an old two-story building and designated it for our program. The barracks was badly in need of repair, so we refurbished the structure ourselves. Through "spiritual networking," volunteers from the AFL-CIO Labor Council provided labor and special tradesmen from the Associated Building Contractors donated building materials and erected a perimeter fence

to prevent those outside the program from looking in to
see the participants.

Initial funding for the About Face Program came from grants from
the Federal Bureau of Justice Alliance, Law Enforcement Assistance
Administration (LEAA), Shelby County, and a $100,000 gift from Memphis
businessman Paul Piper, Sr. of the Christ is Our Salvation Foundation.
The agency always welcomed donations of goods and volunteers from
local companies and organizations. Le Bonheur Children's Medical Center
loaned bed linens and other supplies for the special purpose barracks.
Operating funds were channeled through the Memphis/Shelby County
Juvenile Court since Youth Service was the agency designated by the
Juvenile Court to provide the specialized training.

The original concept for About Face was documented in a "white
paper" drawn up by Don and his staff for presentation to Vice President
Dan Quayle and others at that time. It was technically referred to as,
"A Research and Demonstration Project to Rehabilitate Juvenile Drug
Offenders through a Comprehensive Community Partnership Approach."
Because of this initiative, a group of professional educators, training
specialists, and juvenile court authorities held a series of meetings in
Memphis, Nashville and Washington to share information and explore
possible solutions to the increased drug use among youth. They saw this
destructive environment as a product of accelerated social change, neglect
of public education, the elimination of low-skilled and semi-skilled jobs,
and drug trafficking.

Many of the young people appearing before Juvenile Court judges for
the first time were youth who simply needed a positive direction in life.
Supporters needed bold programs to help individuals develop productive
life styles and return them to their communities. Many of these supporters became positive change agents for these wayward youth.

The About Face boot camp format used "shock incarceration" and
was considered as a path to emphasize discipline, education, exercise,
and hard work. The long-range objective exposed young people to skills
needed to monitor their own behaviors and make conscious decisions
about choices, learning to accept responsibility for the consequences of
their own actions. The team concept served as a constructive replacement
for the proverbial street gang mentality. All of this dovetailed into a nationally replicable program called "Project 1990s: Save America's Youth."
The program encompassed basic educational remediation, job training,
employment, and even involvement in community projects. It contained

the assessment/selection phase, the residential treatment program phase and the aftercare program phase.

About Face was a low-cost way to reduce overcrowding of juvenile detention facilities caused by increased drug arrests and to reduce crime in the inner-city areas. Many people marveled how such a program cost so little. There were no utility bills, food costs continued to be $1.50 and insurance coverage only 5 cents per day, per participant. The counselors' training, wages, and the child's camp T-shirt were only modest costs.

John Edwards, Bill Holmberg, and Don introduced the program to Vice President Quayle at a meeting in Washington. The vice president liked the idea enough to send former Education Secretary Bill Bennett to visit Memphis and lend credibility to the project. Bennett had served as Secretary of Education and as director of the Office of National Drug Control Policy, so he was perfect for the job. Bob Jones, assistant Secretary of Labor for Employment and Training and Doug Coe of the Washington Fellowship were also involved in the planning. Don also visited with Secretary of Labor Elizabeth Dole in the Rose Garden of the White House to discuss the Youth Service programs.

David Abshire became very involved in the About Face initiative and was instrumental in setting up meetings with many high-level officials, such as Senator Jim Sasser, Senator Albert Gore, and Congressman Harold Ford, Sr. Senator Sasser considered About Face as a welcome alternative to what he referred to as the "piecemeal approach to fighting drugs, which has failed in the past." Senator Gore saw it as a good way to save costs in the war on drugs. Bill Holmberg, then president of Terra Plex, Inc., an agricultural enterprise, communicated with Gen. Carl Mundy, Commandant of the Marine Corps, to tell him about the program.

Working closely with the Juvenile Court, the About Face project began under the direction of Youth Service, Memphis in December 1990. Most of the program participants were juveniles who had come directly from the Court after they had been processed through its system. School guidance counselors referred others. Frank Dawson was instrumental in writing the operating procedures and spearheading the About Face Program. Frank recalled his role in the About Face Program:

> We hired and trained the About Face staff and had over 300 participants in the program. The University of Memphis conducted a program evaluation and tracked the progress of the participants. The participants lived in the barracks for six months under a "boot camp" style of as military discipline. We also provided excellent

counseling and educational programs to the participants for an additional six months after completing the boot camp. It was very effective and the young people were very proud to graduate from the program.

Not all of the graduates; however, were successful. One 16-year-old participant told me that he was living in his own apartment, had a car, a live-in girlfriend and was selling drugs to regular customers. The young man said that no matter what the counselors told him, it was likely he would return to dealing drugs because that was his life, his business. It was hard to argue with that logic, because when the participants completed the program, they returned to their natural environment of criminal activity and much of the training was lost. It was difficult for some of them to apply their new training on the streets. Despite a few the program failed to reach, About Face changed the lives of many young people with this approach.

Youth Service had also been working with volunteers from NAS Memphis for the Memphis Big Brother program since the late 1960s. The cadre of schoolteacher and military supervisors from that Big Brother program were solid instructors, advisors, and mentors for About Face in Memphis. Trained military personnel were assigned to the training schools for three to four months before their reassignment to other duty stations; therefore, most of them had extra time to help the young people in the program. The About Face "recruits" also had trained Marine instructors who challenged their bodies and their minds with strenuous bodybuilding classes, as well as educational courses to improve the minds of these young men.

All procedures of the About Face program followed military protocol and was led by Ernie Hall, a former Marine who served as head "drill instructor" for the program, along with other former military personnel. As a part of their daily routine, the participants, ranging in age from 14 to 17, would arise about 5:15 a.m. for exercise and a five-mile jog to get their bodies in shape. They would then march to the galley for breakfast, much like in the original camping and vocational exposure program, and attend educational classes for six hours a day. The teacher-student ratio was small to ensure strict discipline. As part of their educational program, courses included reading and mathematics, as well as instruction in the classroom through the vocational trades. Gradually, most of the young men began to have a sense of pride in what they were accomplishing. For some of them, this was the first time they had experienced a feeling of self-worth. They began to compete with Marine and Navy personnel in marching and discipline, and developed pride and a competitive mindset, not to be outdone by the military personnel.

Father Don was well aware that most of the participants lacked emotional and intellectual maturity. This program helped provide that maturity. Don added, "The About Face Program is all about faith in knowing they can turn their lives around. They know if they run away, they will be sent to a more restrictive place when they are caught."

Juvenile Court officials endorsed the program with the hope that it would inspire specially selected young people with multiple arrests to improve their lives by working with society rather than against it. Since they were wards of the Memphis Shelby County Juvenile Court, court officials selected the participants. Participants in the program were chosen because they displayed a level of intelligence and a non-violent arrest record, and because they showed a potential to become responsible citizens if they applied themselves. Youth Service also involved parents in the entire process. Don remembered about the program:

> Some of the young people did not think they could learn and were told by others that they were dumb. Everyone soon found out otherwise. Each day they went to school because they had no choice. However, it became a fun kind of thing for them, too. I must say it was a very effective learning program.

About Face included several weeks of physical and classroom training in a residential environment at the naval air station and six months of post-release follow-up meetings with Youth Service counselors and juvenile court officials. However, the duration of the About Face program often varied with each individual. Since there was no set time for completion, some of the young men stayed until they were declared rehabilitated by the team of experienced counselors in the training program. About Face, in essence, was the last chance for many of these juveniles. The consequences would be quite different if they committed another criminal offense once they turned 18. Counselors would judge the level of remediation and rehabilitation reached, and recommended release dates based upon these criteria. A mother of one of the About Face graduates asked with tears of joy in her eyes, "What have you done to my son? He talks to me now and looks at me. We can carry on a conversation." Mothers such as these were happy to see a turnabout in their boys' lives, especially when other methods failed to show the desired results.

Securing funds for the About Face project was always challenging. Funding included block grant assistance, matching funds from private donations, funds from Youth Service and even the governor's office.

Father Don made a point to invite key funders and supporters to view the program. It was also important for them to see the transformation that was taking place in these young people's lives. Members of the Memphis City Council, Board of Education, Shelby County Sheriff Jack Owens, and other city, county and state officials visited the program on a regular basis and spent valuable time learning about the young men and their progress. Many people from Memphis toured the base in special 12-passenger vans provided by the Variety Club, had lunch with the young people and saw the program first-hand.

Don recalled how the Youth Service programs affected those who witnessed them:

> I received many letters from people about the good things they witnessed and what was accomplished in that program. Visitors toured the barracks had lunch with two or three selected participants in order to learn how they were progressing. We had visitors from all over the country witness the program in an effort to replicate what we were doing here in Memphis. I received more positive letters about the About Face program than any other program Youth Service offered, locally or nationally.

Aaron Long became its program director, and Lillian Martin was director of Counseling Services. Two full-time counselors and two educators assisted them, along with a dozen paid military instructors, and three community aftercare volunteers.

The Bureau of Educational Research Services at Memphis State University produced its own white paper extolling the successes of About Face and noted its reduction in recidivism. The Bureau presented the paper at the 20th annual meeting of the Mid-South Educational Research Association, which met in Lexington, KY. By then, the program had over 130 juveniles in the program.

The program became the first juvenile boot camp to fight drugs to operate within a military framework in the country. Later on, the residential part of the program was extended to several months to strengthen counseling and education. Despite its successes, the About Face program began to wind down and suspended operations in the spring of 1993. What caused About Face to cease operations remains somewhat of a mystery. Some reported that the Juvenile Court officials began to "micromanage" the program; others felt that the initiative was too successful, thereby causing competition between other service providers. Additionally, as with any government program, a certain level of "political wrangling" always plagues even the most successful programs.

Though many who visited the base considered the program successful, some officials of the Juvenile Court questioned the harsh discipline and traditional military training methods. Apparently, these officials, who had been funneling participants to About Face, decided that the training was too rough on the teens. As a result, Juvenile Court began to reduce funding for About Face and the program abruptly, but quietly ended, much to the dismay of the Youth Service officials, after only two years of operation.

Meanwhile, Don was continuing to connect with prominent persons and organizations to further the larger Youth Service, USA outreach missions. One such connection was Ray Chambers of Newark, N.J. Chambers was a business partner with William E. Simon, former Secretary of the Treasury under Presidents Nixon and Ford. Chambers sold his business and began the Amelior Foundation to help those in need of services. Because of this work, President Bush asked him to be in charge of the Points of Light Foundation. Chambers eventually met with Don and the Youth Service board to discuss youth programs in Memphis and around the country, which resulted in additional funding from the Amelior Foundation.

It cannot be underestimated the values that high-level people played in the national organization during the tenure of their involvement. For instance, Gen. David Jones was the one of the most vitally active and long-standing members of the USA board. He was the commander who had connections with the early program at Blytheville AFB and who exported the concept next to Shreveport, LA, as leader of the Second Air Force. From there, he wanted to spread the idea among all of the constituent bases in the command.

Many important contributors to the success of Youth Service were members of the clergy. James (Jim) M. Coleman who, in 1993, succeeded Alex Dickson as Bishop of The Diocese of West Tennessee helped promote the agency. Don and Bishop Coleman had been close friends for many years and attended seminary during the same period; Jim at Sewanee and Don at Berkeley Divinity School at Yale. Coleman previously served as rector at St. John's Church in Memphis. According to Father Don, Bishop Coleman was truly a "pastor of clergy," and was known for his caring and concern for their individual needs. He served as bishop until 2001 and was very involved with helping to promote the programs of Youth Service at every level. Coleman's comments were equally complementary:

> Don is an exceptional priest by being a man of prayer and discipline. He could walk the halls of Congress explaining his programs to people and later that day he might be presenting a magic show to a group of children. He was always thoughtful and caring for the young people whom he served. On a lighter note, I was talking to someone recently who said 'when you shake hands with Don be sure to check to make sure you have all of your fingers' because of his firm handshake.

Dean Charles E. Reeves of St. Mary's Cathedral in Memphis, another one of Father Don's close friends, reflected on Don's work as a minister:

> Don is definitely a priest of the church. He sees the church as his power source. Many people receive the 'call' to serve the church, but very few find themselves in the right pew. Don was certainly in the right pew and he has been able to reach more people, do more long-term good than most clergy. There are very few who minister to people as well as he does."

By the 1990s, the makeup and complexion of the Youth Service Board of Directors began to change dramatically. No longer were board members representing all of the Episcopal churches; instead, the agency took on a more diverse representation. A movement for a name change began in order to create a better understanding of the 70-year-old plus organization. In many ways and for many reasons, the Youth Service, USA program began to scale back and transition into a decidedly different organization than it was in the 1970s. Instead of starting robust new programs, Youth Service, USA continued to act as an advisor for the existing programs around the country, such as those in Norfolk, VA. and Dayton, OH.

The Youth Service model began to change as the military began to decommission and realign bases in the 1990s. However, local communities wanted them to remain open due to their economic dependency on the military. This affected the Youth Service programs directly as some programs changed or closed due to lack of funding. Many programs never had a chance to start because of funding issues and revised military priorities. The Youth Service model continued to influence new programs around the country, but the success of each one was determined locally.

Don remarked, "It would be difficult for NAS Memphis to operate a comparable youth program today because the base no longer has the facilities it did in the 1970s, such as a mass feeding facility or a barracks for civilians, nor does it provide training for servicemen and women as it did years ago. It could happen again, but it would be very difficult to do it the same way."

BRIDGES, Inc.

In 1995, the Youth Service Board of Directors agreed to change the name to BRIDGES, Inc., which suited the new direction for the organization. The name BRIDGES is actually a derivative of the Bridge Builders name had been used for many of the earlier Youth Service programs. Another aspect of the transition to BRIDGES occurred when the organization began to move away from the official association with the Episcopal Church and take a non-denominational course in the mid-1990s.

The years of planning, managing, traveling, and fund-raising began to take their toll on Father Don. He recalled his last days at Youth Service, "I felt that three decades was long enough for anyone at an agency at this level of involvement, so I advised the board that I was ready to retire. They asked if I would remain until they found a replacement." After an exhaustive three-year search, the board found a capable person in The Reverend James (Jim) R. Boyd, who became the next executive director of Youth Service in 1995.

Jim recalled how his involvement with Youth Service began:

> I originally learned about Youth Service when I was the urban missioner for West Tennessee in the early 1980s. I served originally on behalf on The Episcopal Diocese of Tennessee and then The Diocese of West Tennessee. My responsibilities were to organize the social and educational ministries to enable the people and resources of the parishes to be more fully engaged in the ministry of the church and in our communities.

In 1996, the organization known as Youth Service officially changed course under new leadership and with a new board of directors. Boyd guided the organization in a different direction, with a new charter, a new focus and a new name, BRIDGES, Inc. "Connecting People with their Potential." Priorities shifted from a national to a regional focus as Boyd explained in a statement given in May 1996:

> You will see our new direction in a focused and entrepreneurial approach to the fulfillment of our mission to:
>
> • Enhance the quality of the workforce.
>
> • Strengthen acceptance of cultural and racial diversity and the development of skills in youth through the expansion of our Bridge Builders program.
>
> • Provide bridges of opportunity, encouragement and support for at-risk students and their families in our public high schools with our Quantum Opportunities program.
>
> As an organization, BRIDGES is committed to diversity and collaboration. We will work in a way that will produce measurable outcomes of service. We will work along side the Memphis business community as a partner.
>
> Undergirding all that we do will be our commitment to honor God in the stewardship of the lives of the men and women we serve and with whom we work, of the resources entrusted to us and in our desire to be a servant institution.
>
> With your help and support, we can connect youth and adults of the Greater Memphis area with their potential to be leaders and workers that will build prosperity of this region for the benefit of all.

Boyd was also instrumental in securing an important Plough Foundation grant during his tenure, which helped BRIDGES, Inc. achieve sustainability and move forward. His valuable leadership and vision came at a critical time for the organization and allowed BRIDGES to continue its success into a new era. After successfully leading the organization for 16 years, Boyd decided to step down in 2011 to be executive director of the Pyramid Peak Foundation. Boyd recalled as he departed BRIDGES:

> It has been a wonderful experience and I have many rich and great memories. I have learned about the incredible ability of our young people when given the resources and support. It has been an opportunity for young people to use the knowledge they have to discover what it means to be a leader. We are building a community of future leaders.

Brent Alvord, BRIDGES Board Chairman, described Boyd, "Jim has been at the center of defining the mission and vision of Bridges for the last decade and a half, and we are extremely grateful for his service." That mission was to build a community of leaders to advance racial, economic, educational and environmental justice.

BRIDGES completed a new Center in 2004, which housed the BRIDGES activities in Uptown Memphis. Eco-friendly and built with the youth in mind, the building was designed to facilitate the hands-on experiential learning associated with BRIDGES.

In 2012, Cynthia Ham was chosen as President and CEO of BRIDGES and continues the legacy of supporting the youth of the Memphis community. BRIDGES provides youth with high quality, comprehensive programming with year-round programs and specific workshops. Their mission focuses on three main areas: diversity, leadership and community impact.

According to Ms. Ham, approximately fifty full-time BRIDGES employees serve over 5,000 youth within 57 zip codes in the Greater Memphis area. The staff works specifically with public, private and charter schools individually and serves students entering the seventh grade through the twelfth grade. The BRIDGES model provides programs for a diverse representation of socioeconomic backgrounds and utilizes a scorecard to track the progress of their participants. The organization charges a nominal fee for each participant, which is based on the family's income and ability to pay.

Cynthia spoke enthusiastically of her leadership role with BRIDGES:

> Leading BRIDGES has been quite a learning experience for me. The organization is very complex with a well-developed infrastructure and capacity that most people

do not see every day. We have many solid programs in place, which are carefully designed for our young people.

BRIDGES recently revised its mission statement and is now focusing on the collective impact our young leaders have on the community. We are trying to help students learn that it is not 'just about you,' but how you use your leadership skills to collaborate with others to affect change. This approach is a bit of a shift from the earlier days when we focused just on diversity and individual leadership. We try to show our young people the value of their collective voice and how it is heard in the community.

We recently created a group of 15 student interns, who have completed the BRIDGES program. They are chosen from a rigorous selection process and receive support and resources from our staff. The mission of this Student Congress is to collaborate with students and school officials to solve community issues. They provide an official voice about policies that affect them. They have been working on this comprehensive program for almost 2 years. It is more than a service project – it is a great example of making systemic change.

BRIDGES is an exceptional program in its own right and is the most successful outgrowth of Youth Service. It continues to be a vital organization to this day, enriching the lives of thousands of young people around the country.

Tony Graves, president of Wilson Investment Management LLC and chairman of the BRIDGES, Inc. board of trustees, said of his experience with BRIDGES:

I attended Central High School in the late 1980s when it was about 70 percent African-American. Everybody related well to each other and we did everything together. It was a great atmosphere. When I returned to Memphis after college in 1992, the city did not look or feel like what I remembered. Racial tensions and an increasing divide between public and private schools existed – none of it felt like the city I loved. I wanted to change that.

Becky Wilson introduced me to the idea for the Bridge
Builders program in 2006 and I gladly accepted a role on
the BRIDGES board. What I did not know was that the
work that I found so vital had its roots 90 years in the
past.

Whether it is a middle school student summoning the courage to
lead or a group of co-workers learning new ways to be a team, there is
a common thread at BRIDGES; the transformation of lives. Staff and volunteers at BRIDGES, working in a variety of program areas and using a
variety of methods, are all focused on the same thing, helping to uncover
the capacity to learn, the willingness to accept, the strength to change
and the courage to lead. BRIDGES takes people who may think they are
ordinary and shines a light on the parts of them that are extraordinary.

After almost 33 years at the helm, Father Don officially retired on
April 30, 1995, at a celebration held in his honor at St. John's Church in
Memphis. While transitioning into his retirement, Don told Julie, "For
over thirty years I've been asking for money to support a program for
young people that I believe in, but I have the feeling that when people
see me coming, they want to go the other way. I don't want to ever ask for
money again."

In retrospect, Don knew the value of those who helped make Youth
Service a successful organization. He explained:

I can honestly say that I had two wonderful boards, Youth
Service, Memphis and Youth Service, USA. I could not
have had better people who were willing to pitch in with
their hard work, do their share and make things happen.
For that, I am eternally grateful. We were doing the work
of the church and helping people, particularly teenagers
who strive to become better people.

Within a short time after Don retired from Youth Service, he received
a call from Gene Cashman, chief executive of Le Bonheur Children's
Medical Center for many years and presently the CEO for The Urban
Child Institute (TUCI). Cashman asked Don if he would consider becoming a consultant for the institute. Don agreed to the offer to assist in the
fight to help children, but not fundraising. He began working for the
institute in February 1996.

The Institute was formed in the wake of Methodist Hospital's absorp-
tion of Le Bonheur Children's Hospital. It originally operated under the

name of Le Bonheur Health Systems (LHS); however, some confusion with Le Bonheur Hospital raising money and LHS giving to community programs caused a need to differentiate the fundraising entities. The institution was formally renamed in 2004 with the mission of channeling resources to benefit children in the first three years of development. The UCI is vested with the objectives of educating the community to support families of young children and to develop proven interventions that result in enhanced early cognitive learning. The institute works closely with Le Bonheur and St. Jude hospitals toward it mission and has received help and support for many years from these valuable partners.

According to Dr. Henry Herrod, former Dean of the College of Medicine at the University of Tennessee Center for the Health Sciences and Senior Fellow at the Institute:

> The Urban Child Institute focuses on increasing the community's awareness of the importance of brain development during the first years of a child's life. The Institute believes that science supports the concept ensuring that a child gets off to a good start in life is the foundation for individuals to grow up to be healthy, productive, and contributing citizens. Thus, our long-term goal is to make Memphis a better place to live by improving opportunities for our youngest, who will become the workers and leaders of the future. Other studies target women and children, domestic violence, child abuse, substance abuse, and teenage pregnancy.
>
> Don has been an active participant in what is now the Institute since its creation. For a decade or more, he visited organizations funded by TUCI to determine their suitability for funding. Around 2009, TUCI made a decision to enhance its internal intellectual capital and to focus on a limited number of areas to get our message out in a more meaningful way. This resulted in a decline in funding outside organizations and a greater investment in personnel and programs generated within the Institute. These focus areas included collection of data that would influence our understanding of the status of children in Memphis and Shelby County. This enhanced our efforts to disseminate the message regarding the importance of early brain development, and to develop the skill sets to

effectively evaluate the effect of programs we are presenting to the community, such as Touch, Talk, Read, and
Play, and to continue to support the CANDLE project.

CANDLE is a large project funded by the Institute and
carried out by the University of Tennessee's Department
of Preventive Medicine. The project has enrolled 1,500
women in the second trimester of pregnancy and intends
to follow the mothers and their children for the first
three years of the child's life. During this period, intense
evaluation of the social, emotional, and cognitive development of the child is being monitored. By the time the
child enters kindergarten, it is hoped that this research
will be able to identify some best practices for optimiz-
ing a child's upbringing that can then be tested through
targeted interventions within the community.

Since the decision was made to focus internally, Don has
served as our ambassador, representing the Institute and
its message to the community. The vision for the Institute
is that it will continue to reinforce the message of the
importance of early childhood through data disseminated
through multiple modalities. An ideal outcome would be
that all parents in Memphis have the tools to be effective
parents, and all young children will have access to high
quality, intellectually and socially stimulating childcare
services. Father Don continues to be a very visible face
for this message.

The UCI spent years addressing these issues. With this formalized
organization, experts are able to turn to the science of developmental neu-
robiology and interventions in early childhood development.

The Institute has several stated objectives to accomplish its mission.
These include the creation of an annual data book on children and youth
in Memphis and Shelby County. Another goal is to inform parents, professionals, policymakers, and organizations of the importance of early childhood development.

The UCI has developed a close working relationship with the
Neighborhood Christian Center and other groups. The Neighborhood
Christian Center is a longtime service organization that responds to basic
community and neighborhood needs, such as food, shelter, and clothing.

Don related his experience at TUCI to his longtime friend Bishop Don Johnson:

> I really enjoy my work at The Urban Child Institute. I love working with Gene Cashman, Dr. Hank Herrod and the staff as we continue to discover new ways of studying a child's brain from conception to 3 years of age. For the first time in my life, instead of spending much of my time trying to raise money, I now focus on finding ways to evaluate, invest and create new programs.

Today, Don puts forth the same devotion to the UCI as he did with Youth Service. He is sensitive of its mission and strives to achieve its goals. He also works very hard trying help leverage funds to assure the greatest payoff for the UCI.

Memphians may disagree on many things, but there is a near consensus that the status of the community's race relations underpins serious social problems. Differences in racial perspectives and attitudes influence the people of this community primarily through local politics, education, economics, and the criminal justice system. Programs such as Youth Service and BRIDGES have addressed these and other challenges faced by young people for over 90 years, beginning with the Church Mission of Help, but more work is required to build positive and lasting change for progress to continue.

From 1963 to 1995, Father Don, Youth Service, Memphis and Youth Service, USA, helped initiate four major groundbreaking programs that have been life changing for thousands of young people across the country.

1. The Camping/Vocational Exposure Program

2. The Job Skills Training and Employment Program

3. The About Face (Drug Intervention Program)

4. Bridge Builders

Father Mowery's initial work with Youth Service continues through BRIDGES, Inc., providing a sterling example of how the commitment and effort of one individual with the assistance of others can make a profound difference over time. He continues to host his *Talk-It-Out* radio program, now remarkably in its 44th year, by connecting people with resources that will enhance their lives. Father Don remains active in the church and the community – always reaching out to help someone and serving those in need of spiritual guidance. After almost 60 years in the ministry, he has helped change the lives of thousands of people – young and old – one life at a time, across a city, and onto a broader national stage.

In his heart, Don acknowledges that it is time to retire, relax and enjoy God's creations, but the work he began in 1963 continues to be acknowledged. On January 20, 2014, Father Mowery received the 2014 "Be The Dream" MLK Legacy Award, given at the Mason Temple in Memphis – the site of Dr. King's last public address before he was assassinated the following day in April 1968. Among the many who honored Don on this day was Becky Wilson, Memphis Mayor A.C. Wharton and U. S. Congressman Steve Cohen (D-TN), who read an official proclamation that was recorded in the Congressional Record. A portion of Congressman Cohen's statement reads:

> This special award is given to individuals whose lives have embodied the spirit and legacy of service, sacrifice and hope that characterize the work of Dr. Martin Luther King, Jr. As an agent of change during the Civil Rights Movement, it is fitting that this award be bestowed upon Father Mowery in recognition of his accomplishments and contributions.

As he accepted the award, Don caught a glimpse of several of his associates from The Urban Child Institute who came to honor him on this special day; Eugene and Cathy Cashman, Dr. Henry Herrod and his wife Ann, Barbara Holden Nixon. Bishop Don Johnson of the Episcopal Diocese of West Tennessee also was present among the guests.

This ceremony was an appropriate recognition for Father Mowery's life-long devotion to the youth of America and serves as a reminder of how Youth Service, USA began, in large part after Dr. King's death. Don's spiritual network, built with Dr. King's vision of unity and racial reconciliation in mind, endures. From the early days of Youth Service, USA to the BRIDGES program of today, Father Mowery's ministry continues to influence countless lives of young people in need of support, direction and inspiration.

All effective ministerial work stems from a heart inclined toward service to the Lord, therefore, it is fitting to sum up the life of The Reverend Don Mowery with his favorite prayer. The prayer is the first utterance recited or sung as a part of the Eucharist or Holy Communion. Don has read and recited this prayer throughout his life, which gives thanks and exalts his relationship with the Lord for his service to others.

YOUTH SERVICE BOARD MEMBER MIKE HAAS VISITING
THE BRIDGE BUILDERS PROGRAM

VISITORS VIEW ABOUT-FACE PARTICIPANTS IN
PHYSICAL TRAINING DRILLS, 1982

SHELBY COUNTY MAYOR BILL MORRIS TALKS WITH
ABOUT FACE PARTICIPANTS

FRANK DAWSON, DIRECTOR OF OPERATIONS,
EXPLAINING THE ABOUT FACE PROGRAM TO VISITORS

FATHER MOWERY WITH BRIDGE BUILDERS SERIES
SPEAKER BARBARA WALTERS, 1989

FATHER MOWERY WITH BECKY WILSON AND LOU HOLTZ,
BRIDGE BUILDERS SERIES SPEAKER

FATHER MOWERY ON THE AIR WITH HIS TALK IT OUT
RADIO PROGRAM, 2002

FATHER MOWERY WITH U.S. AMBASSABOR ANDREW
YOUNG AND WIFE

VICE PRESIDENT AL GORE TALKS WITH FATHER DON

FATHER DON PERFORMING MAGIC FOR KERR TIGRETT AND
WOODSON DUNAVANT AT PAT TIGRETT'S FUNDRAISING PARTY

It's All Coming Together!

Art work design by N. J. Woods

The Children in our future INVITE you to a
Groundbreaking BRIDGE RAISING Party for the new

BRIDGES CENTER

4th and Auction Streets

just north of St. Jude

May 8, 2003

10:00 am

INVITATION TO THE GROUNDBREAKING CEREMONY FOR
THE NEW BRIDGES CENTER, MAY, 2003

JIM BOYD, YOUTH SERVICE AND BRIDGES, INC.
EXECUTIVE DIRECTOR, 1995-2012

SALLIE FOSTER, EXECUTIVE ASSISTANT, TUCI WAS
INSTRUMENTAL IN HELPING TO ORGANIZE SUPPLIES FOR
THE ABOUT FACE PROGRAM

AARON LONG, RET NAVY OFFICER AND SUPERVISOR, COUNSELING ABOUT FACE PARTICIPANTS

ABOUT FACE BARRACKS BEFORE RENOVATION AT MEMPHIS NAS, 1990

ABOUT FACE BARRACKS, NEWLY RENOVATED, 1991

ABOUT FACE COUNSELOR EXPLAINING
THE PROGRAM TO VISITORS

ABOUT FACE VISITORS JOEY
AND MIKE JAEGER

BECKY AND SPENCE WILSON

BRENDA AND J. LESTER CRAIN, JR. ON THEIR 50TH
WEDDING ANIVERSARY

BRIAN PECON A LONGTIME SUPPORTER OF
YOUTH SERVICE

CYNTHIA HAM,
EXECUTIVE DIRECTOR OF BRIDGES, INC

DON, 1990s

EUGENE CASHMAN AND DR. HENRY HERROD
WITH THE URBAN CHILD INSTITUTE

FATHER DON (FAR RIGHT) OFFICIATING THE WEDDING
OF KIM CRAIN TO COLLIE LOWRANCE, ASSISTED BY BISHOP
JAMES COLEMAN (FAR LEFT)

FATHER DON'S RETIREMENT SERVICE,
ST. JOHN'S CHURCH, 1995

FATHER LEE STEVENS AND FATHER DON

MARTIN LUTHER KING, BE THE DREAM AWARD
CEREMONY AT THE MASON TEMPLE, JAN. 20, 2014
(PHOTO BY JOHN MATHIS PHOTOGRAPHY)

MEMPHIS MAYOR A. C. WHARTON PRESENTING MLK
AWARD TO FATHER DON JAN. 20, 2014
(PHOTO BY JOHN MATHIS PHOTOGRAPHY)

Glory to God in the highest,
and peace to his people on earth.
Lord God, Heavenly King,
Almighty God and Father,
we worship you, we give you thanks,
we praise you for your glory.

Lord Jesus Christ, only Son of the Father,
Lord God, Lamb of God,
You take away the sin of the world:
have mercy on us;
You are seated at the right hand of the Father:
receive our prayer.

For you are the Holy One,
You alone are the Lord,
You alone are the Most High,
Jesus Christ,
with the Holy Spirit
in the glory of God the Father, Amen

CHAPTER FIFTEEN
Personal Testimonials

Walter Allen
Randy Brown
Phil Burnett
Gene Cashman
James Challen
"Buddy" Chapman
Ken Clark
Phil Claypool
Stuart Collier
Bill Craddock
Brenda Crain
Lester Crain
Frank Dawson
Bishop Alex Dickson
William B. Dunavant, Jr.
Kelli Dunavant
Jay Eberle
John Edwards
Howard and Betty Golwen
Tony Graves
Rabbi Micah Greenstein
Bill and Pam Hickman
Stan Hughes
Joseph R. "Pitt" Hyde, III
John-Paul Jaudel
Bishop Don Johnson
George Klein
David LaBarreare
Curt Ladd
Hal Lansky

Pat Lawler
Chao Lin
Larry Lloyd
Cloretta Yates McCoy
Richard Marsh
Lynda Wyatt Mayo
Jim McGehee
William Morris
Tony Mowery
Frances S. Myrick
Dr. Bill and Tricia Nash
The Rev. Joe Porter
Judge Jim Russell
Jack Sammons
Reid Sanders
Otis Sanford
Sam Scott
Paul Shanklin
J. B. Smiley
Fred Smith
Jim Storey
Ron Walter
Linda Smith West
Becky Wilson

Walter Allen

(former Youth Service Board Member)

I served on the Youth Service Board of Directors for 6 years fundraising and collecting donated items for the annual silent auction. I want to thank Don for helping me.

As a member of Grace St. Luke's Episcopal Church in the mid-1980's, I became aware of the Youth Service's programs and the participation of the Diocese of West Tennessee in this organization. I also grew up in Memphis and listened to WHBQ radio where I heard Father Don talking on his radio program, *Talk It Out*, with kids who shared some of the same problems that I was going through.

The first job-training graduation ceremony I attended was a moving experience for me. The enthusiasm of the young men and women who had participated in the program was shown in their faces. The families of the young people were proud of their children who had gained job experience through working several months, so that they might obtain a career.

Don's positive attitude and energy helped propel him through many challenges that would have stopped most people. I have often said that Don would have been successful in life, regardless of what path that he had chosen.

Don cannot go to a public meeting, sports event, dinner, church, etc. without somebody approaching him and thanking him for contributing to their life. He is an example of how one person who cares can really make a difference to the direction a person takes in life. Don gave me a chance to help identify an interest that I would like to pursue upon my retirement – to work with kids.

Randy Brown

(Director of Operations at BRIDGES)

I began with Youth Service as a part-time photographer for the camps. Over the years, I have done a little bit of everything. Mrs. Myrick was there when I came onboard. Don was very innovative and took to the streets. He went to the folks that needed the services as opposed to everybody coming in for counseling. I think you can say there is an under-served segment of that population here because there is such a huge poor population in Memphis.

Father Don wore his collar almost every day he worked. I have only seen him twice without the collar. That made an impression on me.

In the 1980s, Youth Service, USA began to scale down due to cutbacks in federal funding. Chuck and Ruby Novak were the only ones left running Youth Service, USA with Ruby doing the financials. We used the Army Depot, the Navy base and the VA hospital. Some of these sites were profitable and some were not. All this was performance-based back then. By the early 1990s, Youth Service, USA was losing momentum, and Youth Service, Memphis, handled most of the programs.

Bridge Builders, in those days was summer camp and not a year-round program. It was a rocky road internally for a while. Bridge Builders was different from anything Youth Service had ever done before.

Lee Wakeman was the board president at that time and facilitated the transition of Father Don retiring and Jim Boyd beginning his tenure. Lee had the patience, persistence, and the people skills to make things happen.

Jim Boyd wanted things to be less Episcopal-based and more community-based. The original Youth Service charter specified that the director had to be a priest or had to be Episcopalian, but that is not the way Jim or Lee wanted to set up the new entity.

Don and Jim Boyd were both Episcopal priests, but Jim very seldom wore his collar. Working for Don and for Jim Boyd certainly gave me two different perspectives on the clergy. Nevertheless, the impact that Father Don had on the many lives he served while at Youth Service was amazing.

Phil Burnett

(Former Youth Service Board Member and CEO of the National

Cotton Council, currently President and CEO of the SEAM)

I served on the Youth Service board from 1982 until 1990. What impressed me so much about Don was his imaginative approach to solving problems. For example, he realized the power of vocational training, which grew into practical and successful job training programs. The programs emphasized mentoring and helping kids improve their social skills, so they could move into the world of work. With crime and the cycle of poverty, training and employment was a path out of that kind of life. In the process, young people also learned someone cared.

Don was a master of working with powerful and influential people to gain support for his training programs. He understood how to draw on people with resources. He is a wonderful sales person and is such a committed man of integrity and honesty.

I recall at one of the graduation ceremonies at St. Mary's Cathedral, a young woman told of her life being changed in a positive way by Youth Service. It certainly affected everyone in the audience positively. It was worthwhile to share in his vision of what Youth Service could be. There is a lot of potential in youth going down the drain in many major cities because they do not have someone like Don Mowery there. Not only would he teach them job skills, but also social skills.

Gene Cashman

(Founder and CEO of The Urban Child Institute)

The Urban Child Institute gives money in the community to non-profit organizations specifically focused on children in Memphis. What we do here at the Center involves caring for poor people, underserved people, having a faith, having a trust, having a hope – all these attributes and virtues Don uses as our ambassador. He does not miss an opportunity to discuss the goals of TUCI and what it means to the community. Most people who get to those levels of accomplishment fade into the sunset, but he never stops extending compassion or concern.

In this modern day, few know the name Youth Service, but they know BRIDGES. Because Don was in the business of helping kids and we were in the pediatric health business at Le Bonheur, we needed to know each other. Initially, I did not realize that Youth Service extended well beyond Memphis.

Don received the Le Bonheur Concern for Children Award that recognized individuals working in the community doing things to benefit children. He had a stellar background and it revealed to a large audience what his life-long work had been. Don Mowery has a gift of connection. I don't have a better word for it.

Don has a gift, which is his ability to communicate, to network and to align the best in people. He is also a caring person and will always follow up about somebody's illness. He never misses an opportunity to seek or find a way to help somebody, usually through his network of friends and associates.

I often ask Don for insight and advice. We were aware of his knowledge about youth and activities in the community, so we retained him at the Center. Don is still very connected in the community. There no one he cannot reach and influence. One board member told me, 'Mowery gives the board instant credibility in this business!' He is a trusted advisor. He not only gives you insight into things that are going on with youth and individuals, he has a real sense of value to how important that is. Don has become a mentor to my son-in-law, who is growing in the ministry and is an instrumental part of his growth and development.

James Challen

(Former District Attorney and Youth Service Counselor)

Don and I met in the summer of 1968 when Youth Service started the summer camps at NAS Memphis. I planned to start law school in the fall and was looking for a job for the summer. Youth Service was seeking camp counselors, and I applied for the job. I had enrolled in the ROTC program and had been commissioned, so I was allowed to go to law school and then return for the camps.

Every week we had a different group and we used the wooden barracks with bunk beds, but I felt the campers really enjoyed it. We taught the kids how to swim and gave them the responsibility of keeping the barracks clean. Don and I flew with other campers on a military plane to look at the Pensacola Naval Air Station to help expand the program in Pensacola.

We hit it off and kidded with each other a lot. I remember one time we had an older camper picking on some younger ones. Father Mowery found some boxing gloves and asked him if he wanted to go into his boxing room. Don told him, 'Pick on me if you want to pick on someone.' That worked, and there were no more problems.

Don was effective in talking with a wide variety of different people and in persuading the military that it was beneficial for Youth Service to use the base facilities. He was passionate, sincere, and believed in his work. I also believe that we were doing something positive for racial reconciliation, and the kids learned many valuable life lessons. It was an overall positive experience for these kids and for the counselors.

E. Winslow "Buddy" Chapman

(Former Director of the Memphis Police Department,

currently CEO, Crime Stoppers).

Don and I met during the mid-1960s. Don was one of the healing agents during those times of racial turmoil. He was a 'big idea' person who was totally dedicated and driven. I left the Navy in 1964 and returned to Memphis for family and business interests. I began working at the Shelby County Sheriff's Department as a reserve commanding officer under Sheriff Bill Morris. It was a time of upheaval in Memphis and the nation, with street riots being a common occurrence.

As a graduate from the Naval Academy at Annapolis, I was very involved in the Navy League in Memphis and began to work with Don in his desire to use the Navy base in the early 1970s. Once the program was established, I helped from time to time with logistical requests and tie-ins with the Navy.

Don and his programs were very beneficial in helping with racial reconciliation. His program was effective in helping children early in their lives and in their overcoming adversities. His valuable program embraced them in new ways that they could feel part of the system as a whole.

Don was never deterred from his mission. If a door was blocked, Don would find another door around the corner. You could tell him a hundred times that something would not work and he would come back and try again. He always saw the possibilities with his visionary capacity. I would therefore call him a persistent visionary.

Ken Clark

(Memphis Attorney)

I was very active at Calvary Episcopal Church and became fully vested in Don's idea of Youth Service. I remember helping to fund the Youth Service Camping Program while representing the Theodora Trezevant Neely Foundation. The mission of the Foundation coincided remarkably well with Youth Service's early version of providing camping experiences for children in the great outdoors. Ms. Trezevant was an avid adventurer herself, and she wanted others to have that opportunity as well. She had as a testamentary directive that the estate be used for such experiences for boys and girls, both white and black, and it was very forward thinking in its establishment. Her money helped to purchase camping equipment in the early 1960s, well before the camping program at Millington. This gave Youth Service early confidence and seed money. I thought Don was the real deal when it came to the priesthood. As a member of the cloth, he wears it with great sincerity.

Phil Claypool

(Songwriter, Country Music Artist)

I met Father Don (Doc) through my friend, David LaBarreare. We used to hang out at Father Don's house and assist him with odd jobs for Youth Service. Don was a great supporter of my music. I know Doc thought I was a knucklehead, which I am!

We used to cut up a lot. One time, my friend Bob Laster and I were riding around and had just picked up some of Don's clothes at the cleaners. We decided to dress up as priests, so we changed into the collars and rode around town for a while. We were just being young boys. We reached the backside of Colonial Country Club when it started raining. A woman in front of us hit her brakes and we slid into the back of her car. Bobby jumped out of the car and ran to Father Don's house. When the police came on the scene, he asked for my identification. I did not have it on me at the time, so I told the police officer that I knew Father Don. There I am wearing a priest's shirt and collar, my friend had run away and I was scared to death. When people started asking me, 'Father, are you alright?' I immediately took off the shirt and collar. Father Don finally appeared with Bobby, who was scared to death. The officer said 'Father Don, do you know this young man?' Father Don looked at the officer and said, 'I've never seen this young man in my life.' Don was a funny, honest, straightforward, "straight-shooting" guy. I have many fond memories of those days.

Stuart Collier

(Former Youth Service Board Member)

I worked several summers as a Youth Service camp counselor when I was in high school at Millington and Blytheville. My father, John Collier, was active for years in the early development of the organization.

My dad felt it would be good for me to see a different side of society since I grew up in an East Memphis upper-middle class neighborhood. He felt like it would be good for me socially and spiritually and help me to mature. I knew Father Don through his radio show, which was very popular because it was out of the ordinary. At that time, there was a lot of social upheaval in the late 1960s and 1970s and there was a very broad generational gap. He was one of those who said, 'Let's bridge the gap.' It was an important factor to reach out to young people, especially young people with family, law, and drug problems.

I was a Youth Service counselor during the summers after ninth and tenth grades at Millington and Blytheville and learned many life lessons. I had never been exposed to African-Americans, so it was an interesting and valuable experience for me personally. We had both white and black counselors, but I gravitated toward the African-Americans because of their candor and talent. They immediately became my best friends. Some of the white counselors did not have the same personality and charisma. It immediately changed my attitude during this time of the civil rights movement.

These kids, mostly from public housing projects, had never had three meals a day, but at camp they could have all the food they wanted. It was interesting to watch them devour that food. They were involved in many sports activities that they had not previously had the opportunity to enjoy.

The focus was to give these kids an opportunity, even for a short time, to leave their old environment. This involved reaching into the toughest economic areas of the city to expose them to a different path that they could pursue. Father Don was unafraid and courageous in those days. He was reaching out across generational and racial borders. I do not know anyone at the time doing the same thing. It sure changed my outlook.

I asked him to speak at a Memphis University School event once because I had learned so much from him. He brought a bag with some of the weapons that he had taken from the kids he had worked with. He passed around brass knuckles, guns and knives and explained to the audience what he was dealing with. It was compelling.

Bill Craddock

(Executive Director, Episcopal Clergy-Centered Care, CREDO)

I became connected with Don Mowery at Youth Service over 20 years ago when began a discussion of the future of the organization. I recall that he was an open-minded entrepreneur with a compassion for underprivileged youth and established a very effective network of resources and people. His positive energy and creative approach to challenges certainly paved the path for Youth Service and BRIDGES, its successor.

Brenda Crain

(Youth Service Supporter)

Don came to speak to a group of ladies at Holy Communion Church shortly after his arrival in 1963. I liked what he said so much that I invited him to my home for dinner the following weekend to meet my husband, Lester. They immediately formed a lasting friendship. I remember the two of them meeting with others at our home on many occasions to discuss plans for upcoming youth programs. However, it was really Don's drive and energy that made these programs work. After seeing what Don could do, many people naturally joined in the effort to help.

On a personal note, Don enriched the lives of our entire family. He christened all of our children and grandchildren, officiated at the marriage of our children and conducted the funeral service for both of my parents. He is also a magician and entertained our children who were four and seven years old when we met. He came to all of their birthday parties and fascinated them with his magic tricks. They just adored him and he became our dear friend.

One of the greatest qualities I found in Don was that he genuinely cared about people, particularly disadvantaged people. Countless lives have been changed as a result of Don's influence. He did so much for so many. Most of the kids who attended the summer youth camps came from such horrible circumstances. They arrived hostile, angry and disappointed, but they walked away thinking – I can do better; I can have a decent life. Youth Service camps offered those children hope.

Lester Crain

(Attorney and long-time Youth Service Supporter and Board Member)

One of the few things I did that I'm proud of is introduce him to the right people – people that could help Youth Service. That is really all I did. He had to sell it because I am not a salesman. When I introduced Don to someone that was like putting a "bird on a hunt" and he would take it from there.

When I introduced Don to Admiral E. E. Christensen in 1968, I thought he could help Don with the youth camps. However, the Admiral immediately informed him that any civilian use of the base was against military regulations. Fortunately, his wife Marge discussed the matter with him and convinced the Admiral to give Don's program a chance. Don apparently had the same positive affect on Marge as he did own my wife, Brenda.

I also introduced Don to Bill Morris who was Shelby County Sheriff at that time. The next thing I know, Don has Sheriff's deputies volunteering in his programs.

Don became very good at networking and loved his work with youth. He knew that he was doing something good. One time General Jones flew us to Washington D.C. on his plane to meet with Tennessee Senator Howard Baker who we thought could connect us with the right people. Don usually did the talking in these meetings and I usually kept my mouth shut. Don was the expert on youth programs and I didn't want to mess things up.

We worked with people from all cultures and walks of life to benefit Youth Service. Don spoke once about the program at an African-American church. His message was well received and everyone was sold on Youth Service programs serving the black community. As we walked out after Don's address, I reached in my pocket and pulled out some money to give to the pastor to help support his church. I thought it was a $10 bill, but it was actually a $100 bill. The pastor said, "Brother Crain you can come back any time." I was reminded of the old saying, "When you gives while you lives, you knows where it goes."

Youth Service gave young people a chance in life that they never would have had otherwise. The program gave them ambition to go forward. I attribute Don's personality, desire and drive to make this program grow and spread. His leadership created a competitive environment where each one tried to outdo the other. Of all of the people I have known personally, socially and professionally, Don Mowery did more to give more people hope than anyone. The only way you could replicate that program today is to replicate Father Don. You have to have a person who not only knows how to do it, but is also a leader who can get it done.

Frank Dawson

(Retired Colonel, USAF, Former Youth Service Board Member)

One of the things I admired about Father Don was his unique networking skills. Had I worked for him before going into the military, I would have become a general instead of a colonel because I have never seen anyone work a room as he did. During meetings, he would often have a conversation with everyone in the room. Don's leadership skills and superior memory were notable. He does not forget anyone. He not only knows the individual, but the members of the family as well. He interviewed thousands of people on his radio show and was very interested in them and their projects. People had a great admiration for Don because of his many successes.

In today's terms, he would have been a great asset to the CIA. You build your influence by the people you know and your connections.

Father Don and I often traveled together to set up new programs for Youth Service. Don would memorize his presentations and used them effectively in every community he visited. He showed them how to make the most of excess capacity on military bases for these programs for underprivileged kids. He has a special entrepreneurial instinct of building something and making it better. Many people like to build things, but then sit back on their laurels. Don is always thinking about ways to make things better. Not everyone is like that.

Don is great at taking ideas and changing them around and making them better. He is the best networker I've ever met. He was fearless in his approach to recruit top-level people. From a spiritual sense, I believe Father Don was chosen for this role. His sense of timing was incredible. He recruited Gen. David Jones, the Chairman of the Joint Chiefs of Staff, to serve on his board of directors from 1978 to 1982. This was huge in my mind because he also recruited Gen. John Vessey and ADM William Crowe – the top military leadership in the country to back his programs. He then hired a retired Navy Captain to help him spread these programs. He was a Pearl Harbor veteran and a very competent man. Together, he and Don started 83 camping programs around the country.

Bridge Builders was also unique. Becky Wilson saw the poverty and devastation in the communities and developed ideas that she and Don together refined. Youth Service hired Bill Snodgrass and Troy Gafford, who became the architects for that program. Troy had a PhD in sports and recreation and used his experience to promote experiential learning, placing people through spiritual and mental teambuilding exercises. Snodgrass and Gafford designed the formal model for Bridge Builders from scratch through a unique set of partnerships and skill sets. It was Becky's idea, but it was their inspiration that made the program work. They put the procedures and operational components together and Becky provided the spirit that kept it going. Bridge Builders showed the power of building something person by person.

Some of the finest people I ever met served on the board of directors at Youth Service. Many of them went beyond the call of duty, including Lee Wakeman, John Collier, Ewing and Jane Carruthers, Jacquelyn Hughes, and Mike Haas.

The Rt. Rev. Bishop Alex Dickson

I met Don Mowery when I was elected Bishop of West Tennessee. I was consecrated as Bishop on Saturday April 9, 1983. I officiated at the wedding of Don and Julie in April 1983 at St. Mary's Cathedral, which was my first official act as Bishop of West Tennessee. Julie told me that the only way she could get Don to leave Youth Service long enough for them to have a honeymoon was to have the service early in the morning and leave immediately.

The Lord blessed Don because of his effectiveness with 'hard-to-reach' people. Through his Youth Service ministry, he was able to reach African-Americans in Shelby County beginning in the 1960s and following the murder of Martin Luther King. He also was able to work together with the Department of Defense to multiply opportunities to teach and minister to the youth. Don's wonderful personality enabled him to focus on the mission and get others involved.

We helped establish good working relationships with all of the citizens of Shelby County. This all helped develop and demonstrate the way the military, the church, and the private sector could work together for the good of the citizens.

The support of local churches showed the community the enthusiastic involvement of the followers of Jesus as our Lord and Savior in bringing all people to faith together. The work also enabled congregations of various racial and ethnic backgrounds to work together.

William B. (Billy) Dunavant, Jr.

(Retired International Cotton Industry Executive and co-

Chair of 1988 Youth Service Capital Campaign)

My original introduction to Don was through Phil Burnett who told me that Youth Service needed some extra funding. I then met with Don and Julie in the mid-1980s, and we started the ball rolling to raise funds for the organization. I knew Phil Burnett at the Cotton Council and that he only referred quality people. I donated money to the organization, but more importantly, I led a capital campaign for Youth Service in1988. I also attended the graduation exercises at St. Mary's Cathedral, which I thought were very well planned and arranged. Every time I encountered Don, I became more impressed with his ability to get the job done. He has a dynamic character and is known for being persistent and never shirking his duties.

Kelli Dunavant

(Founding COO, No One Without)

Bridge Builders is an incredible program committed to change. Young people are motivated and guided to become leaders in their community. The idea that you are a literal bridge builder and a committed member of the community is exhilarating. Students come together with young people from all across Memphis to build a bridge between the cultural gaps. The program can be ultimately challenging, but also completely life changing.

I am privileged to have been selected as a young leader participating in Bridge Builders. I learned so much about my fellow group members and myself and wanted to be a part of positive change in my city. We challenged ourselves to build deep friendships with people completely opposite from ourselves. In the end, we realized how special our city was and embraced the differences with open arms.

The beauty of a program like Bridge Builders is that it can cross cultural divides. More cities could benefit from this program and I would love to see young people empowered across the country. The future of our world lies in the hands of our youth. By promoting love and acceptance, they can literally challenge the course of life, as we know it. Without love and compassion, we are nothing.

Jay Eberle

(Journalist and former Youth Service Board Member)

I became involved after being introduced to Youth Service by the rector at Calvary Church. Bob Atkinson introduced me to Don at a meeting at St. Mary's Church in early 1969. Don and I became big friends over time.

I became a member of the USA board when it began and was part of the 'brains' behind Don's active leadership. The kids who in the Youth Service programs had no idea of the real working world, but the doors opened and they were exposed to it. It was fabulous.

The camping program on the Navy base was a perfect place to get this started. The kids were exposed to all kinds of technical training and jobs. They were given free medical treatment and a chance to improve their personal habits. This environment gave them a new horizon and something else to shoot for other than what they were living in.

Don carried tokens in his pocket called 'Round Tuits.' If someone put him off, he would hand them the token, a wooden slug, and said, 'I hope you get Round Tuit.' He was always coming up with unique things to get people involved.

John Edwards

(Retired Air Force Lt. Col., former Deputy Director of Youth Service)

I was a Youth Service staff member and maintained programs at the bases. We set up job training programs and worked with kids all through the year when summer camps were not convening. We dealt mostly with disadvantaged kids. Some of them barely attended school, and others had a hard time even finding something to eat.

Much of what I did early on involved marketing communications, getting the newspapers involved, and helping Don communicate with different organizations. The *Talk It Out* radio show was the greatest tool in terms of Don's exposure. He knew how to work people, and he never quit. Once he had the Navy involved, he knew he could gain an edge with Gen. David Jones, the Air Force base commander. He had no idea at the time that David Jones would become the Chairman of the Joint Chiefs of Staff.

Don was always good at doing dress rehearsals. If he attended a meeting, he would plan the most effective way to network the crowd. He was always thorough, spending time seeing that everything was set up correctly. He was very organized and had a calculated agenda of what he wanted. He did not operate by serendipity. That really is leadership. Don had the personality to tolerate people making mistakes and could see connections between things others did not see and had a vision and a faith and commitment to do God's work. Most importantly, he did not care who received the glory.

In April 1986, the board members of Youth Service met near Washington with Tom Palnell, chairman of Martin Marietta Corporation and a friend of Air Force Gen. David Jones. Because of Gen. Jones' influence, Martin Marietta wanted to help with the youth programs. Even though the U.S. was experiencing problems in Libya at the time, Gen. Jones attended the meeting because of his strong commitment to the Youth Service program. Interestingly, that was the weekend President Reagan decided to attack Muammar Gaddafi. Throughout the meeting,

Gen. Jones was in communications with the bomber wing over Libya. When he found out the bomber group missed Gaddafi, everyone in the room heard about it. The Youth Service board members were exposed to the world stage for this brief moment. Father Don had the military connections and used it to do good work for these kids.

Howard and Bettie Golwen

(Youth Service Supporters)

I (Howard) was quite impressed with the early programs on the military base. It was a perfect place to introduce young folks to a new way of life. Father Don saw it as a way to teach kids how to fish, which was a better alternative to giving them the fish. Don never took 'No' for an answer. He was persistent with carrying out his vision.

When I was with Memphis Bank & Trust, we gave Youth Service a line of credit at a time when federal funding sources were drying up.

We were also impressed with the graduation ceremonies at St. Mary's Cathedral. Don's mission of building self-esteem and teaching youngsters how to function and prepare resumes and for job interviews was wonderful.

I attended board meetings at Old St. Paul's Church in Baltimore, which were also attended by the Defense contractor Martin Marietta and Gen. Vessey, Chairman of the Joint Chiefs of Staff at that time. The general always had the red phone, known as the national alert hotline connection, with him at all times and was always surrounded by Secret Service men.

Don and Julie were visiting at my home one night. As we prepared to go out to dinner together, a young man who attended Don's Nashville church called and was contemplating suicide. Don stayed on the phone with him for over an hour, reassuring him and talking him out of the urge to take his life.

Bettie was active as president of the board of the St. Augustine Guild. I witnessed the effect of the radio show and Youth Service on the lives of many people. While having dinner one evening with Don and Julie, one person after another came up and told Don how he had changed their lives. I knew that gave him a wonderful feeling.

Tony Graves

(President of Wilson Investment Management,

Chair of BRIDGES Board of Trustees)

I attended Central High School in the late 1980s when it was about 70 percent African-American. Everybody related to each other well; we did everything together. It was a great atmosphere. When I returned home from college in1992, Memphis did not look or feel like what I remembered. Racial tensions and an increasing divide between public and private schools existed and none of it felt like the city I loved. I wanted to change that.

The Kickoff Classic in Memphis, which brought public and private high school football players together to learn about each other on and off the field, was my first BRIDGES event. My friend Becky Wilson introduced me to BRIDGES, a program that helps high school students work together to develop leadership skills among these future leaders.

Father Don took the work to the streets, taking the bold step to be the first youth agency around to integrate its programs. He was an advocate for all youth in Memphis throughout the civil rights era and during the time of unrest that followed.

In 2006, I accepted a seat on the BRIDGES board. What I did not know was that the work that I found so vital had its roots 90 years in the past. When Don left, Jim Boyd brought a new energy and vision to the agency. Today, under Cynthia Ham's leadership, it is poised to serve more young people in high quality, comprehensive programming with an increased ability to track progress. The Memphis that BRIDGES is building looks more like the Memphis of my youth.

Rabbi Micah D. Greenstein

(Temple Israel, Memphis)

Someone else built the houses we live in. Father Don Mowery is the unsung builder of the houses we live in today as a multiracial and multicultural society. The renowned BRIDGES, Inc. for youth was an outgrowth of his Youth Service USA program in Memphis. His pilot youth service program at the Naval Air Station at Millington, TN became a national model for tens of thousands of youth at numerous military bases around the country.

When I met 'Father Don' for the first time at a Memphis Ministers meeting in 1991, I wanted to reach him, but I realized that I did not know his last name! Like Moses or Jesus, 'Father Don' was all I knew. Through the years, he has epitomized the best definition I ever heard for a healer. A healer is anyone who is able to elicit the power to live in others. A leader is anyone who is able to elicit in others the power to move forward. Father Don is a healer and a leader whose legacy will be felt for generations through the lives of the youth he changed forever.

Bill and Pam Hickman

(St. Andrew's Church Members)

When Father Don came to our church in the late 1950s, he brought a dynamic approach with him. We needed transportation for the young people, so Don helped the church acquire our first bus, which became one of the more important facets of his outreach ministry. Other forms of outreach were innovative as well, such as acolytes in the float in the Christmas parade with parishioners singing carols and walking alongside.

One time, my wife Frances and I took several underprivileged boys to St. Louis for the weekend. We told everyone about the good food we enjoyed on the trip, which only raised eyebrows. The main thing is that we became very concerned about young people who are deprived of certain things in life, and we felt exposure to these things would give them a good incentive to go forward. Father Don was the leader for many of these ideas.

Something we cannot forget is that Father Mowery was tasked with the responsibility of getting St. Andrew's Church out of debt, and you can rightly say that he was responsible for St. Andrew's being here to this day.

Stan Hughes

When I was 14 years old, I was in Youth Service. I remember touring Air Force One, Air Force Two and the Air and Space Museum with Father Don. He knew I had an interest in aviation and wanted to support me. My mother was a Youth Service board member and a member of the St. Augustine Guild. I have fond memories of listening to his *Talk It Out* radio show as a young person.

Joseph R. "Pitt" Hyde, III

(Auto Zone Founder)

It was Lester Crain, who introduced me to Don and Youth Service. At that time, they were using the Millington Naval Base training facilities for their program. I was very impressed with Don and we started supporting him through Malone & Hyde and the Hyde Foundation. I began to know him better over the years and was impressed with his commitment to youth and his service to the community in general.

He had the capacity to engage people and made favorable impressions on them with his passion and commitment. His spiritual quality was very evident in his work and actions. He was always a member of the clergy who was trying to build bridges throughout the community, and I always appreciated his efforts on that front. Over time, I observed his networking capabilities in bringing people together. He was always there helping to bring people together from all denominations, as well as ethnic groups for the good of the community, and I greatly admire him for that.

One of the significant things he did for my wife Barbara and me is to preside at our wedding at my home. He also baptized Susannah, our oldest child.

John-Paul Jaudel

(International Studies Graduate)

I grew up in Paris, France and attended college in Montreal. Finding work in Memphis was not easy, and I had trouble finding direction. I lived for a while with my uncle in Memphis and worked as a handyman.

I met Father Mowery at St. John's Church where I tried to motivate myself and rediscover my faith. He helped me find work and direction in life. I have met many interesting people because of Don. I also had a chance to learn about his youth programs and of his work in Washington, D.C. He connected me with William (Bill) Holmberg, who had assisted Youth Service in securing military base facilities for the programs. Bill gave me an internship at the American Council on Renewable Energy, a non-profit organization in Washington.

No one is more giving than Father Mowery. The life that I have now could have never happened without him. It was at a time when I was unsure of what I was going to do. He never asked for anything, but always wants to help.

The Rt. Rev. Don Johnson

(Bishop of The Episcopal Diocese of West Tennessee)

Three things come to mind when I think of Father Don. First, he is known for his thank you notes and thoughtfulness. Many times I have heard people speak of how that was a part of his way of building relationships. He always calls me to congratulate or remind me of something. Don is always on top of those details and is tenacious. If he gets a project or an idea in mind, he will track it down until it is complete or someone finally says, 'Don, we just can't do that!' That is a wonderful quality of his because it is always in the service of a greater good. It's not about him. I admire how everything he does is always done in the service of what he believes is of value.

He loves his position working with The Urban Child Institute. He uses those same qualities of care and discernment in disseminating the monies relative to its mission. He is very involved in trying to help leverage those funds to get the greatest payoff for that group.

Don's ministry aligns with the Anglo-Catholic side of the Episcopal Church, which is known for outreach to the community, the poor, and to those who were in need. St. Andrew's, where Don served in Nashville, is an Anglo-Catholic parish. There are not many of these churches around. It is not a 'run of the mill church' – it is working with the inner city, which brings special concerns. You have to have a heart for that kind of ministry, and Father Don definitely has the kind of heart for the person in need.

Don is clear about what he is trying to accomplish and is creative about getting it done. He will be tenacious about staying on it until something changes. He is good at painting a picture of the need, so that you could put yourself in that situation. As a result, you become inspired to act on it.

Once Don knows the problem, he looks for a solution. Sitting behind a desk would not be his approach, and he is certainly quite comfortable rolling up his sleeves and getting in with everybody to do the face-to-face kind of work that is needed. He is willing to walk along aside everyone in accomplishing that ministry.

BRIDGES became a successful spin-off of Youth Service and took a different direction after Father Don left. Emmanuel Episcopal Center in the Foote Homes community was also successful during Don's tenure at Youth Service. The Center is an Episcopal inner-city outreach ministry and it, in some ways, is comparable to the old Youth Service. While it has Episcopal roots, the Episcopal Church became an incubator for this ministry, not unlike MIFA.

We live in a different world now from when Youth Service began. In some ways, the world seems less hopeful now than it was in the 1960s. People seemed to be more willing and wanting to help the needy in those days. To begin the same Youth Service in today's world would be very difficult. Don could not come in and set up a youth organization the same way he did in 1963. However, knowing Don as I do, he would find a way to meet the need. Don might even have to take his collar off if necessary. He wore his collar most of the time because it opened doors. When he was clear on the need, he was not wedded to the methodology. He was wedded to meeting the need. He would find a way to make it happen with his helpmate Julie.

George Klein

(TV and Radio deejay, friend and confidante of Elvis Presley)

I met Father Don around 1970 when I was working as a deejay and program director at WHBQ. He and Jim Bedwell, our General Manager, had just agreed on a format for the *Talk It Out* radio show.

Don and I participated in many community events – walk-a-thons and charity fundraisers. He would call me to go with him and go speak at many of them. When I ran into kids who needed to be in his program, I directed them to him, and he took them under his wing and helped them out.

Father Don has one of those God-given characteristics of being real, not phony. He was always pleasant and friendly to all. When Don approached someone, whether it was a teenager in trouble or an adult, they would calm down and listen. When they saw that collar, they knew he was going to be straight up with them and talk their language. He stayed in contact with the kids on the streets and knew what was going on. Don commanded respect. I do not think he would have received the respect from the young people if he had worn a coat and tie or a sport shirt.

I think Father Don had a way with young people that some preachers and dignitaries just did not have. Many of them tried to get involved with youth by making them go to church and forcing religion on them, but it did not work. Father Don had the personality and the magic of getting them to stay on the positive side of life and out of trouble. For the same reason, he encouraged them to have some religious activity in their life, but he did not push them into it.

I visited the Youth Service program at the Navy base in Millington and at one of the Air Force bases in the region and was impressed with what

I saw. Youth Service had the right person in the right place because he could open doors and get through them. He had an impeccable reputation and he was doing something good for Memphis.

I had some problems of my own and called on Don for advice. He was very calming and very interested in what I had to say. He gave me some great advice and we have stayed in touch over the years.

David LaBarreare

(Former Youth Service counselor, currently owner of Memphis Motor Werks)

I met Father Don when I was in the ninth grade. My uncle was an Episcopalian and I started going with him to Holy Trinity Church.

I remember one evening when I was young, I was out with a bunch of older guys and was caught stealing a bottle of drink mixer from a 7/11 store. The police officer wrote me a juvenile summons and took me home to my mom. I felt very low because I had never really been in any trouble before, though I was heading in that direction. My mom sent me to my room that night and I turned on the radio. I heard Don for the first time on his *Talk It Out* show. It was February 14, 1971.

Joe Bean, one of the Youth Service probation officers, came to my home to counsel me. When he saw that I repaired motorcycles, he said his boss (Don) had two motorcycles that needed to be fixed and it would be good for me to help him out. The motorcycles were at Lester Crain's house, so I went over there to fix them. The next day Father Don called me to thank me and arranged for a meeting to discuss my case. He wanted me to work at the upcoming Youth Service Summer Camp at the Navy base. I agreed since I did not have a job for the summer. At first I didn't want to do it. I had motorcycles to work on at home and it was summer time; however, I agreed to work at the camp for two or three weeks helping set up the programs and getting the barracks ready for campers.

I was a very hard worker and Father Don knew it, but after about four or five weeks I decided to quit. I did not show up for work the next Monday, so Don called me and asked why. I told him that I quit, but he said, 'No, you don't. That's not the way you quit a job.' He had me work the rest of my time at the Youth Service office instead of the base. I kept the storeroom organized, ran errands, attended meetings with him, sat in on many board meetings and watched him raise money for the program. Actually, that is where I learned about business, but I did not realize it at the time.

In the summer of 1971, Don decided to take seven or eight kids dirt bike riding on the weekends. We went to Southaven Kawasaki and Bob McLean gave us a couple of Kawasaki motorcycles. We tied the bikes on his car and rented cabins at Sardis Lake in Mississippi. We rode the trails and cooked out at night. When the summer was over I was prepared to leave Youth Service, but Father Don had other ideas. He wanted me to work with him on the radio show. I quickly learned how to engineer the show and ran the phone board. I would answer the phone calls and screen the people before they could talk to Don on the air.

Don also had me call prospective guests for the radio show and arrange for interviews. Some of Don's guests included wrestler Jackie Fargo, the Memphis Police Chief, Ed Sullivan, Arthur Godfrey, Bob Hope, and Shelby County Sheriff Bill Morris. I sometimes worked seven days a week, attended church and helped him with weddings.

We taught many kids how to ski at McKellar Lake and later at Horseshoe Lake. Altogether, I worked for Youth Service about three years. Father Don treated me like a son and we became very close friends. We both worked extremely hard for Youth Service. He is a charismatic man and an incredible speaker and fundraiser. When he gets in front of a group, he's magic. He knew how to approach people in Memphis and obtain their support. He also knew how to apply and receive federal grants. He was incredible.

I was elected to the Board of Youth Service in 1992 and was on the board when Jim Boyd became executive director. Becky Wilson was very involved spearheading the Bridge Builders Program during this time. When Jim Boyd came aboard, things began to change. Father Don loved what he did and sacrificed a lot for Youth Service. He is a first-class guy and a real gentleman. I owe a lot to Don and in many ways, he is the reason I am successful today.

Curt Ladd

(President, First Financial of Dallas)

When I was a sophomore in high school, I was your typical wild kid and found myself in a little trouble. My parents were separated and they thought a meeting with Father Don would be good for me. He took me and some of the guys water skiing, and we had wonderful times. He is fair, kind and understands where kids are coming from. He is a person you respect and do not want to disappoint. He is a moral man who inspired me to do better. Because of his influence, I became a Christian when I was a senior in high school and committed my life to the Lord. I was also on his radio show.

Hal Lansky

(Memphis clothier and retailer to Elvis Presley)

I have known Father Don for over 40 years and he is a mentor to me. I cannot explain the connection, but Father Don has always been a spiritual leader to me even though he is an Episcopal priest and I am Jewish. I could talk to him about anything. Father Don always was concerned about my well-being and wanted to know about things that were important to me. I considered Father Don as my third father.

He attended all my daughters Bat Mitzvahs and two weddings. I have also been a guest on his radio show three times over the years. He has a knack to make everyone feel very comfortable and special when he is interviewing them. I feel Father Don is very proud of me. He has seen me grow up to be a responsible family man, business and community leader.

Pat Lawler

(CEO of Youth Villages)

My relationship with Don began when I heard his voice on the radio. I was in the seventh and eighth grades when I made it a point to listen to his The *Talk It Out* radio show every Sunday night. He is a great interviewer and always gains the kids' confidence. He was the voice of responsibility that you could relate to on the radio. He was older than we were, but he seemed to be in tune to what kids were thinking and what was going on in our lives. All of the questions he asked were relevant to young people and we wanted to hear the answers.

He was the first grown-up administrator I knew who could actually relate to kids. He enjoyed sitting down and talking to them and was sort of a personal advisor for me. It was important to me to see how he built his network. I wish I had been able to get to know him better in those days. Don was the most famous person to kids my age in the Memphis community.

I remember we were roommates at a youth retreat when I was a young administrator in my twenties from 1983 to1985. I remember sitting on a hill with him overlooking the lake, just talking. I remember thinking it would be great if I could have the same kind of relationship with young people, the reputation in the community and his passion. You didn't find many people in their '40s and '50s that really cared that deeply about young people.

Don had the ability to relate to all people extremely well and always cared about what you were doing. He gained respect from everybody because of what he had done for the community. There were very few people like that in those days.

Chao Lin

(Bank of Bartlett)

I work in marketing as a special assistant to the president of the Bank of Bartlett. I joined Bridge Builders during my sophomore year at Frayser High School. We had a very diverse group – kids from all of the inner-city schools. In my junior year, we had a Bridge Builder get-together of alumni. That is where I learned that they had a scholarship available. When I applied, I was asked to write a 500-word essay on why I thought I deserved a scholarship. The subject of my essay was community involvement and my tutoring work, as well as my involvement with city beautification projects.

Because of that essay, I became the first recipient of the Father Don Mowery Scholarship that Bridge Builders awarded in 2002. Father Don and I didn't actually meet until after I had been awarded the scholarship, but after we met, he became like a father figure to me and we have kept in touch ever since.

I learned a lot from Don's ability to network effectively and became a listener of his radio show. He taught me good business practices and how to properly meet people. He also taught me how to write thank you cards.

I visited with Don and Julie often. They would cook me meals at their home even after I graduated from college. Father Don taught me about investments and always taught me to not put all my money in one place. When I graduated from college, I began running investment programs. Currently, I own numerous investment properties. All of this came with the help of Father Don. He mentored me in networking and working hard, but still enjoying life and learning how to interact with people.

Larry Lloyd

(Founder of Memphis Leadership Foundation and the

Neighborhood Christian Center and Streets Ministries)

I first heard Father Don on his *Talk It Out* radio program in 1970. I used to listen to folks who called in and I thought it was an interesting show. I never was involved in Youth Service directly, but I was active in the Civil Rights Movement and with an organization called Young Life.

I became acquainted with the vocational camps at NAS Memphis when I was working with the students at Rhodes College from 1970 to 74. I met Father Don in 1978 and soon realized we were involved in the same type of work with young people, many of whom would be considered at-risk. I remember being amazed at what he had done. I was very impressed and became a supporter. We agreed to work together to help kids in any way we could from our respective organizations.

In those days, other organizations were working with the disadvantaged, such as Youth for Christ, Youth Service, Neighborhood Christian Center, which I founded, and Young Life Urban Ministries. Father Don and I realized that we were networked with the same web of folks, doing work in the inner city.

I consulted with Don before I started Memphis Leadership Foundation (MLF). I remember he encouraged me to start MLF and we became more involved from 1987 to 88. Even to this day, we get together regularly with our wives for dinner.

There was very little Christian ministry to African-American youth outside of the African-American church in 1968. Prior to Dr. King's assassination, programs like Young Life, Youth for Christ and Youth Guidance were working predominantly with white kids. Father Don and Youth Service were instrumental in getting that changed. He was a pioneer for bringing together black and white young people before other non-profit groups took on that responsibility. Dr. King's assassination is what began the ball rolling to change the consciousness in this country. Young Life made a similar move, albeit a little later in Memphis, but nationally in the '60's.

I remember when I moved back to Memphis from Los Angeles and visited the program at the Navy base. It was incredible to me how he managed to place his program there. Don was way ahead of his time in terms of collaboration and partnerships. He introduced me to that concept. At first, I thought this program was only at the NAS Memphis until I went to his office and realized the programs that he had started were going on all over the country.

I thought it was ingenious when he collaborated with the Department of Defense. This is how you do ministry. There are assets out there and if you can create partnerships, you have synergy. No one had used a non-profit organization, particularly a faith-based non-profit organization, to do what Don was able to do with Youth Service. In many ways, Don was a real renegade and entrepreneur.

In the 1980s, Don became very concerned with the government closing of military bases all over the country. When that happened, the direction began to shift toward the Youth Service program that Becky Wilson helped start – the Bridge Builders program. This program exposed kids from public and private schools together for bridge-building opportunities. I was impressed with all of the schools that wanted to participate with this non-profit faith-based organization. The program became very popular and kids would line up to be nominated by the school principal. It was a great program.

Don has the most impeccable Christian character, and I have met Chuck Colson and Billy Graham. There is no guile in the man. He is humble – probably to a fault. If you wanted to model what a Christian man is supposed to be like, Don would be one of those I would want to emulate. Don is also a quiet leader, though he would plow ahead and get things done in ways that would astonish many.

I think you gauge leadership by who is following. The legacy he has left with Youth Service (now BRIDGES) is a testimony to his leadership abilities. He is not a coercive leader, but one who leads by building consensus. He knows how to do that and to do it properly. He is not manipulative. You never feel badgered by Don.

Now in his eighties, he has not stopped working. There is no true retirement in this business. Abraham never retired, Moses never retired and I do not think Don will ever retire in the real sense.

I know that the financial difficulties and the leadership transition weighed heavily upon him when he retired, but he has persevered. There are many lessons I learned from Don, one was hanging in there when the going was tough and the support you need is hard to find. Nevertheless, God was calling him to do this, so he did not give up. Moreover, he is still going!

Cloretta Yates McCoy

I say it was by divine appointment that the Christian Brother's College work-study program placed me at Youth Service in Memphis during the summer of 1973, where I worked until I graduated in May 1976. I worked in the Youth Service office after school, during the summer and worked as a camp counselor at NAS Memphis. Youth Service was a perfect fit for me. After graduating from Central High School and participating in their Junior ROTC program, my mind was set on entering the military service. For Youth Service to be so connected with the military was more than coincidental for me. I gleaned a lot that helped me throughout my twelve-year career as an Air Force officer. I learned to say, 'Yes Sir;' 'No Sir,' 'Thank you,' and 'Please,' And to always give a firm handshake and look a person in the eye when meeting them. I am forever grateful to Youth Service and everyone at the agency who instilled so much in me.

Richard Marsh

(Bank Executive, SunTrust Bank)

My behavior was not very good during my teenage years, which stemmed from my dysfunctional home environment. When I was 13, I had some delinquency issues and my mother arranged a meeting with Father Don to see if he could be a mentor to me. He helped me acknowledge the fact that my behavior needed improvement.

Don became my mentor and, in return, I helped him from time to time with jobs at Youth Service. I did not realize at the time that he was helping shepherd, mentor and cultivate a positive relationship with me in ways that my parents could not do.

I felt comfortable talking to him about what was going on in my life. Don was a levelheaded, right-thinking adult who was objective and with whom I could talk and share my struggles and issues.

Father Don was the first person I called when something bad happened or I had a fight with my parents. During the early part of my first year in high school, I had a problem with drugs and alcohol. I would get myself in trouble and would be frustrated and leave home. I could always talk to Don and he never passed judgment. He made me think about how I handled a situation and told me often that my parents really loved me. I left home a lot during my sophomore year because I did not want to be there. I spent the night out with friends, slept in the park, and if I did not have a place to go, I would sometimes call or knock on Don's door late at night and stay with him. He was always understanding of me.

The summer between my sophomore and junior year was probably the peak of my bad behavior and I found myself in trouble with the authorities. A friend of mine who was with me at the time was caught, but I was not. I considered leaving town and I wandered around thinking about what to do next. My parents were worried and no one knew where I was. I called Don and told him that I was in trouble. I met with my dad and Father Don and we discussed my options. They convinced me to stay and do the right thing. I turned myself in and my dad gave me a ride downtown to the police station. The intake process was embarrassing, but it gave me a new perspective on what lay ahead if I did not change. I was officially assigned to Youth Service, partly because Father Don had a very good relationship with Juvenile Court Judge Kenneth Turner. Youth Service worked with the court to try to help kids like me.

Since I had not been in any serious trouble before, I was assigned several hundred hours of community service. I remember vividly my experience in court and since then I was able to counsel with other kids in the same situation. Every time I walk down the hall at Juvenile Court, I remember sitting in the office with my parents. Fortunately, I had a better direction in life after I completed my community service.

Don taught me many things about life, but also how to water ski at Horseshoe Lake in the Youth Service Program. That was an enriching time. I also listened to his radio show every Sunday night.

In 1979, Father Don taught me how to drive a stick shift, so I could drive an old International Harvester truck and move things around for Youth Service. My dad was a good man, but I did not have much of a relationship with him. He was very stoic and a very typical WWII-type of guy. I had a real need for encouragement that he could not provide, so Don served as a surrogate dad in many ways. He would always finish the conversation with a positive thought, telling me how proud he was of me. It meant a tremendous amount to me when I was younger and it still means a lot to me today.

Our capacity to understand what a Heavenly Father is like depends to a significant degree on the experiences we have in this life with our earthly fathers. It involves the whole concept of what that relationship is supposed to be. My faith is a very important part of my life today. I'm a Christian, but I was not at that time in my life. Don did not talk about the Bible all the time. He just lived it. As I grew older and explored what God and faith were all about – I definitely know that Don's influence in my life helped me to have an openness to Christianity and to faith than I would not have had otherwise.

Lynda Wyatt Mayo

(St. Andrew's Church, Nashville)

My family and I were members of St. Andrew's Church in Nashville when Don began his ministry in 1956. I was 11 or 12 years old at the time and vividly recalled waves of young people being drawn to the church because Don brought a youthful attitude to the congregation. He brought a lot of energy and awakened us to a new interest in the church. He was able to get many students to visit through his church bus ministry. I attended Cohn High School, which was about two blocks from the church.

With the big local interest in football, Don decided to use the church bus on Friday nights to take students to and from the games. My mother served as coordinator for the bus reservations and rode as a chaperone. Our phone would ring all week for reservations to ride on the church bus. This indirectly developed a new interest in St. Andrew's for many people. There was much energy and laughter there. Almost everyone in West Nashville seemed to know Don. He visited with my family often and we had him over for dinner many times. My mother and father were the first family he ever met in our church.

Jim McGehee

(Owner McGehee Realty)

I served as the treasurer and chairman of the finance committee for The Episcopal Diocese of West Tennessee. I also served on the board of Youth Service for many years.

There was a need for coordination between the diocese and Youth Service, which required us to meet frequently. Don saw unprecedented success first in Memphis and then drew upon an obvious need to take the concept nationally.

Don had an incredible ability to turn around a young person's life with good communication and leadership. He is a gifted communicator whether you are seven or 77 years old. His work with the Department of Defense became a classic example of the way that the military and private sector can work together.

Don and Youth Service were also unifying factors during the civil rights upheaval because Don is 'color blind.' As a result, the organization was able to make great strides. It was critically essential during those tense times that Don leveraged his networking ability. There was at first the usual skepticism among churches and people in the community, but when the success of Youth Service became obvious, it became easier for him to build upon that success.

William (Bill) Morris

(Former Shelby County Sheriff and Mayor)

Don Mowery was the first person I remember involving the community and that of our younger generation on a large scale. He was a genius with program development and responded to the dynamics of changing demographic groups.

I remember our conversations about how the breakdown of the family unit was progressing at a rapid pace. I had learned from my experience in law enforcement and social programs what worked and what did not. I could see that Youth Service displayed a high-level of integrity. The Sheriff's office and Mayor's office had a direct involvement with Don and Youth Service. He was inventive and created programs in response to the immediate needs of youth. You learn from people like Don Mowery to stay with something for the long haul. We also worked together trying to break the cycle of poverty with the Free the Children program.

Judge Kenneth Turner of Juvenile Court was very involved with Youth Service. We would talk about the triage of the Sheriff's Department, Juvenile Court and Youth Service as a binding strength to deal with youth when needed. That created a heavy group of footprints working together. Don instilled an awareness of individual involvement to help sustain others in this society.

Tony Mowery

(Adopted son of Don Mowery)

I did not have a very good childhood. The court took me away from my parents at an early age and placed me into Monroe Harding Children's Home in Nashville where I lived for about 11 years. I did not look at my natural parents the same way as they looked at me. That blended as one big hate. Being at the Children's Home kept me out of trouble. It was a time in my life that there were many bad people out there.

When I met Father, I was playing football for Hume-Fogg High School and he was helping coach the football team. We became good friends. I began living with him to avoid staying at the Children's Home. After the Children's Home suggested that he legally adopt me, we moved from Nashville to live in Memphis after he took the Youth Service job.

I joined the Army in 1966, served two tours in Vietnam, returned to Memphis for a while and then moved to Houston, TX. Father had obtained a job for me with HIA International there, and Mrs. J. B. Cook paid my plane ticket to Houston. I met my wife in Houston and we have been married for 43 years. We have a grown, married daughter and now a grand daughter.

During the years of Youth Service, Father dealt mainly with delinquents. Seeing how people can be hurt mentally and physically can set you straight for what not to do. Because of this, I learned a lot of what not to do. Don has led others like me throughout his career to get back on the right path.

Father works well with others. That man has worked hard to get where he is. I say that as a son and as a friend. He has earned what he has and is as close to being perfect as anyone I've ever known. He really helped me to be where I am with his fatherly advice all these years. I've taken advantage of his knowledge and respected him for that. He has taught me a lot over the years and means the world to me. He took me when nobody else wanted me and we have been together for a long time. Everybody laughed at us at first – I was a poor boy from a children's home – but it has been a great positive experience for me.

Mrs. Frances S. Myrick

(Former Youth Service Office Administrator)

I arrived in 1953 to work for Youth Service and served as administrative director. I hired Mary Frances Greer as our secretary. I learned how to help young people through social work from Ms. Agnes Grabau, the former director. We received referrals from churches, juvenile court and the public school system, and established a wonderful working relationship with all of the social agencies in Memphis. I wrote many guidelines for Youth Service counselors, so that they could offer counseling to the whole family not just the individual child.

St. Augustine Guild members were very important to the growth of Youth Service. Their constant prayer focused on the spirit of love. Dues to join Youth Service were just $10 per year, and it seemed as though we were on a shoestring budget every year; however, our service work went far beyond the dues.

Father Mowery always wanted to help others and started every meeting with a prayer. He was wonderful working with the women of the church and they were very fond of him.

Dr. Bill and Tricia Nash

(Nashville friends of Father Don)

We became associated with Don during his outreach to the Nashville community and specifically to the students at Cohn High School around 1960. Don had an indelible impression on our lives. He was like an ideal older brother who looked out for you and would help you in any way he could. Not only did Father Mowery help us out during our high school years in Nashville, but in like fashion, kept up with us over time like he did with many others. He also assisted us in Memphis when I (Bill) was attending dental school. We would have fun get-togethers at the church; it was just like a community center. Don was very innovative and came up with the idea of going up in a private plane and distributing leaflets all over West Nashville when the church was planning a special event or bazaar.

When I, who had only a modest household income then, expressed a desire to go to college, Don reassured me and discussed his situation with his Episcopal friends. Indeed, through his acquired contacts, I managed to attend Sewanee on a work-study scholarship. Years later, when we were living in Memphis and had a young child, Father Mowery let us reside in his home on Peabody Avenue for four months until we were able to obtain an apartment of our own. He also talked with his friend, Mrs. J.B. Cook, about our situation, and we lived in her guesthouse for three years while I was in dental school.

Father Mowery made the Episcopal Church in our community an attractive place where people could go and practice their religion. He allowed us to freely express ourselves. He was not one to be daunted or intimidated by controversy either, as is attested by the way he handled things very well while he was making changes in the church.

Don was the most influential person in my life. He also gave us hope for the future and expanded our horizons. He provided exposure to a different way of life to many young kids like us.

The Reverend Joe Porter

(Episcopal Minister)

Father Don Mowery has such faith and is authentic with everyone. It made no difference if you were from the streets, the presiding Bishop of the Episcopal Church or the president, Don shares his faith with all people, equally. He has proved that by his work through Youth Service, with retired priests and people from all occupations and life-styles.

When Father Mowery retired, I was living and working at a church in Dyersburg, TN. I remember I could not come to his retirement dinner, so I wrote him a hand-written letter. I told him after all these years, what he had meant to my life and about how it all started from the *Talk It Out* radio show. I did not meet him until his retirement, but that was a perfect time to tell him. It's never too late to tell somebody what they have meant to you.

I was not acquainted with Don until I became a priest. My wife and I would ride around on Sunday nights and listen to his radio show. I appreciated the things he had to say. I remember discussing what his programs meant in the development of my own faith. Later, when I was serving at my church in Dyersburg and involved in community life, I started several organizations and became aware of the Youth Service program at NAS Memphis, a boot camp program for young offenders. I brought a busload of people to witness that program, so we could try to make it happen up in Dyersburg.

I always had a very high regard for Don and his work. He was a gentle figure who encouraged and helped people realize their potential. The programs he developed testify to this ability to lead and influence others. He developed good friendships and supporters in all walks of life. Don had integrity, which would have made him equally successful in the business or political world.

Judge Jim Russell

(Judge and former Diocesan Deputy and Vice Chancellor)

I worked with Father Don in the 1980s within the administration of the Episcopal Diocese of West Tennessee in Memphis. I met Don when I became involved at the diocesan level and had been a delegate to diocesan conventions going back as early as 1976. I became involved from a canon law standpoint and a legal standpoint. In that capacity, I was called upon to get involved with Youth Service and its board. Don and I began to work more closely together after I attended several Youth Service meetings.

Don had a marvelous command over administrative things. That is when I began to think he would make a good bishop. I tried to convince Don to be open to the call to become the Diocesan Bishop; however, he quickly let me know that he did not feel the call, and we had to respect that.

His resonant voice and presence caused a person to do anything in the world he would ask them to do. He knew in his own mind what needed to be done. He was incredibly creative with the Boot Camp Program, using buildings and classrooms that would not have been used any other way. The way he took the program to Washington, D.C. to make that a reality was impressive. I also listened to his radio show in the early days every time it came on. I was captivated by that rich voice of his, but also the things he had to say on the program itself – things with which a young person could identify.

Jack Sammons

(Former Memphis City Council Member and current Chairman

of the Memphis-Shelby County Airport Authority)

I heard about Father Don in 1970 through his WHBQ talk radio show. I was a student at CBHS and would always have WHBQ radio playing in the background. When the radio program began in 1970, I was in the ninth grade. Kids would call into the show and share their troubles and concerns with Father Don. I put my book down and found myself leaning toward the radio as he spoke and became a regular listener every Sunday night.

I was a young man when I entered politics. As a City Council member, I quickly noticed Youth Service and the role they played. I met Father Don when he invited me to attend one of the Youth Service graduation ceremonies. I spoke to the group because I was the 'kid' in government at the time. I was in my late 20s and most of my colleagues were in their 70s in city hall. I attended many of the graduations and soon discovered that Don really carried the hand of the Lord. He influenced everybody he touched. The faith community has historically played a role in the social and political history of Memphis. We certainly had our challenges, including the lingering effects of the assassination of Dr. King. Don and I shared common interests and began to see our community prosper as we tried to create opportunities for people on both sides of the economic strata.

I spent a significant amount of my life studying leadership. There is an ongoing debate about whether leadership can be taught or whether it is innate among some individuals. I can argue it both ways, but if there is anyone I have ever met that has leadership in their soul it is Father Don Mowery. I am one who believes school is never out for the professional. You continue to learn, and Father Don personifies that theory. He is continually learning how he can perform his assignment in life better than he has in the past.

Don Mowery earns the trust of others as rapidly as any human I have met. He can take his priestly collar off and he is the same guy. Don is what we perceive to be very 'Christ-like.' He truly walks in the shoes of others. To Don, all glasses are half-full, not half-empty, and he is an eternal optimist that has a contagious enthusiasm for life. I have spent a lifetime trying to surround myself with people who have a contagious enthusiasm for life, people who are living every moment to the fullest rather than those sitting around waiting to die. Don is certainly in the 'living' category.

I never served on the Youth Service board, but anything Father Don ever asked me to do, or if he needed any assistance from City Hall, I was sort of 'Johnny on the spot' and was happy to help.

When I was married over 20 years ago, I inherited my wife Jennifer's family of aunts, uncles and grandparents. Her grandmother, Sally Hook (mother of Fred Smith of FedEx), was a close friend of Father Don and his wife Julie. Father Don became sort of our family priest. When we had family occasions, he would join us. I always thought that was a treat because he is such a great person to know. There are a few people around town that I am always glad to be with, and Don is one of them. When you talk to Don, you would think that you were the only person in the world that he knew. I always had the impression when I talked to him that he is an attentive listener.

I would attribute 100 percent of Youth Service's success to Don's networking ability. He was the face, mouth and the ears of the organization

– he personified Youth Service. Father Don Mowery and the name of the organization were interchangeable.

Working with or for a philanthropic group can be challenging. You are constantly engaged with a few people that you do not particularly care for. They may have money, but some are arrogant and overbearing. He is a role model for all of us who have been in community service at any level, whether you are a philanthropist or a Boy Scout volunteer. He has treated people with dignity no matter what their station in life and taught people to be optimistic. He has instructed them on the value and benefits of education and having a spiritual dimension to their lives as well.

Father Don was way ahead of his time. During the '60s and '70s, much of youthful America looked at older people in positions of authority with disdain, but he was greatly respected. Those kids who were joining the protests about the war and the civil rights movement might have been angry with their government, but they were always glad to see Father Don.

Reid Sanders

(EVP, Southeastern Asset Management, Inc.)

My long relationship with Father Don began soon after he moved to Memphis in the early 1960's. My stepsister, Nancy Smith, had returned home from Wellesley College for the summer and was busily engaged in developing the world's first computerized motel reservation system for a small, but fast growing local company, Holiday Inns. A family friend made the introduction and Father Don soon became a regular visitor around our house - either courting my sister or becoming the new best friend of a slightly obnoxious 12-year-old boy. I felt certain it was the latter, but strangely, when Nancy went back to school, Father Don became only an occasional visitor.

Even so, I never lost that feeling of having gotten to know someone very special. Over my teenage years, I managed to keep up with Father Don from a distance, as he immersed himself in the most troubled parts of the inner city Memphis community and began trying to make a differ-ence. When Martin Luther King Jr. was assassinated in Memphis, Father Don knew that something more had to be done for the youth of Memphis. He soon developed the vision for the remarkably creative, efficient and effective program, Youth Service USA. This program used underutilized land and facilities at military bases, first around Memphis and then all over the country, to provide much needed secure recreational outlets and educational enhancements to thousands of disadvantaged young people. With boundless enthusiasm, tireless effort, and surely a vision from above, Father Don and his great friend, Lester Crain, who generously served as Chairman of the Board (while maintaining a demanding "day job" as head legal counsel for Malone & Hyde/AutoZone), built Youth Service USA into an organization that was sponsored in part by the Joint Chiefs of Staff.

This remarkable organization operated successfully in more than 30 states and 125 military bases and was an incredible accomplishment. Youth Service would have been more than enough for most overachievers – but not Father Don. During this same time, he began a platform for a "talk radio" program on radio station, WHBQ. This program invited an often-disaffected young audience to call in and discuss their thoughts and frustrations with the sympathetic and always reasoned Father Don, often in concert with other well-chosen guests. Forty-four years later with a somewhat broadened format "Talk It Out" is still a Sunday morning fixture on WHBQ radio.

Father Don followed these early initiatives with other programs that offered adult education; job training; employment placement; family counseling, planning, and conflict resolution; drug and alcohol rehabilitation; and many others, all in a spirit of Christian ministry.

Two of my favorite programs, which exemplify the remarkably creative and resourceful characteristics of most, were:

- "About Face" – designed with the input of forward thinking juvenal authorities and served to separate first-time, not yet hard core, juvenal offenders from those more incorrigible, and place them in a total immersion "boot camp-type" remedial program. This approach was so novel and the results so promising that private equity investment super star and community activist, Ray Chambers, flew his private jet from New Jersey to Memphis to see the program in action.

- "Bridge Builders" – envisioned by Memphis lawyer, photographer, world traveler, community leader, social visionary and super wife/ mom, Becky Wilson, to promote understanding and mutual respect between different racial and socio-economic groups of high school students. This program continues to grow and thrive in the Memphis area and has been successfully transplanted to other cities around the country.

Father Don approached each of his programs with the vision, energy and resourcefulness of a true entrepreneur. He attracted many of the business elite of Memphis – Billy Dunavant, Pitt Hyde, Fred Smith, Spence and Kemmons Wilson, and Lester Crain, along with Elvis Presley, just to name a few – to support and promote these programs. There can be little doubt that had he used his talents to create wealth, he would have been as successful as many of his supporters. But, Father Don's legacy is the many community service initiatives that he conceived, planned, built and staffed, as well as funded, and the untold thousands in Memphis as well across the country, too whom he has dedicated his life's work. I feel touched by God and so very fortunate to have had the privilege of knowing and working with this wonderful man for all these many years and to be able to count him as my close friend.

Otis Sanford

(Newspaper columnist and former editor at the Commercial Appeal)

I started listening to Father Mowery's *Talk It Out* program on WHBQ radio when I was a teenager. I found his shows to be interesting, and I made a point to listen each Sunday evening. I met Don after I became a journalist, and he recommended me for membership in the Memphis Rotary Club.

I consider Father Don to be a Memphis treasure. He has great compassion for human beings, speaks out for the disadvantaged and the downtrodden, and he cares deeply about youth. He made me appreciate the need to give back, and I think I am more community-minded because of him. I have joined a couple of non-profit boards that are committed to helping the disadvantaged in Memphis, and I have Father Don to thank for that.

Sam Scott

(Washington connection, worked for Manpower

Development Corporation (MDC)

My relationship with Youth Service began in the late 1970s. Youth Service, USA received a contract from the U.S. Department of Labor to demonstrate a military/youth job training program concept at 15-20 locations across the country. We found Youth Service, Memphis and Youth Service, USA to be laboratories for demonstrating unique youth programs and concepts. Because of our interest in promoting the South's workforce and economy, that initial work led to an organizational relationship and an appreciation of Don and his staff, which lasted for many years.

My organization was created in 1967 to test and demonstrate programs to move North Carolina's unskilled rural, minority, and impoverished workers into gainful employment, especially through the state's community colleges as catalysts for rural development. Over the years, we expanded our research throughout the South and later nationally.

When we first began working with Youth Service, the National Office for Social Responsibility (NOSR) was acting as administrator of Youth Service's USDOL grant. During the first meeting with NOSR, the Washington staff referred to Don as a somewhat eccentric figure who passed out cookies at our meetings. Don's cookie gesture reflected the genial nature of the man, while at the same time it displayed his wily capacity to influence and motivate others. It was an old marketing tactic that he had honed to perfection. Long before NOSR came into the picture, Don had been using the 'cookie ploy' with Army, Navy, and Air Force base commanders and with the Joint Chiefs of Staff in his successful and unprecedented effort to have them open their bases to kids to provide summer recreation programs that would keep them off the streets and out of trouble. Father Don understood that no military person could turn down a cookie, or the person who offered it.

Don is one of the good people whose heart is centered on service, yet also one who is focused, goal-oriented and has a keen understanding of people and how to get them to do the right thing. He possesses the skills of a good leader and fund-raiser, staff developer and developer of community support and involvement. His greatest leadership characteristic may be his sincerity, honesty, and trustworthiness. People tend to believe in him and what he is striving to accomplish.

Paul Shanklin

(Conservative political satirist, impressionist and comedian)

Father Don had known my father and brother before I met him in 1974. My father died when I was young, therefore, having a male example to display leadership and character was a big deal for me. I began running errands at Youth Service and was glad to be there. Don always had something for me to do and was not shy about asking me to do any job within the organization.

I attended the NAS Memphis summer camp and was able to see how he worked behind the scenes leading Youth Service. He was good at using resources and doing as much as he could with whatever he had. I also accompanied Don when he received the first Freedoms Foundation's award.

Don reads people very well. He always taught me to step up and ask for what I wanted and expect to receive it. He asked people to be at their best and always treated us as young adults instead of kids. He made us take personal responsibility and to think about our course in life. No one had ever challenged me like that before. When I was around Father Don, I felt that I could dream bigger. Many kids came from backgrounds that were less desirable, and they didn't know any other way. He tried to show kids there is a better life, and I admired his leadership qualities. Father Don and I have continued to be good friends through the years.

I also worked with Don on his *Talk It Out* radio show on WHBQ, which was the most popular station for young people in Memphis. It was cool to work on the show, and I was fortunate to arrange for and meet many of his interesting guests.

I became a successful political satirist and I am still in radio, partly because of the *Talk It Out* experience. In May 1993, I sent three demo tapes to Johnny Donovan with the Rush Limbaugh Show. After getting no response, my friend, political cartoonist Mike Ramirez, suggested I call Donovan using Bill Clinton's voice. As Clinton, I told Donovan, *I don't feel Rush and I are as close as we used to be. Can you work things out between me and Rush? I do not think we're really that far apart on the issues.* Donovan liked my impression of Clinton, asked for a demo tape and national exposure followed.

J. B. Smiley

(Memphis Military Entrance Processing Station)

In 1981, Father Mowery hired me as the counseling director for Youth Service, Memphis Jobs Skills Training and Employment Program (JSTEP). Years later, I was promoted to Program Manager of the Youth Service Vocational Exposure Program.

Father Mowery was always interested in the welfare of the under-privileged, disadvantaged, and unemployed. He respected my work ethic, ability to supervise the JSTEP employees, communicate with worksite supervisors, administer the counseling training curriculum and provide directives to trainees. He trusted me to implement and select eligible young adults from the community for training and employment in local, public, private, and government jobs.

Don is grounded in Christian principals and is a calm, easygoing person who has a vision and plan to influence and help others. If a young person was arrested and went to jail, they often called Father Mowery for help. He did not give up on them. His connections and rapport with the police director and juvenile court often secured the best for the youth.

Father Mowery gave me an opportunity for employment and experiences that improved my self-confidence and ability to provide counseling services to employees and students.

I was able to give back to Youth Service by helping reinstate the Youth Service Job Skills Training and Employment Program as a training site at the Memphis Military Entrance Processing Station. I hired a former Youth Service trainee, who became our Test Score Technician. She has a 17-year tenure with the federal government and is another Youth Service success story.

Frederick (Fred) Smith

(Founder, President and CEO, FedEx)

I have known Father Don Mowery for over 35 years. FedEx supported Youth Service for many years and Father Don gave the inaugural prayer in 1978 when we christened our first Boeing 727 aircraft. He also christened our first DC-10 aircraft. Don's ability to work with government officials to establish youth programs on military bases was something no one else had done before. His unique people skills helped Youth Service change the lives of countless youth across the nation.

Jim Storey

(Member of St. Andrew's Church, Nashville)

I grew up in a middle working-class area of Nashville and attended art school before I went into active duty with the Army Reserve. We were lifelong members at St. Andrew's, which had an older priest before Don came to the church.

There was not much youth outreach prior to Don's arrival, but that soon changed. Everyone loved Father Mowery, and the congregation began to have a sense of excitement. He was full of life and ideas. I remember he drove that old 1941 Dodge, which was installed with the cowbell that you could hear a mile away. Kids in the neighborhood thought he was 'cool.' He changed many things at the church.

Father Mowery set to work making physical changes to the inside of the church, much to the dismay of the 'Grande Dame' of the church who wanted to keep the traditional style. He had the finishes stripped off the pews and rounded off the fleur-de-lis's. The altar previously had a lot of elaborate wooden scrollwork, which was removed and replaced with a huge crucifix. He also began moving the church toward a more Anglo-Catholic tradition, while at the same time, making use of modern contrivances. Don installed a special switch under the carpet and could, at the right juncture of the liturgy, tap with his foot to ring the bells during the Eucharist.

Father Mowery had a broad influence among the parishioners, particularly the young adults and tried to expose them to a better way of life.

My most vivid memories of Father Don was when he was young, full of energy, handsome and forged ahead – never looking back. He would determine something was the right thing to do and he did it. He was very decisive about change. On the human side, he made you feel relaxed. You didn't feel like he was judging you.

Ron Walter

(Former Congressional Aide to Harold Ford Sr., currently President

and General Manager for WREG-TV News Channel 3 in Memphis)

I first knew of Father Don around 1977 when I was working for Congressman Harold Ford, Sr. in Washington. Don was a friend of the Congressman, and I met him at the dedication ceremony for the christening of the first Boeing 727 that Board Chairman Fred Smith acquired for

Federal Express. From that moment on, we became good friends. He was somebody that I called on for important local contacts in the congressional office.

Don performed the marriage ceremony for my wife Marianne and me in 1987. It was a religious ceremony and fairly theatrical, since we conducted the event on the stage of the Orpheum Theater. There were a couple of thousand in attendance, and Don helped with everything, including musical selections for our wedding. We borrowed an altar from St. Mary's Cathedral and made the stage look and sound as much like a church as possible. He also performed the baptism for our first child at Calvary Episcopal Church in 1992. He has been a very important part of my life and my family's life.

I served on the Youth Service board in the 1980s and was among the few non-Episcopalians who contributed to that board. He challenged me personally to be involved and to meet our goals. It is something I will never forget. Don is a role model and teaches people how to get along. He lives up to his word and as a result, you feel like you must live up to yours as well.

Don's networking ability was invaluable for Youth Service. There is no way Youth Service could have prospered without the connectivity that Father Don provided because people liked and respected him. Don is a visionary and a leader that inspires people and is always actively involved even behind the scenes.

During the 1970s, many African-American youths and low-income families had some hesitancy about affiliating with a predominantly white-run agency. I think Father Don used his open arms style and understanding of displaced persons to make them understand that he was trying to help. His solid religious background and his friendship with people from all backgrounds helped propel that organization.

In the 70s, not many religious leaders were part of activities outside of the church. The collar he wore created an air of trust; a person whose agenda is to heal rather than to divide. Father Don has the ability to interact with people of all walks in life. He is able to look them in the eye and bring them together to work for the good of Memphis.

Linda Smith West

(St. Andrew's Church Member)

Don was the only churchman in Nashville who reached out to my father, Wendell Smith, who had a liquor store, restaurant and market just two blocks from the church. My father often gave money to area churches, but never attended them. He rightfully thought it was a little offensive that some of the churches would take his money and then send him pamphlets about the sins of drinking. On the other hand, Father Don invited my family to church. After I attended for a while, I noticed that he never preached down to us. He was like a son to my parents, and we all loved him. He made my dad feel welcome at church and we even had a glossy framed photo of him in our home.

I recall when Bishop Vander Horst was visiting town during my confirmation. We were having a reception in the family living room when Father Mowery dared the Bishop to perform a stunt. The next thing I knew, the Bishop was turning a somersault in our living room just for fun and because he could do it.

A number of years later, when my husband and I were in Memphis attending a party, Father Don searched the city and found us to relay an important message. He had the band announce my name over the PA system. At first, Bob thought the bandstand leader was just getting fresh with me, but I soon learned the sad news that my father was dying. Don stayed with us that evening and flew with us from Memphis to Nashville to conduct the funeral service after my father passed away. Father Don played a big part in my life. He also christened, confirmed, and married Bob and me.

Becky Wilson

(Founder of the Bridge Builders Program and BRIDGES, Inc.)

In January of 1988, Shelby County Mayor Bill Morris organized and led groups of people he thought might be able to address the social problems that plagued Memphis at the time. This was part of an initiative that he began called Free the Children. I, along with Gary Shorb and many other interested citizens, were given a bus tour of the city, thereby receiving a crash course in societal issues. We drove through areas of poverty and blight across the city, visited a food stamp office and saw premature babies that needed critical care. I immediately began to understand the difficulties these families were experiencing.

We concluded the tour with a meeting to discuss what we had learned and what could be done to help. Mayor Morris emphasized that cooperation between the public and private sectors was essential or these problems would become severe and threaten funding for essential city services. The seriousness of this situation really hit me hard. The Mayor asked us to help wherever we felt compelled to be involved. That is when I thought of the concept for what became the Bridge Builders program. Mayor Morris advised me to share my idea with Father Don Mowery who had worked with children's programs for years. I didn't know Don very well, but my husband Spence Wilson had served on the Youth Service board for several years.

I was no longer an assistant U.S. Attorney and had more time to devote to helping the community in other areas. I first thought that the Youth Service staff would see me as a busybody housewife, but that was not the case. My first meeting to discuss the idea with Don was in March of 1988. He and his staff were very enthusiastic and I was very pleased and surprised that they accorded me respect and interest. We brought experts who were outside Youth Service on board to brainstorm and help put the program together. Some people advised us to wait and study the idea before we launched a program, but we proceeded quickly and had the first Bridge Builders camp in July of that same year. Don and I both believed that it was important to begin this program immediately.

I was pleased when Don and I visited Tony Walls, principle at Northside High School and Joe Clayton, principal at Briarcrest. I thought it would be difficult to convince these two principles to try something that had never been done before – specifically to pair black and white kids together in an experiential learning model. Once everyone understood the concept, they were all willing to give it a try. However, it took a couple of years before the program really began to pick up steam.

My children had grown up in a segregated world like I did in Jackson, Tennessee, with so-called "legal segregation." I felt that if this program could work at these virtually segregated schools, it could work anywhere. The parents from both schools realized that their children were living in a bubble – with people just like themselves and not experiencing how other people lived, but nobody knew how to change that. This was just one small way of trying to make a change. Everybody seemed ready for it and became anxious for their children to have that opportunity.

Had Don not been willing at that time to discuss the concept and take the risk with an untried idea, Bridge Builders would not have existed and BRIDGES, Inc. in its present form would not be here today.

CHRONOLOGY

1909 – Church Mission of Help (CMH) established at Trinity Church Wall Street in New York City

1917 – The National Episcopal Church placed CMH under the social services division and established the work in several dioceses around the country

1922 – CMH established in Memphis by the women at Calvary Church and St. Mary's Cathedral

1947 – CMH name changed to Youth Service in Memphis

1953 – Don entered seminary at Berkeley Divinity School at Yale

1956 – Don graduated from Berkeley Divinity School at Yale

1956 – Don ordained a Deacon at St. Paul's in Chattanooga

1956 – Don assigned to St. Andrew's Church in Nashville

1957 – Father Don ordained an Episcopal priest at St. Andrew's Church

1960 – St. Andrew's Mission church is accorded full parish status

1961 – Youth Service began providing services to Hurt Village and Lauderdale Courts

1963 – Father Don hired as executive director of Youth Service

1963 – Guild of St. Augustine founded at Holy Communion Church to raise funds and support Youth Service

1963 – Elvis Presley began donations to the Youth Service program after introduction from Mayor Henry Loeb

1964 – First African-American community caseworker hired by Youth Service

1967 – Youth Service received funding from the Office of Economic Opportunity and the Mayor's War on Poverty Committee

1967 – Youth Service began servicing Orange Mound, Hollywood, Whitehaven, Gregg School and Lamar Terrace communities, reaching more than 11,000 young people

1967 – Camping program expands to Shelby Forest, Sardis Lake and Natchez Trace state parks

1968 – Dr. Martin Luther King's assassination and resulting civil turmoil in Memphis

1968 – Sheriff Bill Morris recommended discontinuing camping program in Fuller Park due to civil unrest

1968 – Father Don persuaded NAS Memphis officials to provide temporary grounds for a Youth Service camping program

1968 – Youth Service Memphis program formally began at NAS Memphis

1968 – Over 700 young people attended the summer camps at NAS Memphis

1968 – United Way's Project Extend funds Youth Service camping program

1969 – Blytheville Air Force Base youth camping program began

1969 – First Youth Service Job Training Program began at NAS Memphis

1969 – National Counselor Training Program began at NAS Memphis under Youth Service direction

1969 – Secretary of Defense Melvin Laird forms Domestic Action Council. Youth Service only non-federal agency as a member

1970 – Youth Service, USA, Inc. program officially launched

1970 – *Talk It Out with Father Don* radio show débuted

1970 – Youth Service, USA started programs with Second Air Force

1970 – Peabody Hotel opened for special Youth Service presentation

1970 – Father Don assisted in launching Navy submarine USS Groton

1970 – Air Force Academy Youth program launched

1970 – Camping programs for school aged children expanded to over 20 military installations

1970 – Junior League of Memphis provided funding for the first African-American female caseworker for the Orange Mound community

1970 – The Office of Economic Opportunity provides funding through the War on Poverty Program

1970 – Over 200 Youth Service girls attend camps at Pinecrest

1970 – Charles Allison, Chairman of the Presidential Classroom for Young Americans Program and a White House representative, visited the Naval Air Station for talks with Youth Service

1971 – Youth Service receives its first Freedoms Foundation Award at Valley Forge, PA

1971 – Assistant Secretary of Defense Roger Kelly spoke at Youth Service annual meeting in Memphis

1971 – Pentagon officials commend Youth Service for camping programs on military bases nationwide

1972 – Father Don received George Washington Honor Medal of the Freedoms Foundation for Youth Service

1972 – Youth Service sponsored March of Dimes Walk-A-Thon in Memphis

1973 – Navy produced a documentary film of Youth Service, *Promising Young Americans*

1973 – Father Don appointed Chaplain for the Memphis Police Association and Memphis Fire Department.

1973 – Youth Service received Freedoms Foundation Medal for Good Citizenship

1973 – Father Don and Youth Service receive George Washington Honor Medal Award for Vocational Exposure (camping) programs and *Talk It Out* radio program

1973 – Youth Service received Sertoma Club's "Service to Mankind Award."

1973 – Father Don received congratulatory letter from President Nixon for leadership and youth guidance

1973 – Department of Defense Domestic Action Council members visited Memphis NAS

1973 – Father Don appeared as a guest on NBC's *The Today Show*

1974 – Air Force produced a documentary film of Youth Service, *A Week of Summer*

1975 – Bicentennial Liberty Celebration kicked off at Mid-South Coliseum

1975 – Father Don received The Freedom Leadership Award at Valley Forge, PA

1975 – Father Don assisted in launching submarine USS Memphis in Newport News, VA

1975 – Father Don received congratulatory letter from President Gerald Ford

1976 – Youth Service, Memphis received funding from City Council and Quarterly Court

1977 – Father Don celebrated 20 years in the ministry

1980 – Youth Service, USA peaks with approximately 120 programs established on military bases nationwide

1981 – CETA funds Youth Service JSTEP and Vocational Exposure Programs at NAS, Memphis and 10 other military bases

1981 – Father Don and Youth Service, USA received the Outstanding Public Service Award given by the Secretary of Defense, Casper Weinberger

1983 – Governor Lamar Alexander expresses interest in using the Youth Service Job Training Program in Tennessee schools

1983 – Don and Julie Bailey married at St. Mary's Cathedral

1984 – Father Don met with Martin-Marietta Corp. and other private corporate donors for funding support

1985 – Father Don named first recipient of Bishop's Award for Ministry for the Diocese of West Tennessee

1988 – William (Billy) Dunavant, Jr. and Lester Crain led the capital fund raising campaign for Youth Service in conjunction with Don's 25 years with Youth Service

1988 – Becky Wilson proposed idea for Bridge Builders leadership program to Father Don

1989 – Bridge Builder Speaker Series began

1989 – Father Don delivered invocation for President Bush's first Points of Light award presentation in Memphis

1989 – Father Don met with Vice President Dan Quayle in Nashville to review Job Training programs

1990 – David Abshire, John Edwards and Bill Holmberg begin planning for About Face program

1991 – About Face Program launched at NAS Memphis and ends two years later

1995 – April 30, Father Don officially retired from Youth Service

1996 – Father Don began as a consultant for The Urban Child Institute

2014 – Father Don and Youth Service received the "Be the Dream" Martin Luther King, Jr. Legacy Award at the historic Mason Temple in Memphis

The Rev. Dr. Charles M. Riddle, III

The Rev. Thomas Roberts

Mrs. Helen C. Shelby

Raymond Skinner, Jr.

The Rev. Ralph W. Smith

Robert A. Taylor

David Thompson

James L. Thompson

Mrs. Walter Ulhorn

O.L. Wakeman, Jr.

The Rev. Noble R. Walker

James C. Warner

Mercer E. West, III

Dorothy Westbrook

Clay Whittle

Ed L. Wilkinson

H. Allen Word

Thomas S. Young

Mrs. Thomas S. Young

Richard Zehntner

YOUTH SERVICE CAPITAL CAMPAIGN
1988 – 1989

CAMPAIGN LEADERSHIP

William B. Dunavant, Jr., Chairman
J. Lester Crain, Pacesetter Gifts Chairman

CORE STEERING COMMITTEE

Bruce Campbell
John S. Collier
Mrs. Ann Dunavant
Mrs. Gail French
Nick French
Mayor Richard C. Hackett
Mrs. Henry Haizlip, Jr.
Henry Haizlip, Jr.
RADM David Harlow, USN

Mrs. Herbert Humphreys
Mayor William N. Morris, Jr.
Mrs. Tracy Plyler
Milton T. Schaeffer
Frederick (Fred) W. Smith
Jon K. Thompson
Richard Trippeer
Mrs. Walker Uhlhorn
Deloss Walker

STEERING COMMITTEE

Arthur C. Bass
Jack Belz
Jack R. Blair
George Blasingame
Ken A. Bouldin
George W. Bryan
Col. C. Michel Butler, USAF
Paul A. Calame, Sr.
Mrs. Ewing Carruthers
John D. Canale, III
Mrs. Charles Clarke
George G. Clarke
Mrs. Sophie Coors
Jack T. Craddock, Jr.
William S. Craddock, Sr.
Les S. Dale
Dr. James H. Daughdrill, Jr.
The Rt. Rev. Alex Dickson, D.D.
Lewis R. Donelson
Joseph Eberle, III
Thomas C. Farnsworth, Jr.
Commissioner Carolyn Gates
Charles C. Gerber
Lucia F. Gilliland
James E. Goodwin, Jr.
Henry Haizlip, III
Shelton Harrison
Virginia Henington
Dr. Willie Herenton
Samuel B. Hollis

Mrs. Frank Jones
W. Neely Mallory
Tom Martin
Charles D. McVean
Henry W. Morgan
The Rev. Donald E. Mowery,
Executive Director
Charles F. Newman
Frank M. Norfleet
Joe Orgill, III
Sheriff Jack R. Owens
Harry Phillips, Sr.
William B. Plough
James C. Rainer, III
Richard Rantzow
Dr. Ellen Davies-Rogers
Charles F. Safley, Jr. M.D.
Reid Sanders
Virginia Self
Harold R. Shaw
Robert Snowden
Jack Soden
Robert A. Taylor
Mrs. Pat Kerr Tigrett
Henry Turley, Jr.
Dr. Walter Walker
Ron Walter
A. L. Whitman
Kemmons Wilson
Walter G. Wunderlich

PARTIAL LIST OF
YOUTH SERVICE, USA PROGRAMS (MILITARY)

U.S. NAVY

Cecil Field NAS, FL
Charleston Naval Station, SC
China Lake Navy, CA
El Centro NAS, CA
Glynco NAS, GA
Groton Naval Submarine Base, CT
Gulfport CBs, MS
Imperial Beach NAS, CA
Jacksonville NAS, FL
Mayport Naval Station, FL
Memphis NAS, TN
Meridian NAS, MS
Miramar NAS, CA

New Orleans Navy, LA
Norfolk Navy, VA
Orlando Naval Training Cen., FL
Patuxent River Navy, MD
Pensacola NAS, FL
Point Mugu, CA
San Diego Naval Training Cen., CA
Stockton Naval Comm. Training Cen., CA
St. Petersburg Coast Guard, FL
Whidbey Island NAS, WA
Whiting Field NAS, FL

U.S. AIR FORCE

U.S. Air Force Academy, CO
Andrews AFB, MD
Barksdale AFB,LA
Beale AFB, CA
Bergstrom AFB, TX
Blytheville AFB, AR
Bolling AFB, MD
Carswell AFB, TX
Castle AFB, CA
Charleston AFB, SC
Columbus AFB, MS
Craig AFB, AL
Davis-Monthan AFB, AZ
Dyess AFB, TX
Goodfellow AFB, TX
Grand Forks AFB, ND
Griffis AFB, NY
Grissom AFB, IN
Gunther AFB, AL
Hill AFB, UT
Kessler AFB, MS
Kincheloe AFB, MI
Langley AFB, VA
Little Rock AFB, AR
Loring AFB, MA
Luke AFB, AZ

Malmstrom AFB, MT
March AFB, CA
Mather AFB, CA
Maxwell AFB, AL
McClellan AFB, CA
McGuire AFB, NJ
McConnell AFB, KS
Moody AFB, GA
Mountain Home AFB, ID
Myrtle Beach AFB, SC
Niagara Falls Int'l Airport, NY
Offutt AFB, NE
Pease AFB, NH
Plattsburgh AFB, NY
Randolph AFB, TX
Rickenbacker AFB, OH
Robins AFB, GA
Scott AFB, IL
Seymour-Johnson AFB, NC
Shaw AFB, SC
Spence AFB, GA
Tyndall AFB, FL
Vandenberg AFB, CA
Williams AFB, AZ
Wright-Patterson AFB, OH
Wurtsmith AFB, MI

U.S. ARMY

Fort Belvoir, VA

Fort Benning, GA

Fort Bragg, N.C.

Fort Carson, CO

Fort Campbell, KY

Fort Gordon, GA

Fort Hood, TX

Fort Jackson, S.C.

Fort McClellan, AL

Fort Monmouth, NJ

Fort Rucker, AL

Fort Stewart, GA

Hawaii Army

Memphis Defense Depot, TN

Sharpe Army Depot, CA

Yuma Proving Grounds, AZ

YOUTH SERVICE OFFICIAL SONG

GRAB HOLD

Written by Danny Greene

We're all working for a common goal
Lord help us to understand
We all need to GRAB HOLD
To the brotherhood of Man
Working together
We can realize our dreams
Let's all make this life better
The first step is you and me

GRAB HOLD – of an education
GRAB HOLD – of a better life
GRAB HOLD – of the situation
And make it turn out right
GRAB HOLD to all your hopes and dreams
Keeping faith along the way
Lord help me to GRAB HOLD
To a better life today

We're building bridges of understanding
And connecting them with love
We can reach out to each other
When the times get rough
If we all keep the right attitude
To make this world a better place
There's no limit to what we can do
So put a smile on your face

GRAB HOLD – to something better
GRAB HOLD – to something good
Grab Hold – to the life you lead
You know you can if you just would
GRAB HOLD – to all your hopes and dreams
Keeping faith along the way
Lord help me to GRAB HOLD
To a better life today

ABOUT THE AUTHORS

Darrell B. Uselton is a biographer for individuals who want to share their personal and business legacies. Whether it is a story of one person's triumph or the historical account of an institution, he emphasizes principles of individual leadership and ensures a compelling account of what makes people unique. Darrell has earned BA and MA degrees in history from the University of Memphis and has been an adjunct history professor at the U of M for 15 years. He was formerly a technical writer with the U of M Center for Research in Educational Policy and has received the Phi Theta Kappa International Leadership Faculty Certification.

David McDonald Yawn is a business writer and editor whose career has spanned three decades. He has worked professionally at the Memphis Business Journal, FedEx and International Paper headquarters in advanced publications roles. In addition, David has edited 12 published books of others and has authored five published books of his own for clients. He is the recipient of numerous national industry awards in the field of communications including the Dalton Pen Award, multiple Communicator Awards of Excellence, Apex awards, and a Tennessee Press Association statewide distinction.

NAME INDEX

Bush, Laura, 223
Butler, Gen. C. Michel, 351
Calame, Paul A. Sr., 347, 351
Callow, Bette Ray, 347
Campbell, Bruce, 350
Canale, John D. III, 347, 351
Cannon, The Rev. Carl T., 347
Carruth, J. D., 104
Carruthers, Ewing and Jane, 307, 347, 351
Carter, Dianne, 222
Carter, President Jimmy, 204, 205
Carter, Ken, 200
Carville, James, 240
Cash, Johnny, 194
Cash, June Carter, 194
Cashman, Eugene (Gene), 40, 274,
277, 278, 292, 296, 299-300
Cashman, Kathy, 278
Castile, Tony, 27
Challen, James, 300
Chambers, Elizabeth, 220-221
Chambers, Ray, 268, 332
Chandler, CAPT Hap, 109
Chandler, Mayor Wyeth, 167, 205
Chapman, E. Winslow
"Buddy", 296, 300-301
Cheek, Dale, 104
Christensen, RADM Ernest E., 90,
92, 93, 99, 108, 109, 110, 138, 149,
163, 170, 216, 223, 304, 349
Christensen, Marge, 90, 91,
92, 110, 156, 305
Clark, Father Charles, 51
Clarke, Mrs. Charles L., 347, 351
Clarke, George G., 347, 351
Clark, Ken, 59, 296, 301
Claypool, Phil, 296, 302
Clewlow, Carl W., 173
Clinton, President Bill, 335
Clinton, Hillary Rodham, 223
Coe, Doug, 160, 264

Cohen, U. S. Rep. Steve, 258
Cole, Gen., 155
Coleman, Bishop James (Jim) M., 268, 269
Collier, John S. 72, 132, 138, 141,
148, 150, 159, 163, 197, 212,
224, 302, 307, 347, 349, 350
Collier, Stuart, 296, 302-303
Colson, Charles "Chuck", 202, 321
Connelly, The Rev. Edwin L., 28
Cook, Everett R., 199
Cook, Mrs. J. B., 62, 80, 91,
106, 152, 326, 327
Coors, Mrs. Sophie, 351
Cosby, Bill, 240
Coyne, Jim, 229
Covington, Pat, 178
Craddock, Jack T., Jr., 351
Craddock, William (Bill), 296, 303, 351
Crain, Brenda, 75, 136,
225, 290, 296, 304
Crain, Kim, 292
Crain, J. Lester, Jr., IX, 74, 75, 89,
103, 112, 126, 132, 136, 138, 150,
159, 161, 163, 199, 225, 231,
236, 237, 290, 296, 304, 305, 313,
316, 332, 333, 345, 349, 350
Crosby, Jackie, 222
Crowe, ADM William J., Jr.,
231, 233, 306, 349
Crumrine, Dr. Robert S., 347
Dale, Les S., 351
Daughdrill, Dr. James H. Jr., 351
Davies-Rogers, Dr. Ellen, 351
Davis, Daniel Lee, 118-119
Dawson, Col. Frank, IX, 226-228,
246, 264, 281, 296, 305-306
Dees, Rick, 121-122
Denmark, CDR. G.T., 160, 167
Dickerson, Warner, 217
Dickson, Bishop Alex, 225, 231, 252,
253, 268, 296, 307, 347, 349, 351

CPSIA information can be obtained at www.ICGtesting.com
Printed in the USA
LVOW07s0537240914

405603LV00003B/3/P